D0503055

CIVIC CENTER

# THE
# ROYAL TREATMENT

# THE
# ROYAL
# TREATMENT

## A NATURAL APPROACH TO WILDLY HEALTHY PETS

## Dr. Barbara Royal

### *with* Anastasia Royal

**EMILY BESTLER BOOKS**
—
**ATRIA**

NEW YORK   LONDON   TORONTO   SYDNEY   NEW DELHI

ATRIA BOOKS

A Division of Simon & Schuster, Inc.

1230 Avenue of the Americas

New York, NY 10020

First Emily Bestler Book / Atria Books hardcover edition September 2012

EMILY BESTLER BOOKS / ATRIA BOOKS and colophon are trademarks of Simon & Schuster, Inc.

For information about special discounts for bulk purchases, please contact Simon & Schuster Special Sales at 1-866-506-1949 or business@simonandschuster.com.

The Simon & Schuster Speakers Bureau can bring authors to your live event. For more information or to book an event contact the Simon & Schuster Speakers Bureau at 1-866-248-3049 or visit our website at www.simonspeakers.com.

*Designed by Suet Yee Chong*

Manufactured in the United States of America

10   9   8   7   6   5   4   3   2   1

Library of Congress Cataloging-in-Publication Data

Royal, Barbara.
The Royal treatment: a natural approach to wildly healthy pets / Barbara Royal, with Anastasia Royal.
p.   cm.
Includes bibliographical references and index.
1. Pets—Health. 2. Veterinary medicine. 3. Alternative veterinary medicine.
I. Royal, Anastasia. II. Title.
SF745.R69 2012
636.089—dc23

ISBN 978-1-4516-4769-3
ISBN 978-1-4516-4771-6 (ebook)

# DISCLAIMER

This book was written and published for educational and entertainment purposes only, and it is not intended to take the place of veterinary care. I recommend consulting your veterinarian for any medical or surgical treatments where necessary. The author and publisher disclaim any liability arising directly or indirectly from the use of this book.

I have included information on doses for medications, herbs, and homeopathics only to provide clarification. This is not meant to diagnose or treat disease. My goal is to provide insight into an integrative approach to veterinary medicine.

Every animal, breed, and species is different, and patients require individual assessment for proper treatment. In fact, that is a major theme of this book. I love my profession and my many dedicated veterinary colleagues. Veterinarians are some of the most wonderful people I know. In this book I hope to add to the already impressive array of veterinary treatment options for patients.

Even with animals there are patient-confidentiality issues. Many names, locations, and details have been changed to protect the innocent, the ferocious, the tame, the wild, and their natural habitats. By doing this, I hope the trail leads away from the tracks of the actual animals to protect their destination. All of the animal cases are taken from my actual experiences, some are composites, and all are remembered fondly.

I have issues with the idea of zoos and animals in captivity. But I try to be a realist. Zoos do exist, and improving the health and comfort of the animals there makes sense. People are encroaching on the wild in every part of the world, and anything we can do to improve the life of any animal seems to me to be the right thing to do.

My experiences with zoos and wildlife, while often wonderful, have not been without their share of angst. I hope to further the overall discussion about animals by sharing what I have learned.

*To my children, Sean and Sophie—*
*your wild happiness inspires me.*

# CONTENTS

# TERMINOLOGY

The word *patient* is used to signify the animals being treated. *Clients* are the humans who bring patients in to vet clinics—they are also called *owners* or the *mom* and *dad* of the pet. The current trend to denote *owner* with the word *guardian* is laudable. While new terms can further the cause of our beloved animals, I do not use the word *guardian* in this book, for two reasons. First of all, I think it is often the animal that is guarding or being the guardian of the person. Second, I am habituated to the words I use daily in my clinic and want this book to reflect that ease of usage.

I use the term *pet* to indicate a family member from the animal kingdom.

*He* and *she* are used interchangeably to indicate various generic or specific pets.

*X-rays* are invisible particles that create images that are seen on a *radiograph*. Even though X-rays cannot be seen and radiographs can, I use both words to signify the same thing. The term *X-ray* is easily understood and current usage allows it, but I still cringe.

*Signs* of disease in animals is the term used for what would be *symptoms* of disease in humans. *Symptoms*, while a familiar term, involves a description of health problems experienced by a person. *Signs* are what we observe as health issues in another species. Therefore, where prudent, I have used the preferred veterinary term *sign*.

# PREFACE

What have we done to undermine the innate health of our pets? Why are the animals in our homes riddled with disease? Why do we have more medicines for them in our cabinets than we do for our aging parents? Why do a record number of dogs suffer from cancer, obesity, diabetes, thyroid disease, and other disorders? Why do we accept this as the norm? Is it logical that a carnivore would be allergic to meat? Should a six-month-old cat be plagued by allergies? Why have we come to expect arthritis in Labradors? Does this abysmally low standard of health make any sense at all? Not in my book.

I have always felt there has to be a better way. This was gradually revealed to me throughout the many years I've spent working with wild animals—treating them in zoos and on their own home ground. In the early days of my career, I was oriented toward disease, focusing on what I believed to be the inevitable progression of pathologies and the intricacies of Western medicine's prescribed treatments. Now, after coming to a better understanding of the way wild animals have evolved to sustain their own well-being in their natural environment, I direct my energy toward thinking about potential. More specifically, the potential for natural health that occurs when an animal's evolutionary needs are fulfilled.

This is what I call wild health.

We have an incomplete understanding of our pets when we overlook the relevance of their ancestry, just as we have an incomplete understanding of our own health when we overlook our personal and genetic histories. As a result, we make misguided decisions and draw wrong conclusions about our pets' essential needs. In the case of dogs, for example, their basic needs are not so greatly different from those of a wolf.

You may scoff and say, "Listen, doc, I've got a peekapoo at home, not a wolf." Fair enough, but it's important to realize that wolf biology has not been fully bred out of dogs—not even in peekapoos. Dogs have undergone a relatively brief period of selective breeding before landing in our living rooms. In fact, wolves and dogs are so genetically similar that when bred together, they can successfully produce fertile puppies. This is a surprising indicator of their great similarity; African and Asian elephants can't even do that—and they're both elephants. Likewise, there are more similarities than you might expect between your pouncing housecat and a stalking Bengal tiger.

The point is, the evolutionary biology of your pet is highly relevant to its overall health—and happiness. Applying that knowledge, with a little common sense along the way, will make life with your pets more of a joy and less of a job. It is far, far easier, more pleasant, and less costly to sustain natural health than to fight losing battles with avoidable diseases.

As an integrative veterinarian, I combine the best of ancient practices with cutting-edge modern technology. I am a firm believer in using modern, state-of-the-art, conventional medical treatment where it is appropriate and effective, and I rely on those in my practice every day. The right surgery and the right medication, at the right time, can work miracles. But an overreliance on medications and surgery to eradicate symptoms can sometimes do more harm than good. I have found that a proper diet, natural supplements, physical therapy, and appropriate exercise are often the best means to support an animal's natural tendency toward balance and vibrant health.

I now consider it my job as a doctor to discern and remove impediments to an animal's natural state of well-being and make sure it has precisely what it needs to thrive. I've seen remarkable recoveries in dogs, cats, rabbits, and other pets because I've learned a little secret from wild animals. When the basic evolutionary needs of an ailing pet are fulfilled, its body's ability to heal and recover is heightened. Recognizing that capacity for wild health is at the core of what I do every day, for every wonderful animal that comes into my practice.

I have learned a great many things from wild animals that relate to the dog in your living room and the cat in your kitchen. However, it is possible to boil it all down to one single principle at the heart of the Royal Treatment. Informed by my experiences working with zoo animals and wildlife—from peregrine falcons to Bactrian camels to silverback gorillas to red pandas—the Royal Treatment works with, not against, nature. It balances the body's organ systems and enhances the efficiency of an animal's healing system. The Royal Treatment is not an elitist plan. It is designed for any species of animal and provides them with the care that nature intended. In other words, your pet can attain true health in a faux health world.

Employing the easy actions in this book, you, as a pet owner, can give your pet the Royal Treatment. Jewel, the camel, will show you what to do for your geriatric dog. Songkit, the tiger cub, will provide insight into your frisky tabby. The story of my own dog Tundra may comfort you when you realize that the time has come to end a terminally ill animal's suffering. Easy-to-follow instructions, tips for everyday care, diet suggestions, and recipes are also included. My clients have found that this prescriptive advice not only improves the lives of their animals, but also saves them time and money. I hope it will do the same for you.

# FOREWORD

Dr. Barbara Royal and I met because I had heard of her reputation to heal very sick or complicated cases, and my beloved dog Duke, a yellow lab/white shepherd mix, was fighting for his life. At only five and a half years old, he was diagnosed with cancer and given a week to live.

Three years earlier, I had rescued Duke after he survived the traumas of being a bait dog in a pit-bull fighting ring, and I witnessed his journey from a dog who was terrified of people to a dog that loved everyone. So when I received the bad news about him, I was devastated. Fortunately Dr. Royal entered the picture. She immediately assessed the situation and guided me to make better decisions, such as discontinuing medications, adding supplements, and improving his diet. Although we were thousands of miles apart—she lives in Chicago and I live in Los Angeles—she took the time to explain her medical protocols via Skype and tirelessly monitored Duke's progress. Dr. Royal individualized a treatment plan that, along with my cooperation and the help of a new local vet, energized us all, including Duke, and he started walking and enjoying life again. Dr. Royal was able to help him when no one else could.

After we started to get to know each other, Dr. Royal and I discovered we had connected for the right reason: both of our lives have always been about healing animals.

In the twenty-five years that I've been working with dogs, I have had the pleasure to meet and coach a wide range of dogs and dog "parents." I have also become friends with many veterinarians, but I have never met anyone like Dr. Royal. Her vast knowledge of conventional and alternative treatments is matched only by her common sense and compassion for pets and their owners.

Establishing credibility as a pioneer in any field is difficult, but Dr. Royal has done just that. With her unique approach and commitment to the animals in her care, it is no wonder that she inspires such love from her many clients, including me. In her I found a kindred spirit who looks at the totality of an animal and understands that its diet, health, and behavior are interrelated. I encouraged her to write a book because I felt that every dog owner should be as lucky as I was to have the Royal Treatment. I am thrilled that animal lovers everywhere will benefit from her extraordinary expertise, practical advice, and hopeful vision.

—Tamar Geller

# WILD FIRE

I'm crawling on the floor in our burning house. The stench of smoke and melting plastic is overpowering. My hand slides along the baseboard in the pitch black, trying to find the doorway to the bedroom. I know my animals will all be there, together. Except for our timid cat, Face, who likes to hide in the closet, on a pile of my scrubs.

I had left the house twenty minutes earlier, with my five-year-old son, when my neighbor called me on my cell phone.

"Your house just burst into flames," she said, "and there's smoke pouring out of your kitchen window."

That is just not possible, I thought.

While racing home in my car, I feverishly thought through different scenarios. What could have happened? Did the fire start in the kitchen? The living room? I tried to figure out exactly what I'd have to do to get my animals out. How would I find them, and when I did, would I be able to carry them all? The cats could be tucked in a curl of my coat. The dogs would be harder. Maybe I could drape my long-legged soul mate Tundra around my neck, while carrying hefty Jake in my arms.

Fire trucks surrounded my house. I rushed my son to the next-door neighbors, hugged him tight, and told him I'd be right back.

I was halfway across the lawn to my house when Tundra jumped out of the bushes into my arms. I have never been so happy to see her. I scanned her body with my hands. She seemed okay. One out of four. Where were the others?

I asked another neighbor, who had come out to help, to take Tundra to his house. Tundra didn't like that idea. Always protective of me, she had to be dragged away.

Without thought or hesitation, I darted into my burning house. Now, three steps in, the heat is intense. The ceiling's on fire and I am already gasping for air. Black clouds of smoke roll at me from the kitchen; eerie flickers of light create quick silhouettes. As I drop to the floor, narrowly avoiding some falling debris, the thought crosses my mind that I might die. But the bedroom where my pets most surely are hiding is only one room away. I have to get there.

I hold my breath. Crouch low. I prepare for one quick dash through the smoke. But there's someone else in the room with a different idea. I hear his muffled breathing through the firefighter apparatus. Suddenly I'm hauled upward by strong arms.

Many people say they would die for their pets. I don't doubt it. I've been there. It's a choice we don't often have to make, but we feel certain we would do it just the same. I've also known pets that have sacrificed themselves for their owners. That's how deep the bond goes.

But are we willing to be proactive and use that loving energy to save our pets' lives a little bit, every day? An emergency exists now—much less obvious than the threat of a fire—but I see it daily. Increasingly, pets are suffering from the same maladies as humans: thyroid, liver, autoimmune, adrenal, and kidney diseases; arthritis; seizure disorders; and cancer. Because they live the way we live and eat the way we eat in the environment we have created for ourselves, they have inevitably fallen victim to the same illnesses that plague us.

The average Standard American Diet (SAD, an apt acronym) has changed radically in the past twenty-five years, almost entirely for the worse. Processed foods make up the bulk of our national dietary intake, contributing to rampant diabetes, cancer, obesity, and arthritis. Our pets' diets mirror this trend. Even when owners are careful to buy the most expensive, supposedly healthy pet foods (even prescription foods), they are often poorly suited to an animal's true nutritional needs. And since many of us have come to believe that these diseases are an inescapable part of modern life, we don't think it strange that the same fate should befall our pets.

As for the fire that day, it continued to rage. My life was certainly saved by the fireman who half-dragged, half-carried me, protesting, back through the hallway and out the front door. Apparently he had dealt with this kind of lunacy before. With surprising forbearance, he quickly and efficiently propelled me into the cool spring air, where he gently settled me on the front lawn and asked another fireman to watch over me. They were very kind. If I were in his shoes, I would have tossed me out the door, maybe given me a swift boot on the way out, and screamed, "You stupid, stupid woman!"

Sitting there, I stared at what would soon be the burned-out shell of my home, watching flames lick out of the windows as it devoured the floors on which I had been crawling moments before. Unable to stop the tears, I sobbed, not even noticing the crowd that had gathered.

I stood up unsteadily, drawing a suspicious glance from the fireman designated to watch me.

"I can't just sit here; I have to do something." I said. "I promise I won't go back in the house." There wasn't much house to go back into anyway.

At the time I could barely come to terms with what was happening. All I could think about was finding my pets. I had already done the few things I could to improve their chances of survival in the event of a household disaster. You can do these things, too:

1. *Put an in-case-of-fire sign on windows or doors that tells what pets live with you. Indicate how many and what types of animals they are.*
2. *Microchip your pets. If your pets escape, an agency that finds them has a better chance of identifying them and contacting you.*

Knowing that I had done what I could was some comfort. But most of my animals were still unaccounted for. The uncertainty of their fate was unbearable.

Circling the house, I called their names—"Jake! Fingers! Face!"— not knowing if they were still inside or if they would even recognize my hoarse, shaky voice. When I finally heard Fingers in the alley, her voice echoed mine with a hoarse, shaky meow. She jumped onto my shoulders. This was her signature move. Her white fur was gray with soot and reeked of smoke.

Besides the brave firefighters that day, our neighborhood garbage man was also a hero. He broke down the kitchen door and released both dogs, Tundra and Jake. By good fortune, Fingers had run out with the dogs. But where was my other cat, Face? And where had Jake gone?

3.   *Be sure to secure the animals that have been rescued so they can't get back into the burning building.*

Jake had been freed, but tragically he'd returned to the house. The firefighters later told me that many dogs, including German shepherds like Jake, often go back inside. It is their instinct to protect.

As I feared, Face had stayed hidden. She never did leave the closet. Jake was found right next to her with a toy in his mouth. My only comfort is that they looked peaceful together—as if they were sleeping.

I need to add one final, cardinal rule here, regarding you, your pets, and fire safety: *Never, never go inside a burning building.*

Do not attempt to rescue your pets. I never should have done it. But for me, I suppose, it was force of habit. I'm a veterinarian—saving animals is what I do.

PART ONE

WILD
HEALTH

# THE PURSUIT
# OF PET HAPPINESS

♛

*If your dog wags his tail in your house and no one is
there to see it, is he still happy?*

"I JUST WANT TO KNOW IF DAKOTA IS HAPPY." I HEAR THIS FROM
owners nearly every day.

Are Simba, Diesel, Oscar, Darby, Ladybug, Numbers, Pippin, Isabelle, or Ariadne happy? How can we know?

When we brought animals out of their natural habitats and into our homes, we formed a partnership with them. The original impetus may have been for protection, but I believe that even in the very first human interactions with a cave-pet, there was an element of joy. We hope their domestication has brought them more advantages than disadvantages. Because we are grateful for what our pets offer us, we want to reliably provide what they need. We are advocates for these silent family members.

Nonetheless, they communicate with their language of wagging tails, purring, and head-butting. We'd like to believe that our pets are at least as cheerful as they might be in the wild. In general we do not concern ourselves with the comfort level of wildlife. However, when I worked in wildlife rehabilitation, I was deeply concerned about this, particularly because the animals were under human care. I was certain that once returned to the wild, they would make their own way. While quantifying the contentedness of a wild animal is difficult, I assess the happiness of pets every day.

Owners wonder if any animal can be satisfied living in an apartment, a small ranch house, a mansion, a farmhouse, or a high-rise. They might wonder if the pet that travels the world with my client Oprah Winfrey is happier than the pet living in a city apartment with my client Sondra, who works as a night nurse. Both pets seem content to me.

Pets keep us grounded in the moment. Despite our busy schedules, the pace of a pet remains the same, and we must become part of that pace, if only for a brief part of our day. A fifteen-minute walk with your dog or a quiet moment with your cat is invaluable for both you and your animal.

Pet owners understandably worry about myriad things: whether they provide too few or too many activities for their pets, whether they are feeding them the best food, if current vaccine schedules are safe, and if alternative treatments really work. Finding the right resources and correct answers is fraught with false claims and vested interests.

In response to all of this, I urge pet owners to not overanalyze. *A pet should be a joy, not a job.*

It is simple. Your pet lives in a safe, secure existence with a loving person. At the same time, understanding the primal imperatives will satisfy the inner wildcat and make the outer housecat purr; it will nourish the inner wolf and allow the outer puppy to grow.

I have noticed clients in my practice becoming more confident about their pet care decisions. They know that the Royal Treatment is not a plan that lavishes pets with unneeded pampering, but a sensible way to treat them. Giving your pet the Royal Treatment can ensure that he or she is not only happy but also wildly healthy. Once I've shown you how to do that, the next steps are a walk in the park.

# THE PERFECT FIT

---

WHY ARE WE SO FASCINATED BY ANIMALS? BECAUSE THEY bring the wild into our living rooms. We want to reconnect with our roots and deepen our sense of where we come from. We reap many rewards from animals crossing our paths. We gain insight into the inexplicable from their truncated lives—insights about joy, love, control, surprise, play, acceptance, giving, letting go, and grief.

Whether they are permanent pets in our homes or brief encounters in nature, animals transport us with their beauty. Many people have fascinating stories about how they found their pets—or more often, how their pets found them. It may feel as if we provide for them, but it may be the other way around. They are more than just a wet nose and some fur. The sheer force of their animal nature can bring out our humanity and, at the same time, preserve a little bit of wildness in us too.

When I worked long hours in a veterinary emergency clinic, our dog, Tundra, got up from wherever she was and ambled over to the door to wait for me—always about twenty minutes before I arrived home. This would be understandable if the time I came home was the same every night. But there were no regular shifts.

It seemed like somehow Tundra always knew when I was on my way. My husband, Matt, and I decided to try an experiment. It took twenty minutes for me to drive home. As I got in the car to start the drive home, I checked my watch. If he happened to notice Tundra going to the front door, he'd check his. These times were always within about two minutes of each other. She knew when the homeward-bound decision had been made. How? I have no idea.

The more I've learned about animals, the more I believe we underestimate their ability to interpret and interact with unseen forces in our world. Could Tundra hear my car start from six miles away? Is there some frequency it gave off or that I gave off when I travel? Or could it be a phenomenon that is not yet fully understood by humans?

I don't know how Tundra knew when I was close to home, but I do know that electro-sensors have been discovered around sharks' mouths. These electro-sensors detect body electricity from several yards away. They can detect even a five-billionth of a volt. Bats can correctly locate and intercept a moving insect from over ten feet away in the dark. Snakes have sensors tuned for heat that allow them to distinguish changes in temperature as little as 0.01 degree Fahrenheit from a foot away. This allows them to follow the heat trail of passing prey in the dark and find warm places to help regulate their own body temperature. Trees have been documented to communicate with each other over vast distances in response to threats from insects. In fact, all living things—animals, plants, and humans—give and receive cues to help us fit together on this planet.

*Pets in our homes can contribute to a better,
more balanced life. From fish to felines,
from cockatoos to canines, animals give us sight lines
back to our evolutionary heritage.*

The original reason that people had pets was that they provided us with something we needed and vice versa. The idea was that they seamlessly fit into the lives of humans. Cats lived in a barn because they took care of a rodent problem. Dogs provided a second set of eyes and acute hearing as an early-warning system, and a sharp set of teeth for protection. They lived on a combination of our leftover meat and whatever they could catch on their own. Up until recently, most leftovers were not grain-based.

It's possible to imagine that, over time, dogs and even cats could evolve to eat as we do, digesting more corn or wheat, or even becoming vegetarians. But that radical a change would require long-term adaptation. An example that illustrates this point is the divergent diet preferences of two animals, both in the bear family, *Ursus:* the largest terrestrial carnivore, the polar bear, and the diminutive spectacled bear that is the only species of bear found in South America. The former, also known as *Ursus maritimus* or even *Ursus arctos horribilis,* is the most carnivorous of the bear family, which is a requirement of its harsh environment, while the latter, also known as *Tremarctos ornatus,* is primarily an herbivore and only about 5 percent of its diet is meat.

These two bears' body structure and organ systems have changed significantly, over tens of thousands of years, to accommodate and survive in their distinct and different environments. Polar bears have long, sharp teeth and their claws are short and stocky to dig ice and drag heavy prey. Spectacled bears have long claws that allow them to climb trees, and their molars are large and flat to enable them to chew tough plants. Polar bears require a large amount of calories provided almost exclusively by the high fat content of marine mammals.

Spectacled bears, however, rely primarily on bromeliads, palms, orchids, leaves, shoots, and fruits, supplemented with nuts, eggs, seeds, and occasional small animals or carrion. The polar bear is so adapted to its environment that it cannot survive on terrestrial food sources alone—the few berries and roots they eat are not a significant part of their diet. The opposite is true of the arboreal spectacled bear, which cannot thrive *without* huge amounts of vegetable matter—the animal protein they ingest is incidental.

It wouldn't work to suddenly change a polar bear's diet to all vegetables, just as it wouldn't be wise to feed a spectacled bear a meat-based diet. Each of them might survive for a while, but they would not be healthy.

For as long as I can remember, animals have been a source of wonder and delight in my life. Growing up as the only nonallergic child in a family of six siblings, I spent years surreptitiously healing injured animals, "hospitalized" under my bed. Thanks to the joy of caring for animals and having my own pets, I am inspired every day to become a more patient and compassionate person.

As humans we can choose to be a part of nature or collide against it. Our pets help us fit in to nature and in turn, we must help them by creating a lifestyle that considers their ancestry.

# ZEBRA

♟

*A "zebra" in medical slang is a rare or surprising diagnosis. A vet may say, "It looked like a typical infection, but it turned out to be a zebra."*

BOBBI REMAINED CALM AS I INSERTED A THIRD NEEDLE INTO HER massive striped neck. I was silently elated. Applying the ancient art of acupuncture to zebras had never been done before, so no one, including me, could have predicted how she would tolerate the treatment.

When the zoo veterinarian had called to ask if there was anything I could do for Bobbi's epilepsy and arthritis, I decided it was worth a try. Acupuncture works well for horses, so I was keen to do it, even though zebras are notoriously high-strung, suspicious, and sharp-hooved, and potentially quite dangerous. After weeks of practice with pretend needles and many rewards for Bobbi, it was time to give the real thing a shot. Bobbi trotted over when she saw I had her favorite brush. Grooming her with my left hand as a distraction, I picked up a needle with my right. This one would be tricky to place—inside her shifting foreleg.

With a quick conspiratorial glance at the zookeeper, I felt for the acupoint. Just where Bobbi's bristly hair changed to the softer undercoat, my fingers found the divot. I inserted the needle knowing that one powerful kick to my head could be the end of me.

With my hand right on her solid, muscular leg, it was easy to imagine this beautiful Grévy's zebra running free on the Serengeti Plain. I wondered, would she have developed arthritis and epilepsy if she lived in her natural habitat? Most animals I've studied in their natural surroundings are chronically healthy. While walking in a forest teeming with robust species, you'd never see diabetic robins, arthritic squirrels, obese rabbits, or asthmatic deer. Part of this may be because survival of the fittest and predation take the weak and those with endemic, species-specific diseases, but the vibrant health of all remaining animals is significant. There is an innate state of healthful equilibrium in every ecosystem, benefiting creatures great and small.

> *Nature effortlessly propagates health, but in our civilized world, maintaining health takes effort.*

A zebra that is wildly healthy is in a balanced state of well-being. But this can only happen if a zebra's basic needs are met. When a zebra doesn't eat zebra food, doesn't run in a zebra way, doesn't live in zebra-like environment, that's when disease can take hold. It's very telling that the healthiest environment for any zoo animal is one that meticulously mimics its natural habitat. This premise is somewhat obvious for wild animals like zebras, but also must be recognized for our dogs and cats.

For our pets to be truly healthy we must recognize the wild in them, too. It's okay to call your puggle Mr. Grumpy and dress him in a sailor suit, but his health depends on your awareness of his true nature and your dedication to making sure his basic evolutionary needs are met.

I once treated a male cat named Toast, who had a history of feline lower urinary tract disease (FLUTD). FLUTD is a chronic, potentially life-threatening urinary tract disease that can affect more than 30 percent of all cats. Toast was urinating on his owners' bed pillows instead of the litter box.

Apparently the female cat in the house felt the need to protect the territory around the litter box. With just a subtle tail flick or a glance—strong language between cats that translates into an aggressive rebuff—she consistently discouraged Toast from using their shared bathroom. As a result, Toast's bladder was not emptied often enough, and this contributed to his condition.

One way to prevent FLUTD is to provide more litter boxes than the number of cats in the house. Then there will always be one free, unguarded box. This was how Toast was eventually healed. If you live in a studio apartment and have twenty cats, hide your bed pillows.

In the wild, no one guards the litter box, and so Toast wouldn't have been susceptible to this kind of stress-induced FLUTD. But does it make sense that *any* cat suffers from chronic, life-threatening urinary tract disease? Particularly since, as far as we know, FLUTD is not seen in wild felines? An animal in a balanced state of wild health will be more adaptable to circumstances that tend to be unnatural for it. In other words, your wildly healthy animal will fit into your non-animal world with fewer health problems if his or her natural constitution is not compromised.

The basic genetics of canine and feline biology has not strayed very far from that of their ancestors. Indeed, part of the allure of having a pet is that they draw us closer to the natural world; so we shouldn't pull them too far away from it.

Zoos are microcosms of the natural world. Because we've removed the animal from the wild, we must reconstruct the wild for each animal in these controlled environments. And it always starts with the fundamentals of a good diet. Zookeepers do their best to avoid feeding animals anything other than what they would eat in their natural habitat. Not surprisingly, the greatest percentage of illness occurs when diets aren't properly formulated and assiduously followed.

The same is true of our pets. No matter how we train, dress, and pamper them, they are still the product of their genetic past. Countless years of adaptation have turned dogs into carnivore scavengers, which means they need meat, but they'll take what they can scavenge and make do until meat is on the table again. Cats have adapted into obligate carnivores, which means that they will become very ill without a primarily meat diet—it is a requirement, not an option. It is more than menu preferences. The triggers and mechanisms of behavior and survival are based on those essentials. If we don't give our pets what they need and they have no other way to get it, they will inevitably grow sick.

> *Nature never breaks her own rules.*
> —Leonardo da Vinci

The following often underestimated maladies may be a sign that your pet's natural constitution is unbalanced. The good news is that they may be alleviated or eliminated, by restoring innate balance.

### The Royal Treatment Warning System

- 🐾 Allergies
- 🐾 Chronic lumps, bumps, and growths
- 🐾 Arthritis
- 🐾 Chronic ear infections, skin infections, and eye infections
- 🐾 Picky eating habits
- 🐾 Obesity
- 🐾 Inflammatory bowel disease, chronic pancreatitis, or chronic loose stool
- 🐾 Kidney disease
- 🐾 Liver disease
- 🐾 Hormonal problems (thyroid, adrenal, pituitary)
- 🐾 Urinary tract disease, urinary "accidents," urinary infections, stones or crystals in urine
- 🐾 Neurologic problems, seizures, cognitive disorders
- 🐾 Dental disease—even dental tartar

The gastrointestinal (GI) tract of carnivores—like lions, wolves, dogs, or cats—has not adapted in a way that allows the systems of these animals to contend with processed grains. Why then are those grains major ingredients in many pet foods? My patients' conditions dramatically improve when their owners follow my advice to gradually change the pet's diet to eliminate corn and wheat. It is easy to check whether grains are included in the mix, by reading the tiny print on pet food labels.

Living in a zoo presents dietary limitations that can affect the many species there. Bobbi had been fed a carefully regulated diet but was occasionally given bread rolls as treats, yet no one had thought about the effect of them. You may be shocked to discover that zebras don't forage for baked goods on the savannas of Kenya. If there is any connection between processed glutens and inflammatory response, it makes sense to eliminate bread rolls from the menu of any arthritic, epileptic animal. Without a good, species-specific diet, no medication can sustain long-term health and even small "treats" can have a very negative impact on health.

Wild health seems a more logical and realistic concept when we're talking about a wild animal such as a zebra. But when it comes to cats and dogs, people and even some veterinarians seem to accept chronic ailments as the price they pay for fitting into our world as pets. But it shouldn't be this way.

I'm in favor of whatever method works best to heal a sick animal. And often that means using common sense. When things seem right, but feel wrong, that's when that internal warning voice pipes up, and I tell my clients to pay attention to that voice. Although the practice of medicine may seem complex and mysterious—especially when delving into the more arcane traditions of Chinese medicine—I encourage my clients to ask questions. When they understand what is happening, we are better able to make a plan that can work to truly benefit their animal, using rational, thoughtful care.

This kind of integrative approach provides me with an array of powerful treatment options—and I need all of them because I deal with so many animals, and different species, each with its own variety of potential ailments.

Wild health is such a powerful concept because it defines the elements that are essential to the way all animals thrive—and illuminates what so often makes them sick.

Mammals breathe in the oxygen that is created by plant life and then breathe out the carbon dioxide that plants need to survive. In this and many other ways, all animals, no matter how evolved, depend on and are sustained by their environment. When an animal is nourished by a natural diet, given a natural amount of exercise, and allowed to behave in a way that is natural to the species, it has a much better chance for health and happiness—the way nature intended.

That does not mean that your pet cannot thrive in your seventeenth-floor apartment. He can, provided you educate yourself on how best to provide for his natural needs and tendencies. Domestication has taken the sting out of leaving nature behind. Being fed and loved is not a bad deal for our house animals. However, don't throw away the owner's manual Mother Nature provided. You'll need it for your pet's sake.

Genetic variations and innate behaviors serve a purpose. For example, stripes on a zebra may seem like an extravagance, but they camouflage and confuse predators that are trying to pick a spot to attack in a herd.

Because of the need to find food, a hunting lion "exercises" during the search and the chase. If dinner is delivered right to them, their musculature suffers. Foot health in an elephant is dependent on long foraging walks to find their food. Elephants that stay too long in one place are found to have foot problems, which can be quite serious.

Every enduring species finds its place and the food that keeps it healthy. Giraffes got tall while monkeys got small—both to get to the top of trees. Each species has a way of life that supports health and reproduction from every angle. With the loss of just a couple of crucial elements from that way of life, a species can disappear. Rhinos in a shrinking habitat are not reproducing well. The river otter could not tolerate the poor

Here's a bunny example. Say you have decided to bring home a cute little rabbit for your children. What could go wrong? The guy at the pet store has probably told you to buy a type of hay called timothy, which has the proper balance of minerals for a rabbit (better than alfalfa, for example), and fresh greens and vegetables for your new pet and provide him with a cozy enclosure. You've got that covered. However, there is a very real possibility that your new bunny, who is by nature a prey animal, will think he is about to be eaten every time you or one of your kids tries to pick him up—until he becomes used to you. Why is that important? Because stress is bad for health and the rabbit could actually break its own back in a panicked attempt to escape.

We must remember that our pets are animals first and they come hardwired with predispositions, traits, and behaviors. Ignoring these can be dangerous and put the health of your animal at risk.

Prospective bunny owners: take it slow, speak gently, firmly support his back and legs when picking him up, nibble a couple of carrots together, then get cuddly.

water quality of our polluted rivers, and was lost in many areas. On the hopeful side, as we reconnect animals with what nature can provide for them, we see some species rebounding.

Determining what is essential for health and what is optional is a large part of wildlife and zoo medicine. It is also integral to my practice.

There are absolute rules and there are optional considerations that do not necessarily have to become part of your pet's daily life. Life with a pet should be fun, allow for playful impulses, and encourage healthy randomness.

> *Nature balances disparate forces. It may be that the struggle itself is what the earth has to offer us—our survival needs and our health may be inextricably entwined.*

So, what does wild health look like? You will know it when you see it. A wildly healthy animal looks bright-eyed, bushy-tailed with a lustrous coat, sleek, and vibrant. The mark of well-being is unmistakable. A wildly healthy animal truly does exude vitality.

I have been visited by a fox several times at my home. It is impossible not to notice his sovereign confidence and vigor when he hangs out in my front yard. Certainly, there is no mistaking him for a tame animal. He had no set mealtimes or fleece-lined bed. Even my five-year-old daughter knew he wasn't a dog. The fluid stride and purposeful gait set him apart. He was unfettered, free, full of life, and wildly healthy.

Bobbi the zebra has since passed away, but I know she benefited from the Royal Treatment. After the fourth acupuncture treatment, I read in the zookeeper's log: "No seizures for over a month."

# WHEN BEST INTENTIONS
# DON'T PAVE THE WAY
# TO HEALTH

— ♛ —

*A myriad of troubling signs in an animal*
*can be 80 percent diet-related.*

JUST BECAUSE WE *CAN* USE NEW TECHNOLOGIES DOESN'T MEAN WE *should*. I know this from years of treating my patients, but it struck home as a result of a personal experience with my own dog, Orion.

Orion was a large white German shepherd/Labrador mix. He looked like a polar bear. Unfortunately, he suffered from hip dysplasia. Before he was even one year old, I had put Orion through three surgeries. At the time, I believed I was doing the best thing for him; after all, I was taking the medical advice from the top veterinarians at my vet school.

Four of the eight puppies in Orion's litter had bad hips. Although they never underwent hip surgery, Orion's brother and sisters had fewer joint problems and outlived him. Their owners couldn't afford the surgeries and treatments. Instead they did what they could to maintain joint health at home—they kept the dogs thin and well exercised.

I, on the other hand, was given a vet student discount for the surgeries. Orion was fed the most current and veterinary recommended commercial dry food. It was very high in carbs in the form of corn and wheat.

He received a procedure called a triple pelvic osteotomy, in which both hips were realigned and implanted with metal plates. I made sure he was vaccinated annually for everything. At the time, I didn't realize that these measures may have been contributing to the inflammation in his joints and actually accelerating their deterioration. Today I would have handled Orion's treatments differently. In retrospect, I suspect that my medical choices contributed to his early death.

My Orion, the white hunter, died prematurely of bone cancer at the age of eight. Realigning bone and placing metal implants is not a benign procedure. There is evidence that implants in the bone affect circulation and healing and possibly contribute to cancer. Back then, I never thought twice about the surgeries, and never considered a less invasive, nonsurgical approach for his genetically flawed hips. Today I would have a wholly different thought process. I would have managed his vaccines, medications, and joint condition using an integrative approach. If I had done so back then, perhaps Orion might have lived to sixteen years old, as his brother did.

In certain cases, however, surgery may be the only option. A client came to me for a second opinion after seeing several doctors to treat Bella, her seven-month-old puppy, who had a painful injured leg. She told me the diagnosis was a sprain, but somehow it didn't make sense to her. The dog was in such pain no matter what position she was in—lying down, standing up, limping around—she would shake and flinch if you came near her. Her sweet, happy puppy had changed overnight into this cowering, agonized creature. Sprains can be painful, yes, but not to that degree. The owner's common sense spoke to her and told her it was something more. Watching a dog in that much pain was unbearable to both of us.

> *Serious pain requires serious assessment. A high priority in veterinary medicine is alleviating pain.*

After multiple radiographs emailed from one specialty clinic to another, all the vets still insisted it was a sprain. But I couldn't let it go. Despite test results and the best of intentions, this dog was still in tremendous pain. I made one last-ditch effort. I phoned an old orthopedic vet friend and asked him to look at the X-rays. He called back quickly and said, "It's subtle, but it's a slipped physis. She'll need surgery." I felt a sense of relief. The dog's traumatic injury had displaced the sensitive growth plate (physis) at the end of the femur bone—which is painful but repairable. I could finally relax, as I was confident that the surgery would be successful. Bella would recover and live a normal life.

> *When you have exhausted all possibilities,*
> *remember this—you haven't.*
> —THOMAS EDISON

Exhausting all the wrong possibilities, even with the best intentions, can have a terrible outcome.

The most unnecessarily sick young dog I've ever seen was a German shepherd named Moonshine. Her cascade of serious problems seemed impossible, especially in one so young. She was barely a year old the first time I treated her.

Everything about Moonshine was the opposite of what would be expected in a young female German shepherd. She was a great dog with a great name who had great parents. But she was not feeling great in any way. She looked like one of my geriatric patients instead of a puppy. And her wonderful owners were impoverished by her medical bills. After they left my clinic that first day, I had to go into the back room and weep.

I was reminded of my early days as a veterinarian, when I was distressed about a trauma case. Raf, a senior tech, had taken me aside and said, "Barb, you need to get a man-heart!" He had a strong accent and a kind, man-heart himself. He worried about my ability to be dispassionate.

I knew what he meant. But in this situation, even a man-heart couldn't have stopped my tears.

In the exam room, Moonshine had flopped down on the floor like a marionette whose strings had been cut. She didn't have the energy to be interested in anything, including me. (And most dogs tell me I have a great personality.) The fur on most of Moonshine's face was missing. Her body's hair coat was a patchwork of random dry hair, dandruff, and balding areas. She was potbellied and moderately overweight. Cauliflower-like growths covered her tongue and gums and her feet. Fist-sized calcified lumps on her shoulders and hips had recently abscessed. One was draining a foul-smelling thick tan liquid. Her left foot and ankle were swollen and hot. The fur around her rear end smelled like feces. The owners told me that she had never had normal stools.

The owners were a young, hardworking couple named Sara and Paul. Paul was the one who brought her in that first time. His haggard face reflected the pain of Moonshine's illnesses and his sadness over the fact that he was sure they were losing her. He took a deep breath before starting in on the sad story. They had spent thousands of dollars and seen several doctors, but she was not responding to any treatment. They were thinking seriously about euthanasia when a receptionist at their vet clinic had recommended they come and see me. She had been to one of my lectures and had heard my clients describing how I often helped in situations that seemed hopeless. And Moonshine was the poster dog for difficult cases. "Before you decide," the receptionist had said, "get a second opinion from Dr. Royal."

We discussed Moonshine's medications, including an immunosuppressive medication, steroids, antibiotics, and pain meds. Paul described the taxing schedule of waking up at 4 A.M. every day so that he and his wife could give the drugs to Moonshine according to the prescriptions. Paul, a fireman, and Sara, a radiologist, both worked full days and then struggled to keep up with the care of this dog that they both obviously loved. Many diets and prescription foods had been tried, but Moonshine never responded to them well. She suffered from chronic gastrointestinal distress.

Paul recited a litany of her diseases: MRSA (methicillin-resistant *Staphylococcus aureus*), osteomyelitis, demodectic mange, inflammatory bowel disease, calcinosis cutis, generalized muscle-wasting, anorexia, arthritis, abscesses, joint malformation, urine and fecal incontinence, and the worst case of viral papilloma anyone had ever seen. This relatively benign virus usually causes small papillomas, or cauliflower-like growths on the gums or tongue, which tend to disappear on their own. In her case, the growths were so numerous that she was having trouble walking. A vet had surgically removed seventeen of them from her feet. Because of the growths on her tongue and lips and the open sores in her mouth, she could barely eat.

MRSA, a frighteningly resistant yet increasingly common bacteria, had led to a serious bone infection in Moonshine's left rear leg. That was the reason her leg was swelling. A bone infection of this kind can be deadly and was one of the reasons for the several antibiotics she was on. As a matter of fact, when I started seeing Moonshine, she was on fourteen different medications/supplements: chloramphenicol (strong antibiotic), enrofloxacin (antibiotic), metronidazole (gastrointestinal antibiotic), omeprazole (gastric reflux/proton pump inhibitor), mirtazipine (antidepressant, used as appetite stimulant in animals), prednisone (corticosteroid to treat her inflamed bowel), azothioprine (an immunosuppressive drug also used in organ transplants), oxychlorine compound spray (against MRSA infections), omega 3 and 6 fatty acid supplement (antioxidant), tramadol (a narcotic-like pain-reliever), ondansetron (to prevent nausea and vomiting caused by medications or chemo), Mitaban dips (baths to kill mites), vitamins, and probiotic capsules.

There were medicines to help her immune system fight the infections, and some that suppressed her immune system. There were medications to kill mites, and some that caused overgrowth of mites. The medication to help her pain and make it easier to walk also caused her to be nearly completely sedated. The extensive medication chart the owners showed me was like something out of NASA. No wonder pharmaceutical companies are thriving.

> *Some medical treatments can exacerbate conditions and suppress normal immune response.*

Her skin had a condition called demodectic mange, which is hair loss as a result of mites. A normal inhabitant of the skin, demodex mites are kept at bay by a healthy immune system. But sick animals and animals on immunosuppressants such as prednisone can develop demodectic mange. The weekly Mitaban dips, used to treat mange, made Moonshine so ill that she was hospitalized for a few days after each treatment. She had already had four dips and vets said she still needed five more. Paul and Sara were terrified about doing them again.

Although Moonshine was on steroids and a chemo drug to decrease inflammation in her GI tract, she had chronic loose stools. Surgical biopsies of her GI tract had confirmed an inflammatory bowel condition. I could have told them without surgery that her bowel was inflamed.

In addition, the medications made her drink and urinate excessively. Keeping up with her need to go out was difficult; she had many accidents in the house. The steroids had also caused calcinosis cutis, or golf-ball-sized firm, calcified lumps, under the dermal layer on her hips and shoulders. Calcified lumps would appear at the site of any trauma to the skin.

> *Faulty thinking can compound signs of ill health.*

Paul and Sara were exhausted and discouraged. The surgeries, medications, and hospitalization were terribly expensive. And no one knew why she wasn't responding to all this medical care. They were not sure how much more they could do. I knew the goal was to do less, much less, and let Moonshine's natural immune system do more. I just had to uncover her immune system.

I went over the multiple diagnoses in my head. It was like recalling a medical textbook. I looked up at them and said gently, "Let's not forget there's an animal here—not just those diseases—and her name is Moonshine." Paul tried to hold back his tears. I felt like crying with him.

We had our work cut out for us. After just a fecal test and an in-house blood test, we uncovered two curable factors contributing to her severe imbalances. We found giardia, a debilitating fecal parasite, in her fecal sample. We also found that her thyroid function was severely low. A comprehensive plan to restore and maintain her health was the next step. And we did have several things in our favor. Youth was on her side, and even in her exhausted state I sensed hidden stores of energy that could be tapped. And we had more tools than the average veterinary clinic.

No amount of antibiotics, hospitalization, or supplements can stop any serious infection if the body's own immune system can't pitch in. The body needs soldiers to fight the war. Without a defensive army, there may be plenty of ammunition but no one to guide it. Restoring health requires appropriate nutrition and all systems go—endocrine, circulation, and immune—as well as a working metabolism.

Moonshine may have started out with a bad genetic throw of the dice, but she was also being hobbled by a parasite, and the side effects and secondary diseases from a poor diet and all the medications she was on. In addition, she had none of the advantages of her own natural healing powers because of her undiagnosed, severely low thyroid function. Normal thyroid function would work to help fight these infections and regulate her GI function and development. The side effects from the medications to treat those infections were also taking their toll on her compromised immune system.

*Healing is all about timing.*

I decided which medicines I could safely wean her off of to improve her immune system. We needed to rebuild this puppy from her scarred toes to her naked nose. Unlike conventional medicine, integrative medicine adroitly manages Western and Eastern supplements to improve the immune system and support innate healing.

> *Uncovering the onset of disease,*
> *instead of naming the disease, is half the battle.*

## Moonshine's Royal Treatment

🐾 Diet change—from kibble to pre-prepared raw foods (Stella and Chewy's and Darwin's brands)

🐾 Panacur for her giardia parasite

🐾 Bath and sanitary haircut over her rear

🐾 Full Hemopet thyroid panel (Moonshine had never been properly tested) to fully determine her thyroid status

🐾 Acupuncture

🐾 Warm compresses on left rear leg

🐾 Dimethyl sulfoxide (DMSO) absorbs quickly through the skin and is anti-inflammatory, antioxidant, and an analgesic—specifically effective in breaking down calcified lesions

🐾 Discontinue immunosuppressive medication

🐾 Decrease other medications one by one

🐾 Discontinue Mitaban dips

🐾 Add supplements to support immune and liver function, thyroid, skin, and GI health

As it turned out, Moonshine exceeded all my expectations. Literally one week into her new treatment healing regimen, the owners came in with a changed dog. With the new diet of pre-prepared raw food and just a few supplements, she had normal stool. She was much more energetic; she even played with their other dog. And the full thyroid results hadn't even come back. The owners seemed stunned. They almost couldn't believe that a noninvasive treatment, involving fewer medications, had caused such a quick, dramatic improvement in Moonshine. For me the transformation was more than what I had hoped for. It was a great sign. Her body was stepping up to the plate, and the plate was filled with what she needed.

Two weeks later, her thyroid supplement on board, Moonshine bounded into the clinic. With unbridled energy and enthusiasm, she ran back to my desk to find me. My entire staff, while accustomed to radical turnarounds, was astonished. I only had to look at all the smiling faces to fully appreciate the impact Moonshine's recovery was having on all of us.

I was particularly struck with how Moonshine's owners appeared.

## OVERWHELMED WITH GOOD AND BAD INFORMATION?

When evaluating a plan of action for your pet's health, answer these questions:

- 🐾 Is it working?
- 🐾 Do you have enough time, information, and money to feasibly follow the plan?
- 🐾 Is there an overwhelming amount of conflicting information about the treatment?
- 🐾 Does it make sense to you on a basic level?
- 🐾 Are you constantly worrying and wishing that there were a better course of action?

Their haggard look had been replaced with a glow. They were relaxed enough to joke with each other. Their Moonshine was a new dog. She was recovering against all odds—and the odds against her were formidable, and to my mind, almost entirely human-created. She nuzzled her nose into everything, and acted her puppy age for the first time. She had become the bright Moonshine that nature intended her to be.

The owners were thrilled by her progress in the next two weeks, but three weeks later her condition took a new turn. She looked terrific in every way except for her left rear leg, which had an open sore, right over the MRSA-infected bone, oozing blood-tinged, foul-smelling pus. I cultured the sore and found an arsenal of scary bacteria. Was she regressing?

I explained to Moonshine's owners that the body has its own ways to rid itself of infection. The sores could, in fact, be yet another sign of improvement. It was similar to her hair coat growing in, weight loss, improved energy, and normal stools for the first time in her life. In the face of everything going in the right direction, I could not believe this sign was a cause for worry. She was so much better overall. We repeated X-rays to rule out something more sinister in the underlying infected bones. The bone integrity looked the same and maybe even a little better. We would monitor her closely, but we weren't going to add any medications or change course just yet.

Paul asked me a long question that had a short answer. He asked why it was that Moonshine had been treated for so many diseases, biopsied, and shown to have irritable bowel disease and would need to be on medication the rest of her life, but now, within a few weeks of seeing me, her stool was normal without medication, her hair was growing back, her papilloma growths were completely gone, we were weaning her off other medications, and she was a completely different, healthy dog.

My answer was that the body wants to heal. "We gave her the tools it needed to heal itself," I said as I showed him how to place warm packs over the leg where the ulcer was.

Over the next few days, the sore finished seeping. We did one more culture of the areas where the MRSA was. This time there was not a single horrifying bacterium to be found. The MRSA infection seemed to have resolved. However, I still wanted her to remain on antibiotics for a few more weeks.

Six weeks later, Moonshine glowed with health. The hair on her face and body had regrown, her foot swelling was gone, and the calcified lumps on her shoulders were barely noticeable. Today she is beautiful, energetic, bouncy, and affectionate. When her owners Paul and Sara cry, it is for joy.

Moonshine had been on the brink of death, and the aggressive state-of-the-art interventions of Western medicine not only couldn't save her, but they hastened her decline. In her case, it was time to take a step back to activate and support her body's own healing capacity.

## The Royal Treatment Approach

- 🐾 Good species-appropriate diet
- 🐾 Assess the underlying systems that support the health of the pet
- 🐾 Assess all body functions
- 🐾 Assess proper mental, physical, and emotional stimulation
- 🐾 Minimize meds where possible
- 🐾 Weigh treatment options carefully
- 🐾 Use pharmaceutical medicines or invasive procedures only when other options are exhausted or in emergencies

When faced with a medical decision about your pet, ask

- 🐾 What has obstructed the natural wild health in my pet?
- 🐾 What can I provide that will further the health in my pet?
- 🐾 Is medical intervention necessary?

- Is what I'm doing working?
- Is what I'm doing too expensive/time-consuming/ exhausting?
- Would it be better to use an alternative approach?
- Can I improve on my pet's nutrition?
- Do we need to act quickly or is there time for more slow-acting measures?

The more we understand wild health, the more we will be able to discern which medical interventions are necessary, which are not necessary, and what the alternatives are.

> *No intervention can sustain health without a proper foundation that activates an animal's own healing systems.*

On the other hand . . .

Clara and Michael's first words to me were "We came to you because we refuse to use any more Western medicine for Forrest." Their Chinese crested dog had been having fifteen seizures per day since June. It was November. Forrest was frail and nervous and didn't make any eye contact. He had two mild seizures during our initial hourlong visit. Clara and Michael didn't think that I could help, but they were still hoping for a miracle from alternative medicine. Forrest had been given his annual rabies, distemper combo, and leptospirosis vaccines in June. Several days later the seizures started. A neurology specialist started him on phenobarbitol and then recently added potassium bromide (KBr) for his seizures, but they continued unabated. No one knew why they had even started.

I had to explain to Clara and Michael why integrating Western medicine with an alternative approach was the best way forward. I treated him the way I treat vaccine reactions. The thrust of the treatment was to stop inflammation and to detoxify the system. I continued giving the pheno-barbitol but stopped the KBr because it didn't seem that either of them was really working anyway. I planned to slowly wean Forrest off the pheno-barb as well. I added one more Western medication: prednisone, a strong anti-inflammatory agent. It can be used to help decrease an inflammatory response, in this case to vaccines. It had been a long time since June, but I had to try.

From my alternative bag I used: acupuncture, homeopathic detox sup-plements (thuja and lyssin), liver support for detox (milk thistle, turmeric, and omega-3 fatty acid), and an anti-inflammatory diet (Darwin's com-mercial raw dog food).

Within one week Forrest was having fewer than one seizure per day. Within two weeks they had completely stopped. We slowly decreased the phenobarbitol and even then he had no seizures.

His behavior changed, he became more sociable and energetic, and became more interested in playing with his brother. It took a mix of West-ern medications and alternative medicine to help fix the problems caused by Western medications. I believe in using what works.

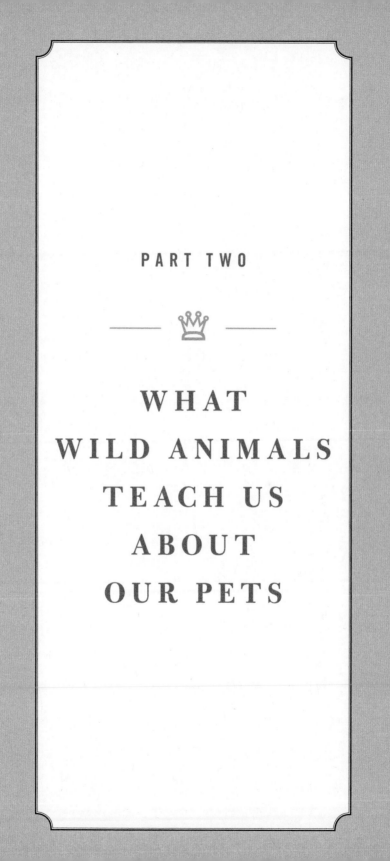

# PART TWO

# WHAT WILD ANIMALS TEACH US ABOUT OUR PETS

# HOOT

♛

W E HAD TO LOCATE THE BABIES BEFORE DARK. THERE WASN'T much time. But we couldn't start our search until twilight because owls are nocturnal. I leaped over mossy logs in the dimly lit forest, barely able to see where I was going, as I ran downhill alternately scanning the skies and the foliage. It was hard to believe, but I was actually following an owl as he flew to his nest, with my mouse in his talons. I panicked every time he darted out of view. The altitude and the breakneck pace at which I ran made it hard to breathe, but I couldn't stop.

I smelled the humid soil and decaying branches under my pounding feet. Everything was a shade of green or brown as I rushed onward. I knew it was dangerous to run while looking upward, but I didn't care. There was no other way to do it.

Earlier that afternoon, the leaders of our group explained our search and banding mission. We were part of a team whose goal was to protect the spotted owl, a highly endangered species, and their whole habitat by registering active nests so that the immediate surrounding area would be considered protected from loggers. Instead of the loggers clear-cutting the whole forest, the trees around a registered nest would be legally protected.

I had imagined that a government program in this day and age would certainly be equipped with some kind of fancy GPS satellite or thermography tools. After all, a forest is pretty vast, and this was an important project, but I was mistaken. The equipment we used was anything but high-tech. We were given a faded and overfolded terrain map, owl banding equipment, a couple of beat-up walkie-talkies, a plastic tub with a few mice in it, and some makeshift ropes on sticks.

The woman in charge, Diane, was surprisingly small for leading such risky business. She spoke softly while we walked, issuing brief instructions in matter-of-fact tone. Her words were clear, the mission impossible.

"We will climb to the densest part of the mountain forest." (Sounds easy.)

"We will call the male owl." (Even owls have cell phones?)

"You will offer him the mouse by holding it on your arm." (Owls take mice from strangers?)

"He will bring the mouse to his family's nest." (What if he's hungry and wants it himself?)

"We will follow him to his nest." (Perhaps a pocket helicopter, James?)

"We will take the birds down from the nest and band them." (Climb a lodgepole pine, with angry parents clawing at us?)

"We will put the birds back." (Back up the tree? Oh dear.)

She paused and started hiking more quickly. She offered one last instruction over her shoulder as she disappeared around a boulder, "By the way, be careful to avoid any loggers." (Noted.)

Yes, it all sounds as easy as falling off a log, I thought, as I hopped over one. I followed Diane up the mountain, too busy trying to catch my breath to ask any more questions, but feeling game for our quest.

Diane carried the small tub of sacrificial mice. I tried not to look, but I could hear them moving about inside. I hoped that they had enjoyed a great life until they signed up for this gig. Since I was a new recruit, I wasn't told to carry much. Still I could barely keep up. The team with all the banding equipment was posted partway up the mountain, awaiting our signal.

Once we were high up in the thick of the mountain forest, we stopped climbing and started calling the owls. Turns out it's called "hooting up" the owls. We were, in fact, pretending to be an interloping male owl trying to establish a territory. The theory is that if another owl is in the vicinity, he will answer vociferously. He will tell the unwelcome visitor to move on. A hooting war will ensue. Diane showed me how to cup my hands to my mouth in order to mimic the sonorous hooting tone. She offered a few other tips and we began hooting.

We'd been hooting on and off for about two minutes when, as if by magic, we heard an answer. I was stunned at how quickly the reply had come. We challenged him again, and he came in closer to explain his boundaries. A few more hoots and we could see his silhouette on a distant branch. We changed languages and started speaking mouse to him, as best we could. This made him forget about fighting. Instead he wanted to be the first owl to get to the mouse.

Diane quickly had me put on the long leather falconer's glove and deftly handed me a volunteer mouse. With the mouse on my outstretched arm, it was presumed the owl would notice that dinner was served.

And notice he did. Miraculously, the father owl silently appeared right above me in a nearby tree. I love how they do that; their wings make no noise. They have evolved a unique interlocking feather system that keeps their flight perfectly silent, even to mouse ears. I could see his dilemma. His head moved slightly left to right as he eyed the mouse on my arm. Mouse, stranger, mouse, stranger. Evidently I'm not that threatening, because the decision was made in a matter of seconds. My breath stopped as the owl swooped down and perched on my hand. Holding perfectly still, I braced myself for impact, but I was amazed at how imperceptible his landing was.

He was smaller than I had expected: only about a foot tall and weighing in at what had to have been less than a pound. But I knew that without the glove, his talons would have made a big impression. The owl wasted no time collecting his prize. With a spin of his agile head, he looked down, grabbed the mouse firmly with his toes, and spread his wings. I was incredulous. Prior training had taught me that none of this should have happened. Who knew that a wild *Strix occidentalis caurina* would accept takeout from a Chicagoan?

There was a millisecond after he took the mouse in his sharp talons—and before he took off noiselessly into the sky—when he cocked his head and looked me straight in the eye. He was less than a foot away from my face. I half-expected him to say, "Thanks, Barb." He was both completely wild and completely comfortable interacting with me. I was riveted by his beauty. His round, brown head was spotted with white and framed at the top by a pronounced widow's peak. Many rows of feathers, circles inside circles, held two shiny black eyes, slowly blinking. His face was expressionless but full of intent.

There is a palpable difference between bird-watching and having a bird watch you. I had thought I was the only observer, but his penetrating gaze gave me much to think about.

As I was drawn into his gaze, I felt a connection with him, the thick forest around us, and everything in it. We were all on the same frequency as the earth.

However fleeting, this moment shifted everything. I was pierced by how perfectly the owl fit into his environment. Looking directly into his eyes, I saw deep into the forest and sensed the profound relation between him and his food, his evolution, and our planet. These elements should not, and could not, be separated from any animal. This moment was quiet and personal and somehow took me outside myself. It set in motion a change in me that I didn't have time to contemplate then. I could only think about the gust of air under his wings as he took flight. The chase was on.

It was quite a scene. Diane and I crashed through the forest pursuing the small, silent owl. Just before it was too late, I caught sight of a stump that would have felled me for sure. I recovered, but I had lost sight of our owl, and worse yet, Diane. Not only was she familiar with the area and more agile than a wood nymph, but she was carrying the maps.

I had to run even faster. But there were two ways down, one steep and one more gradual, and I didn't know which one Diane had taken. The muffling effect of the forest was intense. I opted for the steeper incline, knowing how efficient biologists can be. Careening down, I was relieved to spot the owl again.

I heard a steady crunching of feet up ahead, which I hoped were Diane's and not an angry ax-wielding logger's. The day before, we had found a dead adult owl nailed to a sign that read: "Save The Spotted Owls." Not surprisingly, we were very unpopular in this community because our efforts to save the owls affected the livelihood of the loggers.

The noise was, in fact, coming from Diane. I found her directly under the spotted-owl nest. There on the branch above us were the two parents. The father had the mouse, lifeless now, still in his clutches. Three white fluffy chicks with pointed feet teetered upon the tree limb. Jackpot! Diane radioed our coordinates to the guys with the banding equipment. They arrived in moments.

The instrument meant to bring the baby owls down from their tree was rudimentary at best. It was essentially a long telescoping stick rigged with a sliding noose at the end. When they first described it to me, I misheard and thought they'd said a "sliding moose." Now I felt that neither noose nor moose could possibly accomplish what was required. These were wild birds, and I was sure they would easily evade our caveman tools. But the simple tool was, in the end, the most effective, and the least distressing to the little birds to boot.

The stick was raised up to the branch where the white balls of fluff were lined up. The noose was gently placed under the shoulders and cinched tight enough to hold the baby bird without affecting his breathing. Then, unbelievably, we plucked them off the branch and brought them down, one by one.

The birds sat there, unmoving, wide-eyed and calm at the same time, slowly blinking as if watching a mildly interesting bug crawling by. They did not step away or look alarmed as the noose was lowered over their heads and over their brothers'. They didn't struggle as the crude elevator descended to the ground floor. Slowly swiveling their heads, they observed, but only in an uninterested way. Each retrieval proceeded in this manner. Oddly, the parents were as unconcerned about our presence as their offspring. I suppose it was because we had brought the main course.

All three youngsters had Disney-large eyes and soft, white, feathery bodies. The only feature that spoke of the clever night predator they would become was the large sharp-clawed feet that were much like an adult's. I felt an urge to put a little owl in my pocket and call it a day. But then he vomited.

Vomiting up a "cast" of unneeded animal bits is a normal physiologic function in the owl. These are bits the owl can't or doesn't need to digest—mouse fingers, skulls, vegetation and such—all bound in a neat little package. Evidently, looking at me made this little fellow feel the need to show-and-tell.

The cast was admired by the biologists, who immediately saved it in a baggie. We took several measurements and did a quick general examination. The keel (chest area) was well muscled, indicating that the parents were making a good living in this forest and keeping their kids well fed. A few flight feathers peeked through the fluffy undercoat like porcupine quills held in clear tubes. These owls were basically teenagers. They were not quite ready to leave the nest but were on the verge of gaining the power to glide.

We carefully banded the leg using a colorful blue band with ID numbers on it. Their legs were near adult size, and the band, with a little extra room, would not harm the leg as it grew. Like a clue in a whodunit, the bands would make it easier to trace what had happened to a banded bird if it was sighted or found injured or dead. And we could collect all the workaday scientific information about how they live their lives: neighborhood choices, travel destinations, vacation homes, and favorite dining spots. All part of the small task of saving this species and the entire ecosystem in which they live.

Sporting the new ID tag, each owl was placed back in the noose and slowly elevated back up the tree, where, once his feet hit the branch, he perched again. The other two fledglings, inches away, watched without emotion. I imagined the conversation among them.

*"The aliens took me. Gave me this bracelet."*

*"Big deal. I got one too."*

But this was a big deal to me. A wild owl had just landed on my arm! The experience was exactly the opposite of what I expected. It was extraordinary. When I was hurtling along, up was down. The unexpected, ordinary. The clumsy humans, gentle. The impossible, easy. The small, infinite. Just when you think you have learned everything, you haven't.

A month earlier I had been working at the Woodland Park Zoo in Seattle, and this expedition seemed to be just what I was looking for. I was always uncomfortable with animals in cages, but I relished the idea of being in their natural habitat. I wanted to be in their world rather than with them in ours. I had anticipated a distant view of mature owls and a lot of work with computers. I knew it was unlikely that I, personally, would actually find a nest in the great wilderness. But I eagerly anticipated the chance to try.

Turns out, it was a mind-bending event. My perspective on the world had been deeply altered. I had an insider's view of the world of the spotted owl, and I was overjoyed.

As we headed back toward the cabin, the disarray of the forest seemed suddenly manageable. We might actually do some good here. My step was light. I was barely aware of the many scrapes and bruises I had accumulated. My neck was stiff, but I hardly noticed it. It was dark now, and even the full moon didn't illuminate our forest path much. It only added contrast and deeper shadows.

We kept our voices subdued, not wanting to provoke any angry loggers, but I noticed my body was expressing my jubilation and delight for me. I was skipping down the mountainside. Did I mention a wild owl had just landed on my arm?

# COCO THE MONKEY
# AND WONDER BREAD

*It makes more sense to prevent crippling diseases
through proper nutrition than to treat them
after they occur.*

I ONCE WORKED FOR AN ADVERTISING OFFICE IN CHICAGO. However, even then my real passion was for animals. I had been volunteering as a docent every Saturday at Chicago's Lincoln Park Zoo when I heard there was a part-time position available in the zoo hospital. I joked about quitting my fancy Michigan Avenue job and working there instead. In addition to being totally impractical (it paid roughly one-eighth of my ad agency salary), the job required substantial zoo experience, and I didn't have any.

On my way home I often chatted with Abe, a crossing guard for the local school. He seemed to be one of the only people who knew I was serious when I talked about the zoo job. I didn't have any plan to apply, but Abe knew it was my dream. One day I said to him, "Well, just two more days to apply!" He smiled, and replied, "You should wake up and make your dream happen."

At work the next day, we spent forty-five minutes discussing whether the umbrella in an advertisement should lean to the left or to the right. Suddenly the colorful storyboards seemed utterly inconsequential to me. I stood up quietly, collected my things, and left the room. I went straight to my boss's office and told him I was quitting.

In the interview, the doctors told me that keeping animal records would be the most important part of my duties. And that the job was part-time, with no benefits and no guarantees. It wasn't glamorous but I wanted it with a passion that surprised me. Almost as much as their decision to offer me the job surprised me.

Magically, the part-time job transformed into a full-time position and became my life. For the next four years, I sat at an old desk in the basement of the bunker-like building, which was built into the side of a hill. My chair faced the iron stairs that the staff used to walk down from the public area into the hospital proper. This gave me a key vantage point for observation.

Watching that downward-marching parade of zoo staff day after day—the feet, knees, bodies, and finally the faces of my colleagues—I learned the gait of everyone at the zoo. I could tell who was coming long before the whites of their eyes came into view. The rhythm of the boots, the way their weight shifted on each stair, hopping, plodding, limping, or marching: everyone was slightly different and singular in the way they moved. It was excellent training for my later life as a vet, in which I would assess the idiosyncrasies of ambulation in animals.

The first time I saw my husband, Matt, his Red Wing boots preceded him as they came down that same staircase. I noticed as he approached my desk that he was ruggedly handsome, but all I could think about was the box of peregrine falcons in his arms. He was bringing two injured fledglings to the zoo hospital for treatment. As one of the founding members in the Chicago Peregrine Release Program, he knew how to protect wildlife, even in a city. My professional and private lives were about to merge.

After our first meeting over the peregrines, we next saw each other at a zoo party. I was on the dance floor, and Matt asked my friend Peri who I was.

"She's too wild for you," Peri replied.

That didn't bother Matt. He was good at figuring out where wild things belong.

But on another day, I saw an unfamiliar pair of boots under two layers of pants coming down the stairs, and I couldn't recognize the thumping clang on the corrugated metal. Even stranger was that this new person—who was out of uniform, by the way—was holding a monkey. If this was a new keeper, I thought, he had a lot to learn.

Bringing primates into the zoo hospital required a special protocol. They could catch many of our diseases, and vice versa, so we were given plenty of advance warning and they usually arrived in a van at the back door. This unidentified keeper had come through a public area holding a brown primate like a baby. A huge zoo no-no. He was also unkempt and seemed to be about forty years old, pale white, skinny, and he wore a hat over his deep-set blue eyes. His clothes hung loosely on his thin frame. His jeans showed through under the shorter pair of torn khaki pants. His arms around the monkey seemed to be shaking.

I jumped up and raced to the door, but he was already inside the hall. He had obviously been crying and before I could ask what I could do for him, he told me his story. The previous fall he happened to be walking by a pet shop that was being raided by the police. The shop owner was releasing birds and animals out of a window. "Take this baby monkey," the owner said to him. I could imagine the mercenary shop owner's panic, considering that the fine for possessing smuggled primates was even stiffer than for other animals. The man who stood before me now had taken the tiny creature and run.

"He was only a baby then. I got him some milk and whatever I could find," he said, trying to smile.

Apparently the man was homeless, living in a cardboard box in the "Emerald City"—the long, winding underground thoroughfare lit with green lights near the Chicago River. Now his baby was a grown monkey and needed a better home. The monkey seemed sick, and the man admitted that he couldn't take care of him anymore.

"I don't have nothing else to feed him; I ran out of bread," he said, trying to pull the hat down to cover his eyes, which were filling with tears.

"What else was he eating?" I asked, looking at the tiny frame in his arms.

"Only Wonder Bread," he said proudly. "It's supposed to help build strong bones and teeth."

I tried to hide my horror. No matter how you may feel about Wonder Bread, it was not designed to fulfill 100 percent of the daily nutritional requirements of a baby monkey.

"He's not doing so well," the man continued. "He got real cold in the box with me at night—slept under my shirt. We share everything, but lately there hasn't been much. He hasn't been out of our box in a few weeks. He's stopped moving around much. Hard winter."

The monkey was in a crouched position, pressed against the man's chest. I saw that all his limbs were abnormal. They were gnarled like little twisted twigs and his joints were as swollen as an old person's, even though he was only about a year old. His black eyes moved quickly in his round monkey face, darting between my face and the man's.

"I love this monkey, but I can't take care of him," the man said. "His name is Coco. Please tell me you'll help."

I didn't see how this could end well, but I promised I would help.

On the one hand, it was a bad idea to take this monkey in and risk losing my job. Our policy was to just say no to any animal that came in off the street and to suggest an alternative solution. Long ago, you could bring an animal to the door of a zoo hospital and it might have been taken in, but things had changed. And I certainly was not the person authorized to make any exceptions for this monkey.

On the other hand, I wanted to help this sick animal as soon as I could.

I wanted to help him and the sad man as well. But before I could even find someone for advice, the man suddenly stepped toward me, pushed the bundle of monkey into my arms, ran out the door, flew up the steps, and was gone.

I could feel the little guy's heart racing, and suddenly he let out a moaning cry—he was staring at the empty staircase, missing his only friend. I thought Coco would try to escape, but then I realized that he was so stiff he couldn't unclench his swollen joints. He was frighteningly weightless and had a sparse hair coat, but his grip on my arm was impressively strong. This gave me hope, despite the fact that I was suddenly responsible for a severely malnourished spider monkey.

Monkeys, like many primates, are omnivorous and eat a mostly vegetarian diet, with several strict nutrient requirements. This monkey, living on only white bread, at a time when he should have been developing his agile body, was lucky to be alive.

Joel, the zoo technician, came out of the lab. With a sigh, and a look of despair, he said to me, "Well, well, well, what have we here . . ."

The next second, the hospital animal keeper, Susan, appeared from the commissary. Immediately she ushered Joel, Coco, and me into the treatment room. We grabbed a blanket and gently wrapped Coco in it. He looked desperate and afraid. As I looked at his knobby joints and nonexistent muscles, I didn't see how this monkey could ever recover his health.

"He's a disaster," Joel said. "It looks like he has scurvy and heaven knows what else."

I'm sure we were all thinking the same thought: that Coco should be put down. But none of us wanted that to happen. Transfixed by the intensity of Coco's gaze and the horror of his physical condition, we didn't notice that the door was open. Our boss, Dr. Wolff, one of the zoo vets, had come in. We were caught. Thankfully, Dr. Wolff took one look at Coco's thin hands clenching the blanket and his eyes wildly searching for help and decided we needed a plan to save the little monkey.

After hearing the full story, Dr. Wolff was suddenly optimistic. She had seen animals with scurvy, the vitamin C deficiency that was causing Coco's debilitated joints. Never this bad, she admitted, but Coco could recover. We didn't know the extent of any other health problems he may have had, but as Wolff examined him, we all felt encouraged.

One of the keepers was married to a woman named Beth, who had a sort of halfway house for wayward, unwanted exotic animals in her home. She had an old gymnasium on her property that she had revamped to keep the animals. She had all the permits and the skill, but would she take on such a desperate case?

Wolff finished her exam of Coco and found surprisingly few other issues—aside from the life-threatening emaciation and scurvy-deformed joints. We called Beth, who said she was willing to take Coco and would come to pick him up right away. Coco was fed and medicated, so we placed him in a cozy carrier and he was all ready to go.

We used our own moral code, and certainly bent or broke a number of rules that day. But we all felt how strong Coco's will to live was, and if there was a chance for any type of decent life here in an urban world, he was entitled to it.

When Beth arrived, we told her about Coco's initial diagnostics and treatments, including bland foods, probiotics, vitamin C, and appropriate food from the commissary to start her off. We engaged in a long discussion about the best diet, restoring the balance of his GI tract with foods like yogurt, and the need for plenty of vitamin C. We talked through physical therapy and what might be involved.

Beth had all kinds of equipment that would help Coco strengthen his muscles and bones. After six months of intensive physical therapy, a strict workout schedule, and a carefully prepared fresh diet at Beth's nurturing facility, Coco was finally able to walk. He was like a child to Beth and he soon became part of her traveling educational children's zoo.

Eventually as Coco made a full recovery, he became more relaxed and happy, and increasingly playful. He could climb anything, leap like an antelope, and he even learned to act a little silly—like a monkey. He was always gentle and sweet, and the homeless man's decision and Beth's determination had saved his life. And a little rule-breaking.

## CRACKERJACK

I treated a dog named CrackerJack. She was an adorable pit bull rescued from a hoarder. CrackerJack's legs reminded me of Coco's atrophied and clenched body. She had lived many months in a cage, eating only kibble, and not much of it. She was just over a year old and she walked like a geriatric. The foster owners didn't know what to do, and they discussed options with their vet, which included putting the dog down. He also recommended they contact me. After going through the exam, I told them the story of Coco, which gave them hope. CrackerJack's rehab protocol involved walking, while only partially submerged, in an underwater treadmill. This allows buoyancy to decrease weight on the legs so they can gently exercise without causing pain or injury. CrackerJack's diet was changed to raw food mixed with canned food to give her body what it needed to heal. Today, CrackerJack is a happy, social, healthy dog—her legs have straightened out and her joints are flexible. Again, given the proper nutrients, the body wants to heal, and most times, it will.

# WINDTUNNEL

Windtunnel is a sleek greyhound whose owner wishes she had known about proper canine nutrition years ago. This girl greyhound had been taken from the strenuous racing conditions of the track and put in a lovely home. There she was given every comfort and given a veterinary-approved "high-quality" kibble. She was also vaccinated, spayed, and received a teeth cleaning. Despite all of this, she developed many health issues. She became a picky eater, ate very little, and lost weight. She had chronic irritated, dry skin, allergies, dental problems, and a patchy hair coat, and she never seemed to enjoy her walks.

When I started treating Windtunnel, she was thin, nervous, and ratty-looking. She seemed to be an aging fifteen-year-old dog, although she was only seven. After just a few weeks of a high-protein raw food diet, her robust appetite for food and exercise was restored. She soon became well muscled again and regained a healthy hair coat. Her vitality also returned.

"Why didn't anyone ever mention nutrition to me before?" her owner asked me. "I feel bad knowing I could have done something so simple to help her."

Coco's story is a cautionary tale of what happens when an animal is fed a diet disastrously low in required species-specific nutrients, but it is also an encouraging example of animal resiliency. When animals are given the tools to heal, they often can. Even in the face of extreme debilitation, Coco regained his wild health.

> *There were no evolutionary changes in Coco that prepared him for the devalued food in a homeless urban life.*

I treat many patients with crippling joint disease, and it is often caused by a deficient diet. These conditions are no less treatable than Coco's were. With all the wheat and corn we feed our carnivores, it's no wonder our pets are sick. My question is, why are we feeding our pets the equivalent of Wonder Bread?

It's hard not to feel frustrated with the pet food industry and the hidden dangers of ignoring our pet's dietary needs. We can certainly do better. A rotten diet will spoil all of your best efforts to maintain your pet's health. Animals must be fed according to the requirements of their species. It's not "you are what you eat." It's "what you are dictates what you eat."

The power of an animal's biological determination to regain health cannot be underestimated. If your pet has health problems—even severe, life-threatening ones—and you make changes to a proper diet, you may see a remarkable turnaround. The prospects may seem dire, but there is hope. Recovery may be possible. And the key is often a proper diet.

# LIFE'S A ZOO

$\diamond$

*Always remain calm in a dire situation,*
*especially when an angry gorilla is in the room.*

I AM AN AVID SAILOR AND LOVE TO BE BY THE WATER. I DON'T LIKE the feeling of swimming upstream, though, and that's how my life felt before I became an integrative veterinarian. Now I am where I belong and I'm doing what I'm supposed to be doing. It took a while, but I realized that being a vet wasn't just what I wanted to do; it was what made me feel like I had a reason to be on the planet.

## Chicago, Lincoln Park Zoo, 1979

One cold morning in early fall, I was driving along Lake Shore Drive in my rusty Jetta. Lake Michigan was throwing a wavy fit to my left and the last tethered sailboats of the season were bobbing up and down frantically in the harbor. I took the Fullerton exit and headed for my parking spot in the back of the Lincoln Park Zoo's Animal Hospital. I felt at home there for so many reasons. Apparently one of my ancestors had designed the expansive outdoor gardens that fanned out from the main entrance, but the real reason I felt a sense of belonging was the animals and the people I worked with. I parked, pulled my sweatshirt hood over my head, jumped out into Chicago's celebrated wind, and headed into the zoo. Walking through the clinic door, I saw the head tech, Joel, walking toward me. He looked up and smiled. He knew what was coming. I did this every morning. "Man," I said, taking off my hood and shaking out my hair, "this place is a zoo."

Zoo work is not for everyone. Caring for these incredible animals is an intense responsibility. The animals can't choose their own food, habitat, or level of exercise, as they would in the wild. So it is the zookeeper's responsibility to provide the very best care in the face of the limitations of captivity. As a veterinarian, I feel a similar responsibility for dogs and cats.

A zoo is a great classroom for anyone who wants a career caring for animals. In the controlled yet unpredictable atmosphere of a zoo, there are lessons about life as well as about medicine to be learned. On one day, a zoo tech may have to fashion a breathing tube out of duct tape, straws, or an organ pipe for both a thumb-sized elephant shrew and an Asian elephant. No one makes these commercially, and animals in captivity need them. A zoo tech just has to do it.

Many zoo employees are torn between love for their work and the animals they care for and a feeling of guilt that the animals are held captive. Knowing that as the world shrinks so does the wild where animals would live helps to ease that conflict and deepens our responsibility for their care. For a select few species there is actually hope they may one day be able to return to the land where their species originally became extinct. Maintaining the health and the environment for captive animals that are extinct in the wild adds gravity to an already difficult situation.

There is always a lot to do on any given day at the zoo. Often keepers or zoo staff will come in on their days off to help with an animal transport or to provide extra hands for a medical procedure. We were happy to have several extra pairs the day we anesthetized Kundu, the largest silverback gorilla in the zoo's collection.

I had seen Kundu many times before. The keepers joked that he had a crush on me. One afternoon, as I passed by his enclosure, my boyfriend on my arm, Kundu went ape. He beat his chest and was clearly upset. The next time I saw him, he shyly averted his eyes, then placed his hand on the glass between us.

On this day, though, Kundu was due for his annual physical exam and blood work. Anesthesia is an extremely important part of safe zoo medicine. Keeping an animal asleep just long enough for the procedure to be finished, but not too long to cause harm, is the key. Generally this happens seamlessly, so we had photographers, keepers, vets, and techs looking on as we were administering anesthesia to this shockingly large, muscular primate.

We finished with the examination, measurements, and blood work. I was jotting down the last of my notes about the procedure for the hospital's records when, a few feet away, Kundu woke up. Dr. Meehan was leaning against Kundu's hip when Kundu suddenly sat up as if he were part of the conversation. He looked deep into the eyes of his vet, the man he hated most in the world, and who had recently darted him with a tranquilizer, and grabbed him by the arm.

Nobody moved or breathed, and I don't even remember being able to form a cohesive thought. In one silent motion, Joel, the head tech, injected more sedation into the gorilla's IV line. Several more motionless seconds passed as the gorilla and Dr. Meehan stared each other down. We all knew that sedative had to work. There was no quick escape from the room. I will never forget that moment. We had controlled the situation, up until that point, but how quickly we had lost it, and with potentially deadly results.

The sedation worked, and the silverback gorilla's eyes glazed over. He let go of Dr. Meehan and slumped back onto the table. Those of us standing closest to Kundu wanted to collapse, just like he had. But our job wasn't done. Without comment or hesitation, we finished our work before returning Kundu to his enclosure. Only then did Dr. Meehan say, "Nice needlework, Joel. I think I owe you a beer—or my life."

Conditions can change quickly during operations on wild animals. That's why it is so important to have a hardworking, trusted team. I learned to remain calm even in the most dire of situations—and to always be extra nice to technicians. These lessons are applicable to pet owners as well.

The greatest lesson I learned, though, from my time at Lincoln Park Zoo, was that I was on the right path in life. I knew without a doubt that I wanted to practice veterinary medicine. I wanted to learn everything I possibly could about caring for animals—of all kinds.

# DON'T MAKE
# THE RABBIT SCREAM

♛

*I have learned from wild and zoo animals—who could
have killed me if I had hurt them—that you don't
always have to cause pain to find the source of pain.*

RABBITS FREQUENTLY SUFFER FROM EAR INFECTIONS. THEIR FA-mous long, cute ears can be a problem area. In the wild, the pre-dominant ear invaders are mites. In pet rabbits common infections include bacteria and yeasts, as well as mites.

During vet school, I learned the typical protocol for dealing with ear infections. Take a sample from the ear; examine it under the microscope to find out what mite, bacteria, or yeast was to blame. Then clean out the crusty brown debris with an ear cleaner and cotton swabs and treat with appropriate medication.

In practice, however, I found out that this is not such a good idea. The action of rubbing and cleaning out the crusty brown debris is not only painful for the rabbit, but counterproductive. It may seem like it makes sense to clean the rabbit's ear. And it certainly provides a feeling of accom-plishment to remove aural gunk. But it really can be a form of torture, and making a rabbit scream feels like a crime. But vets do it anyway, because it is what we are taught to do. Eventually I decided to rethink this practice.

Rabbit ear tissue is extremely sensitive. Cleaning out the infected ear makes the ear, in fact, more raw and painful. The earwax system exists in order to push things out of the ears. The crusts, earwax, and discharge are beneficial because they move the infection out of the ear. I finally realized that it makes much more sense to help nature do its job than to go against it.

Now I rarely clean rabbits' ears, and never dig deep into the ear canal with a swab. I determine the culprit of the infection and start the drops, trusting in the capacity of the medication I've chosen and the rabbit's own immune system to restore equilibrium.

Whenever I am training a new tech, I teach them to go against their need to fully clean out the ears of dogs and cats. "Don't make the rabbit scream," I tell them. We all use this phrase in my clinic now. Feline and canine ear skin is not as sensitive as a rabbit's, but being gentle is still essential. Judiciously done, ear cleaning when needed can accelerate recovery.

## Cleaning Cat and Dog Ears

🐾 Clean the infected ear every other or every third day.

CLEANING METHOD
1. Apply and fill the ear canal with appropriate astringent ear cleaner.
2. Gently massage the base of the ear.
3. Stand back for a moment, because your pet is going to shake the fluid and some debris out of his ear.
4. Take cotton balls and wipe out what you can see in the ear—gently. Do *not* dig in with a cotton swab. Repeat if there is excessive debris.
5. If you are applying meds or other topical treatments, wait thirty minutes to let ear fully dry. This will ensure that the treatment is undiluted and will be more effective.

🐾 Always be gentle, even though dog and cat ears are not as sensitive as rabbit ears.

Early in my career, I watched an orthopedic specialist confirm for himself—three times—that a dog's lumbosacral pain was real by lifting that region and making him scream. The owner and I nearly screamed as well.

There are much more subtle and comfortable ways to locate pain. My technique is to move my hands along the animal's body, feeling the heat on the skin, and muscles for spasm and tension. It is not as dramatic, but it is effective.

In one clinic rotation we were taught a technique to locate spinal pain that some vets call "white-knuckling." This involves repeated, intense pressure placed on each vertebra. It becomes apparent when the animal screams or flinches which vertebra has an issue. This is a standard of practice, but when I lecture to veterinarians, I beg them not to do this. A lighter touch can often show just as much.

Painful areas are screaming—the animal doesn't need to. As owners and vets, our hands must be sensitive enough to "listen."

## Sign of Painful Areas

- 🐾 Increased heat on the skin's surface suggests recent injury
- 🐾 "Guarding," or when an animal repeatedly tenses the muscle as a hand moves gently toward a certain area
- 🐾 Decreased range of motion or lameness/gait change/weight shifting
- 🐾 Nervous head turn or moving to avoid contact with a certain area
- 🐾 Licking or chewing around the area
- 🐾 With some chronic conditions there can be significant decreased circulation and the affected area will feel cooler than surrounding areas
- 🐾 Note: Sometimes they're just ticklish, so don't overinterpret reactions

If an exam or medical procedure is hurting your pet, ask your vet the following questions:

- 🐾 Is there another, less painful, way to do this procedure?
- 🐾 Will the result of this type of exam/procedure change the treatment or outcome for my pet?
- 🐾 Is everything being done to manage the pain for my pet?

## Giving Medication in Ears and Eyes and Nose

- 🐾 When giving ear drops, don't be tentative: Make sure you have put in enough medication to reach the ear canal, and then rub around the base of the ear (on the outside) to promote circulation and distribute the meds inside. Do not force the drops in. Let gravity work, and the massaging will help.
- 🐾 An easy method of giving eye ointment: Put a small amount of ointment on a clean index finger. With your other hand, pull down the lower lid. Then use the index finger to wipe the ointment into the pocket of the lower lid.
- 🐾 Some nasal concoctions—decongestants in particular— are more easily administered in the eye. Gravity allows the meds to drip down the nasolacrimal duct and end up in the nasal passages. Make sure, however, that any meds used are safe for ophthalmic usage before employing this method. (I have used a single drop of pediatric Neo-Synephrine nasal drops in the eyes of congested pets, but be careful of the concentrations and dosing! Ask a vet before doing anything contrary to the instructions given with that medication!)

It may seem obvious, but don't forget to calm your terrified pet when you are trying to medicate or examine her. Here are a few nonpharmaceutical tips to alleviate your pet's anxiety:

- 🐾 A Thundershirt or a tight-fitting garment or a wrap can ease anxiety in a pet. Highly effective and rooted in neurological science, it draws on the idea that if you are being hugged, you can't be anxious. This works very well for many nervous animals.

- 🐾 During an exam, I sometimes wrap an anxious animal in a towel to calm him down. You can do the same thing for your pet at home during nail trims and while giving them medications.

- 🐾 A T-shirt or boxer shorts worn by your pet can be used to prevent him from nervous gnawing on the skin and fur or from chewing on surgical sites or allergic skin.

- 🐾 An E-collar (or "Elizabethan collar") or muzzle provides gentle control of the head and mouth and serves as a protective barrier between you and the animal's teeth if you have an animal that gets anxious to the point of biting. In vet visits, if the doctor or the tech has control of the head, the animal may feel calmer. The E-collar is also used to prevent self-chewing.

Just before my junior year of vet school, we were told we would be practicing surgical techniques on dogs that were purchased for that reason. We would perform several procedures on them, sometimes with minimal pain medication. They would recover and then be euthanized. Ostensibly, they were dogs that would otherwise have already been euthanized at pounds or otherwise.

Dog theft by dealers had been in the news at that time. The rules against that practice were not very strict. Proof of where they had obtained the dogs was not always clear, and we heard that dealers could profit about four hundred dollars per dog, so I was concerned. Many of the dogs my university bought responded to commands, were delighted to see anyone, and wagged and wagged their tails. I worried that they had been stolen from loving homes. We had seen several upperclassmen crying about these euthanasias and I started to wonder if I could do this.

There were, in the end, eight of us who couldn't. It didn't make sense to any of us that they would require future veterinarians to ignore the grim reality of this situation. In order to further our knowledge, we were preparing to sacrifice the lives of healthy animals in a manner that was painful and prolonged. In addition, we didn't know where they came from or who benefited from their sale. It was argued that there was no other way—that surgical experience with live tissue was essential.

I doubted very much that those poor dogs would find it a compelling argument. The proposition seemed to me to be directly in conflict with the Hippocratic first principle—to do no harm. It was an untenable situation in every way, not the least because of the possibility that we could be supporting or at least turning a blind eye to trafficking in lost or stolen animals.

This issue kept me up at night. I didn't want to begin my fledgling career at the expense of these dogs. There had to be a better way. We told the administration that since shelter animals needed surgery, practicing on them would be a win-win situation. As for the other course-required surgeries, we asked if it would be possible to practice on animal cadavers.

The response was mixed. Many professors were furious. Some insinuated that we were afraid to do surgery. A few strongly suggested we leave vet school. One, in particular, suggested that certain professors who were against the idea of change might take their disapproval out on my grades. Even one failed class in vet school means you're out, and I was diligent in keeping a high grade point average.

This had become a serious problem.

After many difficult meetings, I began to worry that I might never be able to become a vet if the administration didn't come up with an alternative. Many of our classmates even signed a petition against us, publicizing their disapproval of what we were trying to do.

In the end, an alternative surgical track was established for us. All eight of us completed our surgery course with flying colors. In fact, during my surgical rotation my senior year, one of the soft-tissue surgeons commented that my surgical technique was so strong I should consider applying for a surgical residency.

Since then, many vet schools in the country have banned the practice of buying student surgery dogs from disreputable dealers. Veterinary programs like the alternative track we helped establish at our school are increasingly becoming the norm.

PART THREE

WHERE
THE
WILD
THINGS
EAT

# 4,000 PET FOODS
# AND COUNTING

♟

WITH EACH PASSING YEAR AS A VET, ANIMAL NUTRITION BE-comes simpler and simpler to me: feed appropriate foods. This is similar to what Michael Pollan says of human nutrition.

I often ask my clients to bring in the labels for everything they are feeding their pet. It is a fail-safe way for me to assess the animal's functional nutrition. I've even created my own database that helps my clients understand the myriad of foods and ingredients out there.

There were over 4,000 pet foods for dogs and cats from which my staff and I collected data. I was shocked to find that I could not recommend more than 11 percent of the pet foods we analyzed. This, of course, means that a whopping 89 percent of them were unacceptable, and some of those were woefully unhealthy.

Years ago, when I was a new doctor fresh out of veterinary school, a woman brought in her three Newfoundlands for their annual exam. It was the first time I had ever seen them. These dogs were undeniably the healthiest, most energetic Newfies I had ever seen, and their exams only confirmed this. Their coats were positively glowing, their teeth had no tartar, and their weight was perfect. One of the dogs was eleven years old but looked and acted like a puppy.

I had one major concern: their diet. It was a raw-meat based food, prepared by the owner herself. Joan ground bones, added lots of meat, veggies, and a few supplements. My biggest worry was how to convince her to stop feeding the dangerous raw food she'd been using for twenty years. I was certain they needed to be on a "completely balanced" hard commercial kibble, as described in my nutrition class in vet school. After calmly listening to my unfounded concerns, this pleasant woman looked me straight in the eye and said, "Dr. Royal, let's never speak about diet again."

Was it possible that these pets were so healthy *because* of their raw diet? At the time I thought it unlikely, but I felt less certain that what I'd been taught was true. This was the first of many experiences that planted seeds of doubt in my mind.

Most of the 4,000 commercially produced foods in my database have the AAFCO (Association of American Feed Control Officials) stamp of "quality." Package claims like "Our pet foods are made following AAFCO guidelines and must pass *stringent* testing" (italics mine) sound great, until we take a close look at the basics of AAFCO testing. And it *is* basic.

After some preliminaries are followed to ensure that the ingredients aren't overtly toxic and include representation from basic food groups, the food is animal-tested. But, the only requirement is that they test it on a minimum of eight animals. As long as the eight animals don't die of "nutritional causes," they can lose up to 15 percent of their body weight and have significant health issues during the trial, and the food will pass as "complete and balanced." The eight animals' blood is tested for a few basic parameters, and then an average group number for each test is determined.

If the average blood test values show no anemia, and there are normal values for hemoglobin, protein levels, and a liver enzyme, the group is considered normal. These tests are overly general, and too limited to assure a client that the diet is truly nutritious. In my mind, these tests are in no way "stringent."

It doesn't matter if the animals are itchy, lame, unhealthy, downright sick, or hate the food: the food still passes. I'm not comfortable feeding my dog a food every day for the rest of his life based on a six-month, eight-dog trial.

> *AAFCO certification of pet food may be a good place to start, but it is not a measure of excellence.*

As a scavenger, a dog is uniquely suited to "make do" even with poor-quality food for a short period of time. However, a dog that must "make do" long term is headed for trouble. Diet-related health issues may not show up immediately, but they can become serious over time. There is no organized system that evaluates whether food is of high quality and will stand the test of time, but we can use our common sense and knowledge of what animals would eat in the wild when deciding what to feed our pets.

We have changed the outer packaging—size and shape—of the wolf/coyote/fox or lion/tiger/jaguar ancestors of our dogs and cats, but the inner workings of their GI tracts have remained essentially the same. The pet food industry, government agencies, and, sadly, even caring veterinarians will not always warn against foods that are unfit for our pets.

> *Many specialized and prescription diets were created because original maintenance formulas were never really adequate for any pet.*

Owners are increasingly skeptical about pet food claims and desperate for some answers. When a client asks a veterinarian, "What food should I feed my pet?" the answer is often, "Feed them any dog food." Nutrition is not a favorite subject for many vets and just like in human medicine, this attitude only reinforces diet-related health issues.

Pet food labels can be confusing and provide a false sense of comfort. Marketing ploys are used to convince a consumer to buy a product. Catchwords like *natural* or *healthful* make us feel good about buying a bag of dry food for our companions. Manufacturers will split the less appealing components to make them appear farther down in the list of ingredients. The names are changed to protect the undesirable or toxic. Products known by the public to be detrimental will sport a more likable name: it's not wheat or corn; it's spelt, pasta, and maize—which are, of course, wheat, durum wheat, and corn.

> *Many ingredient names are changed to protect the undesirable or the toxic.*

Labels do not have to include ingredients such as *ethoxyquin* (a preservative derived from DDT) that may have been added before the food even arrived at the manufacturing plant. Unhealthy ingredients abound. Poor protein content, inappropriate protein sources (potato, pea, or soy), a too-high percentage of grains, even ingredients like onion, a known toxin to dogs, are found in several dog foods.

When I first started my database, my staff analyzed diets using a few parameters: protein percentage, and the first five to ten ingredients. We were looking for corn, wheat, soy. I also wanted to screen for preservatives and carcinogens like BHA/BHT and ethoxyquin. We screened the nightshade family—potatoes/tomatoes—because of their potential to induce inflammation. We found a lot of powdered cellulose, which is chemically prepared plant material cellulose from pulps. Ann Martin says in her book *Food Pets Die For: Shocking Facts About Pet Food* that powdered cellulose is, "in other words, sawdust." As a veterinarian, I do not favor sawdust as one of the first five ingredients in a pet food.

I anticipated that many commercial foods would pass my criteria. I was naïvely confident that some arm of the pet food industry was watching out for pets. Sadly, that doesn't seem to be the case. Most protein levels hover around 20 percent. With few safeguards and regulations in the pet food industry, unwanted ingredients are a staple in most dry foods. Too many nutritionists and veterinarians obtain their knowledge from information disseminated by large pet food companies, which can be misleading. Here is a sample of how it looks. I've randomly chosen a section and copied it below.

| DRY FOOD | % PROTEIN | INGREDIENT CONCERNS |
|---|---|---|
| Authority Adult Formula w/ Real Chicken | 24 | Ground corn 3rd, corn gluten meal |
| Authority Adult Formula w/ Real Lamb | 22 | Ground wheat 3rd, wheat germ 4th |
| Authority Harvest Baked Chicken Adult Dog Food | 25 | Whole ground wheat 2nd |
| Authority Harvest Baked Chicken Less Active Dog Food | 24 | Whole ground wheat 2nd |
| Authority Lite w/ Real Chicken | 21 | Ground corn 3rd, corn gluten meal |
| Authority Lite w/ Real Lamb | 20 | Ground wheat 3rd, wheat germ meal |
| Authority Puppy w/ Real Chicken | 26 | Ground corn 3rd, corn gluten meal |
| Authority Puppy w/ Real Lamb | 25 | Ground wheat 3rd, wheat germ meal 4th |
| Authority Senior w/ Real Chicken | 20 | Ground corn 3rd, corn gluten meal |
| Authority Harvest Baked Chicken Puppy Dog Food | 29 | Whole ground wheat 2nd |
| Avoderm Natural Brown Rice/Oatmeal/Chicken Meal Lite Adult | 18 | No corn/wheat/soy |
| Avoderm Natural Chicken Meal & Brown Rice Adult | 23 | No corn/wheat/soy |
| Avoderm Natural Chicken Meal & Brown Rice Puppy | 26 | No corn/wheat/soy |
| Avoderm Natural Chicken Meal/Brown Rice/Oatmeal Senior | 20 | No corn/wheat/soy |

| DRY FOOD | % PROTEIN | INGREDIENT CONCERNS |
|---|---|---|
| Avoderm Natural Lamb Meal & Brown Rice Adult | 20 | No corn/wheat/soy |
| Avoderm Natural Vegetarian Adult Dog Food | 18 | Soy flour 2nd |
| Eagle Pack Adult Reduced Fat for Overweight/Less Active Dogs | 20 | Ground yellow corn 1st, wheat germ |
| Eagle Pack Adult Small Bite for Dogs | 25 | Ground yellow corn 2nd, corn germ meal 5th |
| Eagle Pack Holistic Select Anchovy, Sardine, & Salmon Meal | 22 | No corn/wheat/soy, ethoxyquin probable |
| Eagle Pack Holistic Select Chicken Meal & Rice Formula | 24 | No corn/wheat/soy |
| Eagle Pack Large & Giant Breed Puppy | 23 | Ground yellow corn 4th |
| Eagle Pack Maintenance Formula Chicken Meal & Rice | 20 | Ground yellow corn 2nd, wheat germ meal |
| Eagle Pack Natural Lamb & Rice for Dogs | 23 | Ground yellow corn 3rd, wheat germ |

This grouping represents what I have discovered: rarely is any dry food over 25 percent protein and most include grains or other unwanted ingredients.

Here are the most beneficial commercial pre-prepared pet foods (in the order of my preference) for dogs and cats when the option of making the food from scratch at home is unsustainable. Again, food you choose should not contain corn or wheat ingredients.

1. Frozen raw foods
2. Freeze-dried raw food
3. Canned food that is BPA free
4. (A distant last preference) kibble food that is processed using low heat

I prefer raw and canned foods to dry foods (especially for cats) for the following reasons:

- There is typically higher (more natural) protein content in raw and canned foods.
- There are typically fewer chemical preservatives in raw and canned foods.
- Wet food is licked clean off the teeth, which is better for healthy mouths.
- Moisture content is better for regulated hydration for all pets, especially for kidney health in cats that would normally become hydrated from their food, not from drinking water.
- Food with normal moisture content is more suitable for a carnivore's GI tract motility.
- Extrusion (high heat) processing creates two potent carcinogens, *heterocyclic aminos* and *acrylamides,* which are then (in small amounts) eaten with every mouthful of dry food.

MYTHCONCEPTION

*Dogs and cats eat grass primarily to settle an upset stomach.*
**Not true.**
*Dogs and cats may eat grass because the thick blades of grass in springtime smell like protein. However, this protein is not easily digestible for a dog or cat.*

# DIET IS NOT A
# FOUR-LETTER WORD

♛

*Diet turns out to be vastly more predictive*
*of health or disease than any other factor*
*in an animal's life.*

I USED TO HATE TALKING ABOUT DIET WITH MY CLIENTS. THAT WAS before I fully understood the vital correlation between food and optimal pet health. Now diet is my favorite subject. I've noticed from my caseload throughout the years that a discussion about diet figures more and more prominently.

As an integrative vet, I work with, not against, the healing power of the body. Nourishing an animal with what it requires from an adaptive, evolutionary standpoint is paramount. There are many forms of pet food you can consider.

## ROYAL TREATMENT
## FOOD OPTIONS

### Pre-prepared Frozen Raw Food

- A ready-to-feed, complete diet once thawed
- Pre-prepared frozen raw meat is mixed with vegetables,

fruits, fiber, vitamins, minerals, and sometimes supplements

- Provides all of the vitamins and minerals for a complete diet
- Contains appropriate moisture content
- Comes in the form of medallions, patties, bricks, and tubes
- Needs freezer space
- Great nutritional value
- Can be expensive
- Takes slightly more prep time than feeding kibble or canned food

Common questions from clients regarding raw foods:

- *Can't I just feed some ground beef from the grocer?*
  No, that is not a complete diet. Muscle meat should not be the only ingredient in a dog's diet. Dogs do need a completely balanced diet that includes raw meat, but there is more to it than that. Pre-prepared raw food includes the minerals and vitamins needed for the animal to thrive. This includes the proper calcium-to-phosphorus ratio that is so essential for dogs and cats. Raw meat alone does not have a proper ratio. In the wild, an animal would obtain the proper ratio from eating many parts of the prey animal, including feet, eyes, brain, fluids, organs, intestines, and bones. They wouldn't just eat the muscle meat. Typically the patties are frozen and need only to be thawed before feeding.

- *Aren't there more dangerous bacteria and contaminants in raw pet food than in raw grocery meat for humans?*
  Not necessarily. Raw food manufacturers know their food will be fed raw and therefore they take great pains to use quality ingredients and avoid pathogens during processing. The deep-freezing process itself takes care of many pathogens and parasites, and it

doesn't degrade the quality of the nutrients. And freezing affords easy shipping and storing.

Grocers, on the other hand, sell meat that they expect will be cooked to destroy any contaminants. The safeguards against parasites or bacterial counts are different for grocery meat than for a raw food-processing plant. Recent recalls are more often for dry and canned foods than for pre-prepared raw foods. My rule for *all* pet food is to use normal hygiene procedures. If you are concerned about bacteria in the food, wash your hands and bowls after feeding. This will help minimize pathogen transmission.

❧ *Can I let my dog (or cat) lick my face if she is eating raw food?*
The short answer is yes. Bacteria live in all mouths. Bacteria live in most foods in some amount. And, as I said before, raw food isn't likely to harbor pathogenic bacteria anyway. Bacteria are, well, everywhere. Feline and canine saliva contains an enzyme that kills bacteria. It works well as long as the teeth are not covered with tartar, which can harbor the bacteria. Dental tartar is, in my experience, more often found in the mouths of animals that eat high-carb kibbled foods. If your pet is eating a raw diet, you will find that their breath improves. Less dental tartar buildup means a decrease in foul-smelling mouth bacteria. Raw foods, in the end, help foster healthier slobber in all ways.

❧ *Can all dogs and cats eat raw foods?*
Not necessarily. There are some animals with conditions or genetics that require a diet with more processed foods. They may have deficiencies that make it difficult for them to easily digest the raw foods. In some cases, once a deficiency is treated, the animal can then tolerate raw foods well. I recommend cooking raw food in the oven at about 225 degrees just until the meat has changed

color throughout, for animals undergoing chemotherapy or animals that are seriously immunocompromised.

## Pre-prepared Cooked Food

- Packaged whole-ingredient food, available in boutique pet stores
- Contains appropriate moisture content
- Great nutritional value even though the cooking process minimally decreases the nutritional value
- Can be expensive

## Freeze-dried Raw Foods

- Much like the pre-prepared frozen raw but instead of frozen, it is freeze-dried and needs no refrigeration
- Easy to store or travel with
- About 95 percent of the moisture is removed in the freeze-drying process
- Retains much of its nutritional value
- This can be a complete diet or given as treats
- Can be expensive

## Dehydrated Dog Food

- Retains nutritional value well because it is dried (95 percent of moisture removed) by the sun, or wind-dried
- Easy to store or travel with
- Can be a complete diet or given as treats
- Can be expensive

## Home-Prepared Food

- Requires a time investment from the owner
- Main ingredients are cooked or raw meat mixed with vegetables, fruits, and moderate grains/starches
- Must include vitamins and bone meal with correct proportions
- Because it is often fresh, it can have superlative nutritional benefits and has appropriate moisture content
- Can be easy on the budget, but hard on your time

## Canned Food

- Can be a complete and balanced meal
- Some canned foods are meant to be only a supplement
- Has an appropriate moisture content
- Can be easier on an animal's digestive tract
- Great nutritional value
- Cost varies from brand to brand—check the label
- BPA (bisphenol A) in the lining of all steel cans and some small aluminum cans is considered a carcinogen

## Kibble

- Oven baked or extruded dry pelleted food
- Very convenient and stores well
- Originally created to replace canned pet food because of the rationing of metal during World War II, not for the health of our pets
- Considered a complete food
- Moisture content is low and carbohydrate level is high
- Often contains fillers of corn, wheat, white potato, and soy

- Protein levels, ingredients, and nutritional value vary dramatically from brand to brand
- Cost varies from brand to brand
- High heat extrusion can cause two potent carcinogens in the food as a by-product

## Treats

- Protein/meat-based treats are preferred
- Protein and moisture content is not crucial, unless large number of treats are given
- Avoid baked cookie-like treats; they tend to have corn, wheat, and sugars in them
- Freeze-dried lamb lung, chicken, beef, and liver are recommended
- Avoid treats made in China—too few safeguards on import ingredients

## ROYAL TREATMENT DIET GUIDELINES

- No corn, no wheat, no soy, no peanut butter, in any form, in food or treats
- Be aware that glutens, spelt, maize, corn syrups, pasta are other names for wheat and corn

If you are going to feed your pet commercial foods, I recommend pre-prepared raw or canned foods over dry kibbled foods, where possible.

- Protein levels should be at minimum greater than 30 percent, based on dry matter.

🐾 To determine protein levels in canned food, use this dry mattter to protein conversion calculation

1. First subtract the percent of moisture (80%) on the can from 100%. This is the dry matter (DM).

    100% − 80% = 20% (DM)

2. The percent protein on the label is then divided by DM. This gives you a decimal that translates to the actual protein percentage by multiplying by 100. For example:

    6.5% protein divided by 20 = 0.325 or 32.5% (DM) protein in the can.

You can use this calculation to see whether a bag of dry food that has 25% protein listed on the label has more protein than a canned food that says it has 10% protein on the label (with 78% moisture). If you don't like math, you can trust me on this one: the canned food wins! It has 45% protein on a dry matter basis.

Raw and canned foods on our *Royal Seal of Approval* list have appropriate protein levels, so you won't need to do the conversion calculation. You'll find updates about these foods on my website, www.royaltreatment veterinarycenter.com, as food products and recipes change frequently. I have a database where I assess more than four thousand new foods as they become available on the market all the time. The Royal Treatment guidelines here will help you assess them.

Here is a summary of the most important tips to keep in mind:

🐾 Read all the ingredients listed on your pet food label. (It's a page-turner!)

🐾 Avoid corn, wheat, white potato, peanut butter, garlic (depending on amount), molasses and sugars, alfalfa, and sorghum.

🐾 Avoid preservatives such as BHA/BHT, and foods with a large amount of additives and food colorings.

🐾 It's best to avoid foods that are made in China (unless you live in China).

🐾 There are many readily available pre-prepared canned, dry, and raw foods that meet my criteria of an adequate amount of protein, that are processed without corn or wheat, and that have basic, canine-appropriate ingredients.

🐾 Consider feeding your dog or cat a food that is organic, or one that uses free-range meat sources. You will be nourishing your pet from a healthier and more sustainable source and being kinder to the planet.

🐾 Raw foods may be a good option for many pets.

Optimal amounts of protein, contained in most raw foods, keep the carnivore's body functioning properly, at the correct pH for blood and urine, and can improve many body functions. Raw foods have proper moisture content and encourage a proper GI motility. Dogs on raw foods tend to have smaller, less frequent and much firmer stools. I also see a decrease in urinary incontinence in dogs on raw foods because hydration is better regulated.

I have had cases where cats or dogs don't tolerate raw foods well. This is not based on breed, size, or external features. Most animals I have treated do thrive on raw food, but not all. In some cases, the solution is to cook the raw food for fifteen minutes on 225 degrees and in other cases, a canned food proves best. Just knowing your pet has a "sensitive stomach" is not always the main factor in determining the type of food best suited for the pet. This is why, overall, commonsense factors are essential. Try the food and monitor your pet's response. No matter what anyone says, even me, if your pet does not tolerate a certain food or thrive under a health regimen, please reassess the food. Make sure you have allowed an appropriately slow changeover and proper supplements to support the GI tract, such as probiotics and pumpkin, to make the transition smoother.

Because cost is often an issue, here are some cost-cutting Royal Treatment tips:

- 🐾 Feed the best diet you can afford most of the time (e.g., canned or kibble).
- 🐾 Supplement with meat-based table scraps some of the time— remember *no* corn, wheat, white potato, onions, grapes, raisins, avocado, or other toxins.
- 🐾 Provide perfect meals (pre-prepared raw, for example) a few times a week.

Note: As scavengers, dogs, when healthy, are well suited to mixing and matching food types (canned, raw, cooked). Many cats can mix and match too.

## Supplements

- 🐾 Probiotics should always be used during a food change or while using antibiotics.
- 🐾 I recommend regular use of probiotics for many animals.
- 🐾 *Bacillus coagulans,* a beneficial probiotic bacteria, can be added to pet food to support the flora in the distal intestine, and it is useful during a diet change. After being ingested, it can survive the low pH of stomach acid in the dog and cat and can colonize the lower intestines to help avoid loose stool.
- 🐾 Other strains of probiotics are helpful in different circumstances. Because the foods we feed tend to be so carefully packaged to avoid bacterial pathogens, it may be difficult for animals to obtain proper bacteria for their GI tract. A periodic probiotic supplement provides those bacteria.
- 🐾 Probiotics come in many forms. Dairy-free versions are available for sensitive animals. Pets that are already accustomed to dairy products can be given good-quality yogurt from most supermarkets or health food stores.
- 🐾 Probiotics meant for humans can be used as a pet supplement if you can't find the *B. coagulans.*

- Look for good-quality products from respected companies. Generally, a dairy-free probiotic is the most effective.

- Omega-3 fatty acids (fish oil) can improve hair coat, inflammatory conditions, arthritis, and skin problems. Omegas encourage free radical scavenging, which can decrease inflammation.

- Carnivores do not efficiently convert flaxseed, hemp, or borage into a usable omega source, although these plants can be used as laxatives.

- For an animal that has oily/hot skin or loose stools, fish oil may not be recommended. Instead consider DHA from algae (see below), coconut oil, or aloe juice (small amounts) to help the skin.

- DHA from algae sources is more accessible and renewable. It's easy on the stomach, and is bio-friendly. The algae are not killed to harvest it. The manufacturer feeds the algae, and the algae make the DHA.

- Avoid krill oil. It is the only thing whales eat. Let's not be cruel and take it away from them.

- Unsweetened canned pumpkin is a terrific stool regulator that combats both constipation and diarrhea. It regulates moisture and provides a gentle fiber. Use during food changes to regulate stool. Dosage is 1 tablespoon once or twice daily for a 30-pound dog or a ½ teaspoon for an average cat, in food or as a treat. I am surprised at how many cats like to eat straight pumpkin from a spoon. You can also mix pumpkin with meat baby food or yogurt and put it into ice cube trays or Kongs (then freeze) to use as treats.

- Psyllium fiber/oat bran fiber for both loose stool or constipation. Many foods, especially raw foods, may not include enough fiber. Adding psyllium fiber or oat bran (about a teaspoon per meal for a 50-pound dog, or ¼ teaspoon for an average cat) is a great way to improve the fiber content of the food.

✿ White rice relieves diarrhea. Do not use Minute Rice. Cook the white rice with extra water and overcook until it is gloppy. It absorbs better when it is overcooked and sticky wet. Brown rice is not as absorbent for diarrhea/loose stools. The white rice is given for its absorbent quality, not for its nutritive value.

✿ Low-sodium chicken or beef broth or even warm water can be added to food to increase palatability. Pets will drink more water this way because it tastes good.

## Food Vehicles for Giving Pills, Powders, Other Medications

✿ Liverwurst—cover pill completely

✿ Meat baby food—use small jars of a single meat: chicken, beef, lamb and other flavors. Do not use baby foods containing onion or onion powder, which is toxic to pets. Some baby food products contain small amounts of cornstarch, which is okay.

✿ Pats of butter, cream cheese, or other cheeses

✿ Hide medicine in butter, then let it harden in the freezer for a moment to make it easier to give.

✿ Good-quality plain yogurt with active cultures is effective if the animal does not have a dairy sensitivity. Also useful during diet changes or when using an antibiotic.

## For Picky, Hard-to-Pill Dogs or Cats

✿ Many compounding pharmacies will make a pill into a flavored liquid or chewy treat.

## Fun Treat Foods

- 🐾 Use baby foods for versatile meal enhancement and treats.
- 🐾 Dilute baby food with warm water to make gravy and pour over foods.
- 🐾 Add baby foods directly to regular food to improve taste.
- 🐾 Spread favorite foods, as if it is pâté, on plain rice cakes or in ice cube trays or inside a Kong toy, then freeze

## Food-Related Dental Notes

MYTHCONCEPTION

*Dry food chips off tartar and keeps teeth clean.*
**Not true.**

- 🐾 Many veterinarians and dog food companies suggest that dry food is better for the teeth. The truth is, dry food is *not* better for the teeth. Dry food sticks to the teeth. Look in your dog's mouth after he has eaten a meal of dry food and you will see that the dry food is stuck in the crevices. To compress the ingredients in a piece of kibble, an adhesive carbohydrate is added. This makes it more likely to adhere to the teeth and form plaque.
- 🐾 Check your pet's mouth and teeth regularly. This will get him accustomed to someone checking/touching his teeth to assess dental health. It may also make a dental procedure less stressful for your pet.
- 🐾 Brush the teeth two to three times a week. You can even use a piece of gauze and a paste of baking soda and water to help avoid tartar buildup.

Outlandish nonnutritive things I've seen pets eat, many of which I have surgically removed

---

GI Joe dolls, fully intact

Barbie dolls, with clothes

large Nerf balls, gold balls, tennis balls, soccer balls

$20,000 diamond rings, credit cards

underwear, socks, and sock toys

small wooden boxes

forks and knives (all sizes)

rocks, coins, candles, nails, pens, and pencils

fish hooks and needles

rubber duckies

magic wands, batons, drum sticks, two-foot-long sticks

cell phones, remote controllers, batteries

pacifiers, bottles

diapers, tampons

toy dogs, cats, and robots

empty cans

yarn, tinsel

prosthetic limbs

If they can swallow it, they will.

# FUNCTIONAL
# PET NUTRITION

♛

*What you put in your pet's bowl is one of the most
important health decisions you'll ever make.*

I DEFINE THE ROYAL TREATMENT'S NUTRITIONAL CONCEPTS AS functional nutrition. The function of proper nutrition is to promote optimal wild health. The shift to processed convenience pet food has contributed to increasingly overfed and undernourished pets. If food, or the amount of it, is making a pet fat, the nutrition is not functional. An animal with the wrong fuel and too much of it is not fully functioning.

Just because your pet has solid poop doesn't mean his food is suitable. In other words, don't judge a food by the poop. Many owners tell me they don't want to change food because their pet's poop is normal. "Since I started this food," they say, "my dog no longer has diarrhea." This does not indicate the food is the correct long-term food for the pet. While I'm thrilled the diarrhea has been alleviated, the ingredients of the food may not be nourishing other canine organ systems, and the food may still need to be changed.

In a healthy dog or cat, poop tends to be small, firm, and infrequent. They should go once or twice a day, max. Generally the size should be about the diameter of the base of the animal's tail. In the carnivore, huge and frequent stools are not indicative of health.

Now on to a less scatological and a more charged subject: veganism in cats and dogs. If you have chosen a vegan lifestyle, that's great. If you want your pet to be a vegan, too, get a rabbit. Or get a chinchilla, a couple of sugar gliders, a guinea pig, a few hamsters, or certain vegetarian fish. These animals thrive on being vegan: it's their heritage. But dogs and cats do not.

I routinely see many preventable illnesses when people try to make a vegan out of a carnivore, particularly when they use poor-quality vegetable proteins. The digestive system of a dog or cat is not suited to a preponderance of vegetables and grains. Cats are especially at risk for illness from a vegan diet because they are *obligate carnivores*. But dogs are not suited to veganism either.

There may be some future possibilities for a more vegetarian diet that includes excellent vegetable proteins, and perhaps some combination of healthy cheeses, eggs, or dairy. New information and research is on the horizon. I am open-minded to any discussion, or new empirical evidence and research that has long-term tangible results on this subject. The field of nutrition is exciting and we are learning things every day. But I practice what nature intended for my patients and what they're evolved to tolerate today. I believe this minimizes health problems for them in the short and long term.

I have seen several owners who prefer a vegan diet for their dog or cat. I explain the options and why I believe this is a mistake. As long as the owner knows that they may be shortening the life span and possibly decreasing the quality of life for their pet, they can make that decision. As their vet, I try to support the pet's health as best I can. But none of my vegan dog or cat cases are fully, vibrantly healthy. Weight problems, diabetes, heart disease, musculoskeletal problems, vision deficits, and cognitive diseases abound in these animals.

Humans are omnivores and can therefore choose the type of food they want to eat. But we choose for our pets, and it is wrong to feed a carnivore as if it were an omnivore or an herbivore. As much as I enjoy eating a wide variety of fresh vegetables myself, I couldn't have offered that to Songkit, the tiger cub I hand-raised, if I expected her to survive. A carnivore that doesn't eat meat will have health issues.

I agree with vegetarians and vegans that we consume too much meat in our country, torture farm and factory animals, and waste precious resources to raise our livestock. It's a shame that our carnivore pets contribute to that imbalance. However, pets have as much of a right to be healthy as do animals that are raised to be slaughtered for food. Better food practices and improving conditions for livestock and poultry used in pet food are important moral issues for people who love animals.

## ROYAL TREATMENT RECIPES FOR FUNCTIONAL NUTRITION

> *With the foundation of a nutritious diet, you may not need any pet supplements. However, even with exceptional supplements you will always need to provide a nutritious diet.*

### DR. ROYAL'S ULTIMATE CANINE RAW FOOD RECIPE

*For a 30-pound dog:*

Take 1 pound raw organic chicken, no bones, leave on half of the skin, include heart and liver.

Or rotate with 1 pound other raw meats such as turkey, beef, or lamb; or eggs, or sardines.

Cut into pieces (to make about 2 heaping cups).

Put into a large bowl.

Add ½ cup canned or homecooked pumpkin (unsweetened).

Add ¼ cup lightly steamed or cooked vegetables (green beans, broccoli, zucchini, peas, carrots, bell peppers).

Add ⅛ cup fruit, e.g., blueberries or melon (approximately 2 tablespoons).

Mix together.

If you plan to cook this recipe, don't add the fish oil or calcium (next ingredients) until after you cook the meat mix.

Add 400–500 mg fish oil.

Add 2,000 mg calcium from bone meal—depending on the source, this is about 2 teaspoons (this is available online or from your vet).

Vary the protein sources (beef, lamb, venison, turkey). You can follow the proportions below. I find it's easiest to stay with volume to measure ingredients. If you change proteins and vegetables every so often, you are more likely to cover your nutritional bases.

You can include bones if you can finely grind them. Bone meal isn't needed if you add ground bone. If you have bone pieces in the food, don't cook the meat with the bones; they become too brittle and are dangerous when cooked.

## General Diet Rules for Home Cooking

### *Meat—60–75% of Diet*

Types of meats/proteins include: beef, lamb (tends to be high in fat), chicken (use only half of the skin), turkey, fish (sardines are easy, salmon must be cooked), tripe, rabbit, buffalo, venison, eggs (yolks uncooked are best for omega integrity). Meat that comes from organic farms with free-range animals will be better for your pet and better for the earth.

### *Veggies/fruits*
### *(15–25%—at least two times more veggies than fruits)*

Types of vegetables/fruits to include: pumpkin (baked), squashes (baked), sweet potato (baked), carrots (cooked), red or yellow peppers, cabbage (cooked), chard, romaine, endive, cucumber, kelp, spinach, broccoli (cooked), peas, eggplant, zucchini, celery, green beans, blueberries, raspberries, watermelon, cantaloupe, apple, pear, papaya. It's okay to use frozen veggies and fruits. Raw broccoli, cauliflower, cabbage, brussels sprouts, or bok choy should not be fed every day to hypothyroid animals. Unless they are cooked they can affect thyroid function due to iodine uptake issues.

### Fat—10–30% of Diet

Most of the fat is from the meat, chicken skin, or added oils. In nature, this would vary by season—more in the fall, less in the spring.

### Supplements

Add probiotic/enzyme mix during any food transition; for maintenance, most animals benefit from a dose of probiotics given 1–2 times a week.

Add a complete **pet vitamin** tablet at least 3 times per week.

Every meal requires the important **bone meal** (1,000 gm per pound of meat based food) or finely ground bones to provide a proper calcium/phosphorus ratio. In healthy animals I recommend bone meal rather than ground egg shell, which doesn't have quite the right ratio.

### Tips

Make a large amount at one time, but freeze the food in small portions. Freeze with as little air as possible, and quickly and evenly.

Every week, you can add a little iodized salt as a supplement and for a change of taste.

A normal 30-pound adult dog's daily portion can vary widely depending on the activity level, metabolism, and genetics of each pet. It can range between 2 and 5 cups of homemade food per day. Judge amounts based on weight and defecation.

Growing puppies may need double the amount you'd feed to an adult. It may seem obvious, but there is a correlation between amount of food and frequency of defecation. It is normal for a puppy to poop 4–6 times a day until it is six months old.

## Diet for Dogs with Cancer

Start with the Royal Treatment Ultimate Diet.

Increase the fat component to 30 percent fat (add egg yolks, green tripe, fish oil, or DHA from algae).

Decrease the vegetable component to 10 percent veggies with minimal fruits.

### ADD DAILY

- ☐ Probiotic for a healthy gastrointestinal tract
- ☐ Turmeric—an anti-inflammatory supplement (spice) that is also known as an effective anticancer supplement. Doses range from ¼ tsp for a small dog to up to 1 tbsp for a large dog per day. Note: turmeric is indelibly orange and stains fabrics.
- ☐ Mushroom complex (particularly reishi and maitake) to support the immune system. Give ¼ of a human dose for a small dog to up to one human dose for a large dog per day.

### ADD TWO TIMES A WEEK

- ☐ Multivitamin that contains zinc. Give ¼ of a human dose for a small dog to up to one human dose for a large dog each time.
- ☐ B complex—give ¼ of a human dose for a small dog to up to one human dose for a large dog each time.
- ☐ Vitamin C—give ¼ of a human dose for a small dog to up to one human dose for a large dog each time.
- ☐ Selenium—with the dose range of 20 micrograms (mcg) for small dogs up to 200 mcg for a large dog each time.

ADD FIVE DAYS A WEEK

☐   Vitamin A—(dose ranges from 5,000 IU for a small dog to up to 50,000 IU for a giant breed dog). There is toxicity associated with vitamin A and all the oil-soluble vitamins, so giving the right dose and only five days a week keeps the supplement safe.

## *Basic Kidney Support Diet*

Start with the Royal Treatment Ultimate Canine Raw Food Recipe. Add the following supplements:

- A good probiotic—Azodyl or a lactobacillus/acidophilus combo
- Fiber—psyllium husk works well (some is already in Azodyl)
- Vitamin B complex (about ½ a human dose for a 30–50 pound dog)
- Potassium supplement, if blood work indicates it's low. Foods that are high in potassium include bananas, melons, apples, potatoes, carrots, peas, and beans.
- Omega-3 fatty acids from fish oil
- Coconut oil (¼ tsp for a cat, and ½ tsp for a 30-pound dog)

A kidney diet should have limited phosphorus.

- If you are cooking for your pet, substitute ground egg shell, which has less phosphorus, for one-half of your bone meal.
- In order to decrease phosphorus, avoid any grains (wheat or corn), egg yolks, bones, organ meats, and dairy.
- A phosphate binder is recommended such as aluminum hydroxide, or Epakitin (a chitosan-based intestinal

phosphate binder). When phosphorus in the food is bound to a phosphate binder, it does not get absorbed into the bloodstream. This helps control high levels of phosphorus that are not well controlled by the malfunctioning kidney.

* Many animals in kidney failure digest better if their raw food is cooked.

I do not typically recommend lowering the amount of protein in diets of animals suffering from kidney disease. Pet food already contains too little protein, and it is crucial for proper kidney function in carnivores. (See the chapter "Don't Feed an Anemic Hummingbird a Steak" for more on kidney diets.)

A great supplement for animals with kidney disease is green tripe. It can be added to the regular food and even the pickiest eater will perk up for a bite. Tripe is from the intestines of herbivores. It contains a therapeutic combination of easy-to-digest protein, fat, beneficial bacteria, and enzymes. Warning: the smell of tripe is beyond foul. Tripe is available in cans, fresh from a butcher, or frozen. If you don't thaw it completely, it is less pungent. Give ¼ to 1 cup of tripe for a 50-pound dog at least twice a week.

*Liver Detox and Support Diet*

## Liver Detox Diet Recipe

⅔ cup sweet potato

⅓ cup white potato (make sure not to use any green skin from the potato)

2 cups white-colored fish (pollock, haddock, cod, or other white fish—lightly cooked)

Combine potato mix with 2 cups of fish

Add:

⅛ *tsp of chopped fresh garlic (Do not use garlic powder, which is too*
    *concentrated)*
¼ *tsp chopped fresh parsley*

Alternate in *two* of the following:
    *1 tbsp chopped cooked carrots*
    *1 tbsp chopped cooked zucchini*
    *1 tbsp chopped cooked string beans, green beans*
    *1 tbsp chopped cooked celery*
    *1 tbsp chopped cooked summer squash*

Occasionally offer scrambled eggs or cottage cheese instead of white fish.

Five days a week, add one dose of a children's liquid multivitamin (dog ones tend to have flavoring) for a 30–50 pound dog, and ¼ of the dose for a 10-pound cat. Also add the following:

## Milk Thistle (Liver Support Herb)

300 mg twice a day for a 30–50 pound dog
50 mg twice a day for an 8–15 pound dog or cat

## Coconut oil

½ tsp for a 30-pound dog
¼ tsp for a 10-pound dog or cat

## Omega-3 Fatty Acid from Fish Oil or Algae DHA

1,000 mg each of DHA and EPA for the 30–50 pound dog
250–300 mg for 8–15 pound dog or cat

## SAM-e or Denosyl (S-adenosylmethionine)

400 mg once a day on an empty stomach for a 50-pound dog

90 mg once a day on an empty stomach for a 10-pound dog or cat

This diet gives the liver a break. It is formulated using a variation on the basic liver detox diet from Dr. Jean Dodds and is effective for animals that have liver disease, hepatitis, liver enzyme elevation, history of seizures, recent anesthesia, or liver-taxing medications. The whitefish contains an amino acid that helps heal the liver. Feed it to your pet until health is restored. The pet's regular diet should be slowly reinstated.

If your pet is taking potassium bromide (KBr) or sodium bromide (NaBr), the dosage may have to be reduced if your pet becomes wobbly or weak. Low sodium in the diet may make the bromide in the KBr or NaBr more potent. Ask your vet.

### *Diet for Dogs with Seizures*

Avoid these ingredients in food for animals with seizures (read labels carefully, as these ingredients are more prevalent than you think):

- All forms of gluten, such as wheat, barley, rye, bulgur, durum, graham, spelt, spelta, kamut, and triticale
- Casein (cow's milk products) increases the precursors for neuro-excitatory chemicals
- Soy contains estrogen-like compounds that can affect seizure activity
- Corn (inflammatory)
- MSG and its myriad pseudonyms are neuro-excitatory
- Aspartame (NutraSweet) is a neuro-excitatory compound

When preparing a diet for dogs with seizures, start with the Royal Treatment Ultimate Diet and add:

- ☐ Regular-strength multivitamin with zinc
- ☐ Vitamin B complex (¼ of a human dose for small dogs up to a full human dose for large dogs daily)
- ☐ Vitamin C (50 mg per day for a small dog up to 1000 mg per day for a large dog)
- ☐ Omega-3 fatty acids (fish oil, or algae DHA) (150 mg EPA or 100 mg DHA for small dogs and 750 mg EPA or 500 mg DHA for large dogs daily)
- ☐ Taurine (250 mg for a small dog up to 1000 mg for a large dog, once to twice a day)
- ☐ Magnesium (5 mg for a small dog up to 50 mg/kg per day)

## GERIATRIC PET SUPPLEMENTS

FEED GERIATRIC PETS A carnivore diet and add extra protein. Older pets need at least 40 percent protein to maintain and strengthen muscle mass.

Add coconut oil to the food to moisturize the skin and GI tract.

Offer ¼ to 1 cup of green tripe several times a week.

Add warm water to the food to increase the smell for aging noses.

Herbs like turmeric, boswellia, gingko, ginseng, arnica, and other homeopathic supplements can help with inflammation, arthritis, or cognitive function.

Add egg shell/membrane to dog food. For cats, scrape the egg out of the shell. They won't eat egg membrane if it's still attached to the shell.

Egg Shell Membrane (Inner Lining of an Egg Shell) Contains

❧ Collagen—Supports cartilage and connective tissue and promotes elasticity
❧ Elastin—Helps with tissue elasticity and helps tissue to regain normal shape after stretching
❧ Glycosaminoglycans (GAGs)—glucosamine, chondroitin, and hyaluronic acid, which are vital polysaccharides and components of joints, joint fluid, and connective tissue
❧ Transforming growth factor b—A protein that promotes tissue rejuvenation

## ROYAL TREATMENT

### MAYA

Maya, a lovely young black Labrador, was brought to see me for alternative treatment for her seizure disorder. It was deemed to be idiopathic epilepsy. Her owners wanted to avoid treating her with phenobarbital if possible. The seizure activity seemed random and unrelated to any particular event, until we looked closely at her diet.

Once we had changed her diet from food that was high in wheat and corn to a grain-free diet, her seizure activity decreased significantly. But periodically she would still have seizures. One day her owner called me, very excited. She could trace every seizure since the diet change back to times when Maya had eaten corn. The popcorn from her daughter's slumber party, a corn taco on taco night, and some corn-based left-overs on other evenings—all had resulted in seizures. Even some corn on the cob managed to cause a seizure.

Now this household is virtually corn free, but if Maya does get any corn, she has a seizure. Otherwise she is seizure free. No medication. Adjusting her diet was the key.

## DIET CHANGE TIPS

When changing foods, be sure to do it slowly and incrementally. A complete diet change typically takes about ten to fourteen days. Each day, you should increase the new food and decrease the old food. This will cause the least amount of trouble for your pet's GI tract and will cause you the least amount of headache.

| DIET CHANGE CHART | | |
|---|---|---|
| Day 1 | 90% old food | 10% new food |
| Day 2 | 80% old food | 20% new food |
| Day 3 | 70% old food | 30% new food |
| Day 4 | 60% old food | 40% new food |
| Day 5 | 50% old food | 50% new food |
| Day 6 | 40% old food | 60% new food |
| Day 7 | 30% old food | 70% new food |
| Day 8 | 20% old food | 80% new food |
| Day 9 | 10% old food | 90% new food |
| Day 10 | —— | 100% new food |

> ❧ Even with the exciting advances in nutrigenomics (a new field that determines how nutritional components interact with an animal's specific genetic makeup), there are still no tests that can fully predict what food is best for any pet. To conclusively discover what your pet can tolerate, slowly incorporate the new food into his daily diet.
>
> ❧ Monitor for vomiting or diarrhea or other GI signs. If these issues occur, decrease the amount of new food and try again more slowly.
>
> ❧ If the diet is not working for your dog, provide a bland diet for a few meals before substituting another type of food. This will rebalance the GI tract.

A bland diet can help your pet avoid or resolve diarrhea, whether from a virus, bacterial overgrowth, dietary change/dietary indiscretion, or a variety of other causes.

## Bland Diet Recipe

*2 parts overcooked white rice (not Minute Rice) to 1 part boiled meat, tripe, or a meat baby food, white fish, cottage cheese, or scrambled eggs.*
Increase to 1:1 and then slowly return to regular diet.

Add extra water and cook a little longer to make the rice soupy, which enhances its absorptive capacity.

A bland diet should be fed in the same volume as you normally feed your pet, or slightly less. If you feed 2 cups a day of dry food, feed nearly 2 cups a day of the bland diet. This is a transitional diet, formulated to be tasty, easy to digest, and effective in firming stool.

It is not a complete diet. As signs improve, pets should be weaned off the bland diet and back onto their regular diet over a period of three to four days.

Unsweetened canned pumpkin can also be used regularly or as part of the bland diet. Many cats and dogs love it. Feed 1 teaspoon per meal for a 10-pound dog and 1 tablespoon per meal for dogs 30–50 pounds. To keep a large can of pumpkin from spoiling, put it into ice-cube trays to freeze for future use.

If you would rather cook a fresh pumpkin for your pet, steam-bake a cut-up pumpkin in a pan with 1–2 cups of water in the bottom for 40 minutes at 350 degrees. Then scrape out and freeze the cooked pumpkin in ice-cube trays.

Cooked millet (preferably overcooked, with extra water) can also be used to treat diarrhea. Mix in with the food about 1 tablespoon for a 30-pound dog. Be aware that millet can be constipating, so once the stool becomes formed, wean off millet.

Provide a probiotic supplement to help the GI tract restore its normal bacteria. An appropriate complement of "good" bacteria in the GI tract is essential for proper nutrient absorption. Bacterial overgrowth can be a reason for digestive issues. Dogs live in a more sterile world than they would in the wild, and bacteria-free food may not be conducive to optimal digestion. I recommend intermittently adding good bacteria into the food in the form of probiotics. They are available at vet clinics, pharmacies, and natural grocers.

A 50-pound dog would take about half the human dose of probiotics. There is a wide range of safety for this supplement. Adjust dose up or down by weight.

## Oversupplementation

An arsenal of supplements can be difficult for an animal to digest. Upset tummies can be due to oversupplementing. If you are feeding an appropriate food for your pet, supplements may not be required.

🐾 Avoid "diet" pet foods for weight loss—the best diet is less food.

If you are feeding a prescription diet, check the label for undesirable ingredients and discuss them with your vet.

## PROTEIN

☐ Protein must make up a minimum of 30% (dry matter) of the diet—*not* including nonmeat sources of protein such as soy, potato, or pea protein.

Determining protein content of wet foods based on dry matter is complicated. Just remember, canned food labels list percentages that might seem too low. This is because the manufacturers are using a different scale. This is when the conversion calculation (page 80) comes in handy. When protein percentages are measured on the same scale using this calculation, it will be apparent that most canned foods win against dry foods by having more protein.

## CARBOHYDRATES

☐ Minimal carbs
☐ The amount of carbs is rarely listed on the label, but it can be easily approximated by subtracting protein and fat percentages from 100%. For example: 100% total − 30% protein − 10% fat = 60% carbs.

## FAT

☐ Dogs and cats require fat in their diets.
☐ Carbs, not fats, are the main culprit in carnivore weight gain and often in pancreatitis, too.
☐ Loose stool can be an indication of too much fat consumption.
☐ When adding omega-3 in fish oils, decrease the amount if diarrhea occurs.

## TIPS FOR OPTIMAL HEALTH FEEDING

☐ The most common cause of diarrhea is overfeeding.

☐ Optimal weight for dogs and cats depends on good portion control and low carbs.

☐ Dogs have the unique ability to gain and lose weight quickly and safely. As scavengers, dogs efficiently use up body fat when they don't find a meal. With cats you must be more careful.

☐ A normal adult dog defecates 1–2 times a day. An overweight dog should be fed less and therefore defecate only 1 time a day. When their stomach is empty, they use their fat for energy.

☐ It is crucial that feline weight loss happen gradually.

☐ It is best not to rely on the suggested daily amount on food packages or cans. It is often way too much.

☐ Your dog will still love you if you feed him less.

☐ If your dog is constantly begging for food, add plain rice cakes or green beans to the diet to fill up his stomach.

## WET VS. DRY FOOD

☐ As I have mentioned, dry food is not better for the teeth. Dry food, with its added carbs, adheres to the teeth. (See page 85 and the chapter "Going Dental.")

☐ A dog that eats wet food, uncooked soft bones, and a natural diet will easily lick their teeth clean after a meal.

☐ 70% of the digestive system of a canine is taken up by the stomach, which expects to be fed in just one to two daily batches. (A human stomach takes up only 30%—so we need to eat more frequently.) A canine stomach is a strong, muscular sac that mixes the food with hydrochloric acid, digestive enzymes, and mucus, which the stomach lining secretes to protect stomach cells. The food is held in the stomach and broken down until initial digestion is complete. At this stage of digestion, the food changes to a liquid consistency, similar to soup. This soup is then pushed out of the stomach and into the small intestine. Further digestion occurs with more enzymes added from the pancreas and liver.

☐ Dry food arrives in a dog's stomach like a cement block, requiring an influx of water from the body to break it up before it passes into the intestine. Animals that eat dry food must drink more water all at once, resulting in unnatural urination patterns. In addition, for about an hour, while all that water is in their stomach, they can become dehydrated. This is not ideal for the health of kidneys and circulation.

## FIBER

☐ Dogs need fiber in their diets.

☐ Fiber is not the same thing as processed grains.

☐ Wild carnivores obtain fiber from the animals they eat— parts of the carcass that would be hard to digest, like fur, nails, fins, cartilage, scales, hooves, feathers, sticks, dirt, teeth, and/or tendons. Plant matter that is in the stomach of their prey also provides fiber to the carnivore.

This "wild" type of fiber is not easily available for homemade diets. But other usable sources of fiber are unsweetened pumpkin, psyllium (ground husks of a native Indian plant used as a source of fiber to maintain colon health), and fiber from vegetables. Canned pumpkin can be added to the diet at about 1 tablespoon for a 50-pound dog. Or add a teaspoon of psyllium to wet food for a 50-pound dog if more fiber is needed. Adjust dose proportionally by weight.

## Treats

Conform to the same rules when deciding how to give treats to your dog. Commercial treats tend to be very calorie-dense to make them tasty. Don't feed too many per day. Check ingredients carefully and avoid treats made in China.

Great treats directly from the refrigerator include green beans, apples, carrots, celery, cheese, butter, meats, and many vegetables. Avoid raw vegetables in the cruciferous or brassica family, such as broccoli and cauliflower, if your pet has a thyroid problem.

THE DIGESTIVE MECHANICS OF your pet are as immutable as those of any carnivore.

---

MYTHCONCEPTION

---

*Raw food contains more harmful*
*bacteria than kibble does.*
**Not true.**
*There have been more recalls because of harmful*
*bacteria found in kibble food than in raw food.*

# HOW TO READ
# A PET FOOD LABEL

♕

## A Short Course in
## Deciphering Pet Food Products

THE TWO MOST IMPORTANT COMPONENTS ARE *NOT* THE BRAND name, the attractive packaging, or the veterinary seal of approval. The most important components in pet food are

1. **The ingredients list**, which shows, in order of amount by weight, everything contained in the food.
2. **The guaranteed analysis**, which gives, by percentage, the breakdown of the food—although inexplicably it doesn't usually mention the percentage of carbohydrate.

### INGREDIENTS LIST

The first ten ingredients are critical, and every ingredient on the label should make nutritional sense.

1. Read the first ingredient—is it meat-based?
2. Is the meat a by-product or a meat meal or fish meal?

3. What are the first five ingredients?
4. Are there mostly real foods or do you see a lot of chemical names?
5. Does it contain corn, wheat, or their products?
6. Any major preservatives, other grains, or obvious troublesome ingredients like onions, raisins, or preservatives BHA, BHT?

## Pet food labels should show the following information:

🐾 A good amount of meat protein—greater than 30% DM

🐾 No objectionable ingredients (corn, wheat, soy, powdered cellulose, white potato, preservatives like BHA or BHT, or ethoxyquin)

🐾 Ideally, the greatest percentage of the ingredients should not be carbs

## Unnatural Selections

🐾 *Beware of soy as a high percentage in the first few ingredients.* Soy is considered a goitrogen—affecting thyroid metabolism. Soy may be implicated in hyperthyroidism in cats, although this is not yet clear. In addition, soy has high levels of phytoestrogen compounds that play a role in the immune response, sex hormones, and dermatologic conditions. More research is needed on the biological effects of a constant source of unregulated phytoestrogens in animals.

🐾 *Beware of whole potatoes as a high percentage of the first few ingredients.* A carnivore diet should not have carbohydrate as a main ingredient. Another issue is that white potatoes are in the nightshade family. They are considered an inflammatory root vegetable because of solanine (a glycoalkaloid poison that is one of the plant's natural defenses) concentrations. Green under the potato skin and the "eyes" or sprouted areas concentrate solanine, which when eaten can cause painful inflammation in joints and in the body. Animals with allergies, seizures, or arthritis should not eat nightshade for this reason. The storage and condition of the potatoes determine how much solanine is present in a food. To have more control over potatoes with solanine content, avoid feeding potatoes from unknown sources. (Note: If you cook potatoes yourself, use fresh, nonsprouted potatoes.) The word *potato* on the label usually means white potato, not sweet potato. Sweet potato is not a nightshade. If white potatoes are farther down the list of ingredients, you may safely consider using that food.

☙ *Beware of peas or other vegetables/grains used as a source of protein.* This falsely elevates the usable protein levels. The protein percentage entitled "crude protein" may be listed as 34%, but not all of that is meat protein. This is not a travesty if the protein level starts reasonably high, but it's troublesome if there's already a low amount of meat protein, which is commonly the case.

☙ Flaxseed is a source of omega-3 and omega-6 fatty acids for humans but is not as effective for dogs or cats, because they are not efficient at making the conversion from flax to omega-3. However, flax can be useful, not as a source of omegas, but as a laxative and a moisturizing oil.

☙ *Beware of toxins.* It's hard to believe they would be there at all. But whether they are on the label or not, they are often contained in the food. For example, some pet foods contain onion, which is toxic to dogs. If a dog or cat eats too much onion, it causes a blood disorder called *methemoglobinemia*. The blood changes color to blue and can't carry a normal amount of oxygen to the tissues. It can quickly become a life-threatening problem. The toxicity of onions is a dose-related issue. Small amounts can be tolerated. The incremental damage of small amounts of onion in a pet's daily diet is unstudied.

🐾 Avoid monosodium glutamate (MSG), which is neuro-excitatory and causes many health issues. It often masquerades under other terms, such as vegetable protein extract, hydrolyzed vegetable protein, autolyzed yeast, or textured protein.

## Ingredients that may be in the food but are not listed on the label:

🐾 Chemicals used in premanufacturing. One such chemical is ethoxyquin, a pesticide considered by the federal government to be a hazardous chemical, rated 3 on a scale of 1–6 (with 6 being so toxic that just 7 drops is lethal). Human limits on consumption are 0.5 ppm, but a dog eating some foods might consume over 100 ppm in a meal. It is often not listed on the label. But it still could be in the food. Any premanufacture product, by-products, or "meal" can have ingredients that don't have to be listed if they are added before arriving at the pet food company. Be aware that most fish meals tend to contain ethoxyquin as a preservative because, unless companies specifically request a permit to do otherwise, the Code of Federal Regulations requires fish meal to have a minimum 100 ppm of ethoxyquin at time of shipment.

🐾 Pentobarbital is an anesthetic drug used to euthanize dogs and cats. It is not usually used to euthanize large animals, like cattle. However, it has been detected in some pet foods. The Food and Drug Administration claims it's in small amounts and doesn't matter. Therefore, they don't routinely check for it. There is no enforcement to regulate pentobarbital in pet food. I question why it is there in the first place.

🐾 Other chemicals may drift into the food via farming management practices. Chickens may have the lion's share of chemical processing additives. That is one reason I suggest using free-range organic chicken.

The controversy about what dogs and cats truly need to eat to stay healthy has never been fully resolved, even though these animals have resided with us for hundreds of years. We used to know just what to feed them. That's how they came to live with us. They would eat our meat leftovers and table scraps in addition to what they could catch outside. It was a mutually beneficial relationship. As soon as these animals became domesticated,

---

### THE FENNEC FOX

I was asked to consult on a case of a fennec fox that had a chronically inflamed toe. This type of fox is about three pounds, with a caramel-colored coat, enormous ears, and big, dark eyes. I was asked to do acupuncture or laser—I did both. The fox was overweight. This was attributed to his movement being limited by the hurt toe, but it didn't make sense to me that the toe wouldn't heal. It had been infected for over a year. I asked what they were feeding the fox. They said, "Fennec fox diet." I found that this included a kibble food with corn and wheat in it. I brought up the fact that a wild fennec fox would eat insects, rodents, plants, fruit, and reptiles, never grains. Corn and wheat cause glycemic index changes that can contribute to inflammation. When we eliminated grains and provided the fox with a proper diet, along with acupuncture and laser treatments, the animal slimmed down and the toe healed quickly.

though, we began to confine them and limit their ability to catch their own food. The burden of a complete diet fell on us. In the past it was easy—meat scraps and by-products worked well. Soon the pet food industry took over and started putting in inexpensive fillers and that's when pet health went awry. Regardless of a few healthy-looking ingredients like blueberries or flax, many commercial foods may still be wholly inappropriate for your pet.

## GUARANTEED ANALYSIS

In the guaranteed analysis the label will always list percentages of:

Protein

Fat

Moisture

Most labels don't mention carbohydrates. The pet food companies avoid drawing attention to it in print because carbs are plentiful in pet foods, but shouldn't be. The fact is, most dog and cat foods contain *mostly* carbohydrates.

### Note for Raw, Wet Food, or Canned Food Protein Analysis

The percent amount of protein on a canned food label or a raw food label will not be described in terms of "dry matter," so it will look as if there is way too little protein (typically 8–10%) in these foods. But by using the conversion calculation on page 80, the dry matter protein of these raw or canned foods (moist foods) can be more than 4 times the wet matter listed. Most of the canned or raw foods I recommend have 40–50% protein.

Take the time to make other simple calculations: 20% protein plus 10% fat equals only 30% of the ingredients that are accounted for. Plus a small amount of minerals, fiber, and vitamins. The rest are carbs. That leaves nearly 70% carbs! I doubt you want to pay for that. And I don't think you should feed it to your unsuspecting carnivores.

# DON'T FEED AN ANEMIC
# HUMMINGBIRD A STEAK

♔

*Even if the exact food an animal would eat in the
wild cannot be given, the foods we feed our pets should
approximate the nutrient components of the wild diet.*

A PANDA WITH A HEART CONDITION EATS A MAIN COURSE OF BAM-
boo, and a sniffling anteater feeds his cold with ants. As omnivores,
we can choose between a triple cheeseburger and a Waldorf salad, but an
omnivore diet is not optional for some animals, such as cats.

I have this discussion countless times a week with owners and veterinarians whose cat is refusing to eat a recently prescribed (not by me!)
kibble kidney diet and is wasting away. Worried owners are told to resist
offering foods the cat prefers because that food contains "too much" protein. This scenario makes me very sad. Not only are we offering a low
moisture content food (dry kibble) to an animal in need of hydration, but
we also shortchange them of the protein they require.

Low-protein diets mean high-carbohydrate diets. A high-carbohydrate diet is not going to help a cat's body to heal itself. Sick animals still
need to eat the food that is meant for their species. The workload for an already dysfunctional kidney will not be reduced by reducing protein levels
below what's required to support a healthy body.

The kidneys do help process protein. And it may seem logical that the kidneys' workload is proportional to the amount of protein ingested. We could surmise that if protein is decreased, the kidney won't have to work so hard. But by that logic, water should also be decreased, as water regulation is another of the kidney's jobs. We could then suggest that if we decrease water in the diet, the kidneys will have less to do. We know this is certainly not true and that proper hydration is essential in kidney disease.

A hardworking kidney is not a bad thing. It is shown that protein entering the kidney's blood circulation stimulates the kidney tubule cells to open up and start working. Cats, as obligate carnivores (they must eat meat), have a mechanism to metabolize and excrete high levels of protein. If the feline body does not have a lot of protein in the diet, the body, being efficient, will shut down these systems. Tubules can become dormant, because they're waiting for work.

When protein is present, more kidney tubules open up and they work harder. Circulation through the kidney increases in order to perform that duty. This is the principle behind giving extra fluids to kidney disease patients—to increase circulation and increase function of the kidneys. Considering kidney activity in this way, feeding a lowered protein level only perpetuates a cycle of kidney shutdown in the carnivore.

The second reason to rethink protein levels in patients with kidney disease is that feline diets are, on average, already too low in protein. These low protein levels mean that before we start lowering protein, about 70% of the food is already not protein. In the wild the proportions would be more like 70% protein and 30% fat and a little carb. Low-protein food may be creating part of the problem in the first place. Exacerbating the problem with even less protein seems disastrous.

There are researchers who claim that low-protein diets improve kidney blood values, and researchers who say they do not. Unfortunately, funding for studies often comes from the company that has the most to gain by a specific outcome. Sometimes the answer is not so black and white.

More compelling to me than data from laboratories is my personal experience with real animals diagnosed with kidney disease. I started out in my medical career as all vets did, prescribing the prescription kidney diets. The cats' prognoses were poor, and their renal failure and muscle wasting progressed as expected.

Now, on a sensible moist diet, my kidney patients live longer than expected (often by many years), have more energy, keep weight on, sport shiny hair coats, and maintain better appetites than they did on their low-protein prescription diets. I am glad I don't prescribe low-protein diets anymore. My patients love their food and are all the better for their delicious, appropriate diet.

I prescribe herbal tonics and supplements to support kidney function. Kidney dysfunction can cause elevated levels of phosphorus in the blood, making an animal feel ill. There are several supplements (aluminum hydroxide and Epakitin are the most common) that can bind the phosphorus in the GI tract before it is absorbed. Phosphorus comes in many foods, from plant to animal matter, so it is simpler to bind it in the GI tract than to avoid it. However, eating fewer grains helps because phosphorus content in many grains is high.

Iron, raspberry, and parsley help replenish red blood cells if anemia plays a role in that patient. Omega-3 fatty acids (algae DHA and fish oils), selected probiotics (Azodyl), dandelion, aloe, burdock, rehmannia, astragalus, and coenzyme Q10 are all possible supplements used to support a healthy kidney.

Supplements are harder to give to cats than to dogs. They are more suspicious and harder to pill. The first line of defense against disease in a cat is to feed them well. Don't make them waste away with a poor diet that they hate. Let them eat with gusto. Proper nutrition will give the body a better chance of healing. Some vets attribute inappetence, or lack of appetite, to kidney disease's inevitable progression. This can be true. But often the diet is wrong and the cat doesn't want it.

## ARIEL

Ariel the cat was diagnosed with inflammatory bowel disease (IBD) and subsequent kidney disease. Her owner was told to expect this to significantly affect her longevity. She was an eight-year-old cat when she was diagnosed. I saw her after she had been on prednisone for over two years for her IBD and dry kibble kidney diet. She had intermittent loose stool, chronic vomiting, and gastrointestinal issues. After we got her off a carbohydrate-rich (corn and wheat) diet, the kidney disease did not get worse, as her owner had been told it would. She stopped vomiting.

We weaned her off prednisone. She received periodic acupuncture, probiotics, and vitamin $B_{12}$ injections. With her food options improved—she was given canned food and no grains—and the integrative treatments, blood work showed that her kidney disease remained stable for many years. She had no more gastrointestinal signs and lived well until the ripe old age of twenty!

Animals with significant kidney disease can benefit from subcutaneous fluids (just under the skin). Owners can easily be taught how to administer these at home to decrease stress to the cat. I also recommend that owners weigh their cats weekly (a baby scale works well at home).

If your cat or dog does become so ill that it is not interested in eating and is losing weight, ask your vet about assist-feeding.

## ASSIST-FEEDING

Cats need assist-feeding more often than dogs, but it may come in handy for either animal. Remember that dogs can go without food for several days, but cats can become severely ill if they don't eat every day.

### Collect everything
### you need before you start.

If you have to leave in the middle to get something, the cat will think you are finished and try to leave the area.

### Don't choose your cat's
### favorite food for assist-feeding.

If you do, the cat may associate that food with the illness and may stop eating it.

### Items You'll Need

- 🐾 Towels, sheets, bibs
- 🐾 Feeding syringes
- 🐾 Food that is blended enough to fit through a syringe
- 🐾 Any medications
- 🐾 Water and wet towel (for cleaning up)
- 🐾 Dry towel to wrap the cat in or use as a bib

Use the same words every time you assist-feed, such as "It's time to eat," "Open," "Almost done," and "All done." The pet will then learn what to expect during this procedure.

Lift the side of the lip and go between the teeth at the side of the mouth—there's a gap between the long canine teeth and the premolars.

Point the syringe straight across the tongue from the side of the mouth. Squirt a small amount at a time across the tongue. The syringe should be pointed side to side, from one cheek to the other—*not* directly down the throat. The pet will stay relaxed swallowing this way. Wait until the pet swallows the food and then repeat.

Each mouthful can be 1–3 ccs at a time. A cat's stomach can tolerate 10–45 ccs per meal. Work up to a full meal per feeding over a couple of days. It is crucial not to feed too much or too fast because it may cause vomiting. And then you have to start all over again, and maybe have made things worse.

Assist-feeding should typically be done three to six times a day.

Getting a little bit of food into the stomach may jump-start the hunger mechanism. After the first 5 to 10 ccs of assist feeding, offer warm food in a bowl (adding some hot water to canned food) to see if your cat will eat voluntarily.

## PRETTY IN PINK

All species, including zoo animals, are healthier when fed an appropriate diet based on their evolution. Successful reproduction is an easy way to judge how well zoo diets and husbandry are working, because nutritional deficiencies compromise reproduction. Those deficiencies may also be responsible for underlying health problems. The animals may seem properly nourished on the surface, but underlying imbalances inhibit breeding success. Because a majority of our pets are neutered and don't breed, this important sign of a nutritional deficit is often lacking.

The vibrant coloring in a male flamingo attracts the female flamingo. If the color isn't flamboyantly pinkalicious, the female just won't be attracted. This color is directly related to the fat-soluble pigments of carotenoids in their foods. Carotenoids are rich in antioxidants and may be helpful in the general longevity of the birds. A zoo where I worked had trouble getting the supplies for the exact flamingo diet mix. Their color started to fade. Patrons began to wonder if they were sick. Luckily, within a week of correcting the diet, the flamingos pinked up. The appropriate, color-making food may be linked to other underlying body functions that we haven't yet discovered.

Arthritis is a condition that is considered the norm for older animals. Most vets don't question why; we just treat the signs. Early in my acupuncture career, I was asked to treat some camels with arthritis. As the months went on, I heard more and more instances of camels in other zoos needing treatments for arthritis. The camels I treated had responded well to the acupuncture and the word had spread. I received emails from many other zoos asking about our successes and how to treat their ailing population. I wondered why there were so many camels with arthritis in zoos. We discussed substrates, climates, and exercise, and then I looked into their diet.

This was over twelve years ago—basically pre-Google. I was researching old texts that I found in zoo libraries. I read that "without enough salt in their diets, camels develop arthritic joints." There was no other comment as to the correct amount of salt for them. So the search to find out was on.

I spoke to keepers and vets in several zoos around the world that had camels. Most of the camels in question were provided with salt blocks. It had always been assumed that they absorbed what they needed from licking the block, but clearly it was worth checking into.

Further research finally gave me a startling answer. Camels need over eight times the amount of salt that cattle and sheep require. An adult camel should have more than one kilogram (kg) of salt per week in their food. A salt lick is not adequate. In a camel's natural habitat, the plants contain a high percentage of salt. In addition, a camel is not adapted to assimilate their salt requirement merely from a salt lick.

Why their bodies need salt to keep the arthritis—and possibly other conditions—at bay is still unclear. But without the required amount, painful joints appear. With enough salt, arthritis signs decrease. Zoos began increasing the salt in camels' diet, and the arthritis diminished. I consult with zoos worldwide about this issue. It is gratifying to know that this crippling condition can be ameliorated by a simple correction in diet.

> *Zoo and wildlife nutrition can provide valuable information for our pet food solutions.*

Most animals are resilient enough to make do with suboptimal foods for a while, but adverse health signs manifest if the food remains inappropriate. It is in the interest of zoos to maintain healthy, active animals for several reasons, including the fact that lethargic animals do not attract as many visitors.

Many years ago, a zoo obtained a group of wolves from another zoo that had been feeding them only animal carcasses. The zoo "improved" their nutrition by combining a kibble dog food mixed in with raw ground meat. The wolves developed lethargy, ear infections, skin and hair coat issues, and loose stool. In a zoo animal, it is considered unusual to see these problems, so the diet was reformulated to help solve the medical problem. Once returned to a balanced raw food (meat, bones, and organs) diet, the wolves' health rebounded. I see exactly these positive changes in dogs when I put them on balanced diets with appropriate foods, too.

At one time our zoo storks were producing offspring with soft beaks and poor bone density. This sign of a calcium deficiency made no sense because the parents were feeding the chicks well, with their regular diet (they eat, then vomit up the food for their chicks). But someone found out that in the wild, stork parents changed food to an almost exclusively frog diet during chick-rearing. Frogs, as the zoo nutritionists describe them, are mostly bones with skin, providing a higher percentage of calcium for the chicks. When zoos increased the amount of calcium in the parent storks' diet, the chicks thrived.

I worked in the late 1980s at a zoo where the nutritionists were establishing baseline data on gorillas. The zoo's gorillas were suffering from many of the human maladies that were unheard-of in the wild—obesity, heart attacks, high cholesterol, and strokes. Zoo gorilla diets were based on the human version of a primate diet. As soon as meat and eggs were removed from the gorillas' diet, fiber was added, and their habitats were altered to allow more exercise, these problems disappeared.

Poison dart frogs, lethal in the wild, lose their poison in captivity. They produce poison from components in their diets that are difficult to replicate in most zoos.

Even if we can't provide the exact food an animal would eat in the wild, we should try to maintain the nutrient components of the food they are accustomed to eating. At least with our pets, we have many options for good nutrition.

Koalas only eat eucalyptus, and hummingbirds drink mostly nectar. When these animals are sick, they need that food even more. It is their true comfort food. Diet changes in sick animals should be geared toward meeting the animals' evolutionary needs. We're not going to feed a koala a bowl of chicken soup for the flu, or a hummingbird a steak. Even if it's anemic.

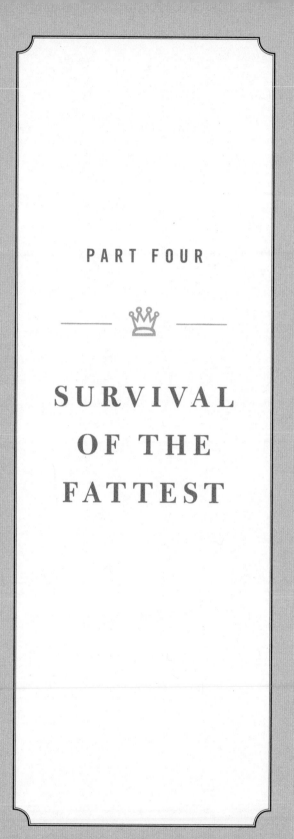

PART FOUR

SURVIVAL
OF THE
FATTEST

# LEAN TOWARD LEAN

♛

*If your pet is fat, your pet is not healthy.*

FAT IS HEALTHY WHEN IT IS A STORAGE RESPONSE TO A TEMPO-rary abundance in the environment. In nature, abundance is often balanced by a period of scarcity.

In the wild, animals put on fat for a reason—to survive the hard win-ter months. Fat squirrels, chubby sparrows, and pleasantly plump pigeons abound by the first snowfall. The pets in our care live in air-conditioned and heated environments, and dinner is delivered regularly in a bowl. For them, aside from the forays to the park, winter is now room temperature. A little extra weight in the winter to take the chill out of the wind is fine, but if that "little extra" becomes year-round roundness, it can be a detri-ment to a pet—unless he is a sled dog. Sled dogs and other pets that are predominantly outdoors in cold weather might need the insulation and en-ergy reserves to get their jobs done.

Over half of the pets in the United States are overweight. We barely even notice because, in this country, it is the norm. It doesn't look like fat anymore. It looks like a dog shape. In actuality a dog should have a defined edge to the rib cage, a waist, and hips. You should be able to feel the ribs without applying too much pressure on the chest. Unfortunately, it is more common to see dogs that look like sausages—no waist and no ribs visible.

> *Feed less than it says on the can or package.*

There are loads of reasons for the loads of fat. Pet food companies routinely recommend feeding amounts that are way too much for the average pet. I have found recommendations as much as four times too high for some of my patients. Feed less than it says on those packages! If you're unsure of the amount to feed, watch how many times a day your dog poops.

I recently talked to a client about her sweet seven-year-old beagle, Tinder. Tinder was obese and arthritic. Her owner insisted Tinder was not fat and was always starving. She was "barely feeding her enough to keep her happy." I asked her how many times a day the dog was pooping. She stopped to count. "One, two, three, four, five . . . six . . . seven . . . well, six or seven times a day," she said.

She was surprised to hear that Tinder should be pooping once or twice a day. With a constantly full GI tract, Tinder's little overweight body could never possibly use up its own fat.

> *If your pet is overweight and you are feeding it "nothing," feed it half of nothing.*

Among the reasons our pets are overweight is that the food we feed our pets is too high in carbs, which causes obesity in carnivores such as dogs and cats. Also, we exercise less with our pets than we used to. We spend more time in front of computer screens, and less time outside playing with our pets. I am looking at my dog right now as I type and I know he's thinking, "Oh, yeah? And you should talk!" And when we do exercise, the choice of a comfortable gym for us rather than a weather-related hike with the dog often wins out.

Cats get less exercise than dogs as they age. Kittens play, play, play, but older cats do a lot of window sitting. We need to remember that they need to run and romp even during their golden years.

Food is too often equated with love. While it would be unloving, indeed cruel, to starve an animal in our care, the opposite is not true. It is not more loving to give so much food that an animal becomes overweight. Owners tell me they can't stand the brown eyes begging for food. They say they must feed them at least one treat, usually several times a day. I tell clients that every treat is like feeding a candy bar to your pet. If you ate candy bars all day, how big would you be?

There are many ways you can show your pet love without overfeeding. Respond to begging with a fun game, or a nice rubdown, or a pleasant, sense-stimulating walk. We shouldn't be afraid of our pets having an empty stomach. From an evolutionary standpoint, being hungry would be more the norm than the exception. The body knows what to do when it is hungry. It becomes lazy when it is full.

I am reminded of what happened in my six-year-old daughter's karate class. One day her instructor, Sensei Rhonda, said, "Great job everybody! Shall we celebrate with doughnuts?"

Sophie's voice could be heard over the crowd shouting with the rest of them. She yelled a resounding "No, Sensei!"

Sensei Rhonda said, "What shall we celebrate with, Sophie?" And to my surprise Sophie said, "Push-ups!" I thought of ice-cream push-ups. But Sophie dropped to the floor and started counting in Japanese with each push-up she completed. She was taught that, while enjoyable, a doughnut would do nothing but unravel the hard work they'd done in class. I try more often now to think of something other than ice cream as a treat. And the same goes for pet treats.

Dogs and cats have evolved from the animals they once were, who ate what they hunted. In our homes, their incentive for exercise and work is gone. In the wild, the need to find food would have been the incentive to get them moving.

Animals in the wild experience intermittent fasting, but we never let our pets get hungry at all. There are actually many proven benefits to going hungry for short periods of time. If the body has a scarcity of

## ZEUS

Zeus, a significantly overweight Rottweiler mix, had arthritis of the hips and was unable to climb stairs. His owners had adopted him when he was quite elderly, and they weren't aware that his weight was an issue. They came to me looking for palliative care. Besides the weight problem, his heart rate was slow. He had chronic skin issues—ear infections and hot spots—that they thought were allergies. We changed his food and I administered acupuncture. I prescribed Adequan, an extremely effective, easy-to-give injectable joint supplement that I teach owners to administer at home subcutaneously, usually just twice a month after a loading dose. I also added herbal anti-inflammatories. In addition, I had his thyroid checked.

On the next visit he seemed brighter, and the owners noticed him playing with another dog. The thyroid test results had come back and his thyroid function was indeed low. We added thyroid supplements, both Western and nutraceutical, and continued acupuncture. After only two weeks, his owners said he was a different dog. He lost weight quickly and could walk up the stairs again. He was more playful. He had been aggressive and barked like mad at other dogs, but now started to be friendly to the neighborhood dogs. Because his thyroid was regulated and he could now move quickly to retreat, he didn't feel as threatened. Zeus's behavior changed as his health improved. His general comfort level contributed to better behavior. This was all-around good news for pet and owner.

food, it will protect cells, conserve resources, and activate the brain and senses to be more aware. It may even give extra help to inflamed joints and stiff muscles, to make the animal a more efficient hunter. Pets don't benefit from this if they are fat.

## SO YOUR PET IS FAT?

I have learned to be careful when I say a pet is fat.

I had a veterinarian friend over at my house several years ago, and I can remember exactly how I felt when she said, in an offhand way, "Hey, your dog is fat." I was so insulted. She could have said, "You're so fat," and I wouldn't have been more insulted. I immediately denied it—even as I looked at my dog and it rang true. Why yes, he had gotten fat in the last few weeks.

There is always emotional baggage when I tell owners their pet is too fat. I try to be tactful and give hope for a thinner future, but for the sake of the pet's health, I have to be honest.

Dogs are carnivores and scavengers, and therefore they are uniquely suited to losing and gaining weight quickly. They expect times of scarcity and times of abundance, and their body mass will reflect those conditions quickly. We can use that information to our advantage by aggressively feeding less to an overweight dog to get him to lose weight fast.

As long as there is fat to metabolize, canines will use it for energy. They do not have to exercise to lose weight, although it can help. The reduction of food will accomplish that, as long as they don't have another medical reason, such as thyroid issues, to retain weight. Thin dogs feel better and handle arthritis, heart disease, skin problems, and inflammatory conditions better.

Keep in mind that every extra *one* pound on your dog becomes—by way of some nifty calculations using physics, gravity, and a slide rule— *four* extra pounds of torque and pressure on each leg joint. This translates into some painful ambulation for overweight arthritic dogs. Get the weight off and your pet will be so much better, you may even be able to decrease arthritis medication.

*Dogs can lose weight quickly.*

## Weight Loss in Dogs

- 🐾 Chubby doggies can and should lose weight relatively quickly.
- 🐾 You can take emergency action to help reduce football-shaped dogs. In six weeks, they can lose considerable weight and look like a dog instead of a not-dog.
- 🐾 Calorie counting is not necessary. Simply use your own informed judgment. How often is your dog pooping? Are they really losing weight? 1% weight loss in 2 weeks is probably too little. 10% in 2 weeks is more like it.
- 🐾 Don't use diet foods. Just feed excellent dog food and much less of it.
- 🐾 Supplement hungry overweight dogs with rice cakes (plain); they are useful stomach fillers, and in this form the carbs aren't absorbed much. Low-sodium canned green beans are also good stomach fillers with very few calories.

*Cats shouldn't lose weight quickly.*

## Weight Loss in Cats

- 🐾 Fat cats can and should take their time losing weight.
- 🐾 Don't force a cat to lose weight quickly. It could result in serious illness and liver disease (hepatic lipidosis).
- 🐾 Just use a great-quality food and rely on the cat to lose the weight slowly.

While impatient with canine weight loss, I am resolutely patient with feline weight loss. A cat should not lose weight quickly. Once you decrease the carbohydrates, make very small decreases (maybe ⅛ less than their normal intake for a while) in food amounts. Their systems are delicate and light-touch changes are best. Cats, unlike dogs, can develop fatty liver disease from a "starvation mode" metabolism if they don't eat every day. This is life-threatening. Feline weight loss takes time and effort. Some cats may take over a year to reach a normal weight once they are on a suitable food. This is fine.

### To Encourage Cats to Exercise More

- Move food bowls to a place where the cat has to make an effort to get to it when hungry. They will be less likely to snack unless they are truly hungry.
- Don't forget to show them where the food is and make sure it is accessible to them.
- Feed twice daily. It's okay to leave a small amount of the food out till the next feeding.
- Play more with your cat—cat dancer–type toys can pique their interest.

# EIGHT ON WEIGHT

♔

## Tips for Shedding Pounds from Hounds

1.  Feed less. Pooping more than twice a day usually means your dog is processing too much food and will not lose weight. The 1% bodyweight your dog lost over six months is not visible on my weight loss graph. It may be just the difference in weighing before and after urination. Feed less.
2.  Choose a low-carb, excellent food.
3.  Substitute freeze-dried meat treats instead of baked treats with wheat or corn.
4.  Fill a begging stomach with low-sodium green beans and/or rice cakes, and other vegetables (no onions, grapes, or raisins). Adding a thin schmear of meat baby food (no onions) or butter to his rice cake can make a dog think his life is grand.
5.  Don't feed high-carb treats out of guilt because you don't have time to hang out. Most dogs love green beans. Freeze-dried meats and rice cakes are crunchy fun for them (I asked them). They snap them up so quickly, they hardly know what they are. If they don't like the treat you're offering, fine. You are not trying to convince them to eat!

6. Change your behavior. When dogs beg for food, offer playtime and petting instead.

7. Consider using supplements or herbs to help with joint function and appetite. Seek good veterinary advice before trying them.

8. Have your vet do blood work to check thyroid function, which could reveal other problems relevant to diet and weight loss.

# EIGHT ON WEIGHT

—— ♕ ——

## Tips for Fat Cats

1. Start with a low-carb food. This is even more relevant for cats (the "Catkins" Diet). They are obligate carnivores and carbs can cause obesity, diabetes, and other health problems. Find foods that are predominantly protein, with a normal amount of fat and low carbs. Don't try to look for low-fat foods for cats. They need fat in their food to lose weight. Again, they must lose weight very slowly.

2. Cats must eat every day or they can get seriously ill. Offer a preferred dish if your cat won't eat a new food within an hour or so. Even if it's just what the doctor ordered, it may not be what the cat would have ordered. They would rather starve than munch on something unpalatable to them. And even the best cat foods in the world can be considered yucky to some cats. You can't force them by waiting them out.

3. Add warm water to wet or raw foods to increase volume of the food filling the stomach, improve aroma, make the food stay moist longer in the bowl, and help hydrate your cat.

4. Don't make the food *too* easily available. A cat that sits by the food bowl and can take a mouthful whenever the mood strikes is more likely to be fat than a cat who has to leave a favorite cozy spot, hike

up some stairs, and head to the back of the house to get to the food bowl. If it takes all that fuss to get to it, they will more likely eat only when they are hungry. For physically challenged cats, make sure food is accessible, and do your best with the exercise part. Cats' bodies are built to be active hunters. Getting food should require motion. It keeps them healthy.

5.  Consider twice-a-day feeding instead of free feeding. If your cat will eat canned or raw foods, this may be easier to do than with dry foods. A cat may nibble on dry food because it's not that tasty, and they don't want to eat a lot at once. If a cat will eat canned or raw food, he may eat a full meal in one sitting. When the food is gone, the food is gone. This is a good way to regulate amounts of food.

6.  Play games with your cat. Even older animals will play if you find the right toy or game. Some food-motivated cats will even chase a piece of kibble or a dried meat treat down a hallway. The urge to hunt/play is never fully dormant in a cat.

7.  Make sure treats are carb-free where possible. Remember there's a sensitive carnivore in your cat.

8.  Keep track of how often your overweight cat defecates. If it's more than once a day, you're feeding too much. The body won't lose weight unless it feels the need for the fat.

PART FIVE

WILDEST
DREAMS

# THE UNLIKELY ZEN DOC

I ALWAYS CONSIDERED MYSELF THE MOST UNLIKELY OF EASTERN medicine practitioners. During my years as an emergency veterinarian, I was fueled by adrenaline and the immediacy of critical care. The finality of any incorrect decision was daunting. My minute-to-minute mission was keeping pets alive, each case centering on the question "Did I fix it?" I still retain that did-I-fix-it mentality. But now I add these caveats: how will I fix it, prevent it in future, *and* do the least amount of harm.

When I graduated from veterinary school, I never anticipated becoming an alternative practitioner. Having studied at the College of Veterinary Medicine at the University of Illinois, I was all about hard science and modern technology. A published researcher, I was heading into my residency in zoo pathology with a strong background in chemistry and no-nonsense medicine. Why would I step off the beaten path and possibly expose myself to ridicule? For a very good reason, as it turned out. Much to my surprise, alternative medicine proved capable of generating unexpectedly positive results. And positive results are what it's all about.

Years ago, when I started doing acupuncture, someone jokingly asked me whether an animal has to believe in acupuncture for it to work. I quipped that my needles would make an animal believe in anything. Even

Chinese medicine. Animals obviously are not influenced by placebo effects. Their response is determined 100 percent by the effectiveness of the treatment. I am happy to say that acupuncture has been tremendously effective for my patients.

I began to look for alternative options when I started working with racing greyhounds that had been retired from the track—often with severe ailments. Greyhounds are a uniquely sensitive breed, with hair-trigger reflexes. (Thus their suitability for racing; although, in terms of temperament, they are quite happy to live the life of a couch potato.) They also are highly sensitive to many medications, which can make traditional Western treatment problematic. As I became more aware of the problems faced by these cast-off former athletes—and became increasingly anguished about their plight—I decided to explore the possibility of treating them with acupuncture. This was the first step down the road that eventually led to profound changes in my practice and in my life.

I remember a pivotal case early in my integrative career. It involved a greyhound named Lightning, just retired from the track. He was emaciated and anxious, and suffered from dental disease and a broken foot. His overall health had been compromised by the constant demands of racing and by poor medical care.

I began by providing Lightning with the best practices of traditional Western medicine. His foot was set, he was neutered, and his teeth were cleaned. He was also given several vaccines, medication for pain, and a balanced meal of kibble for the first time. But despite all of that, his condition worsened and his leg was slow to heal. He lost his appetite and became increasingly anxious and difficult to approach.

My training at that time was leading me down blind alleys. I considered adding more drugs to treat anxiety in this unhappy fellow. Instead I decided to give my new alternative tools a try, and that new approach proved to be a lifesaver for Lightning.

One of the most basic principles of Chinese medicine is that food is medicine and body type determines the proper prescription. Although

Lightning's most obvious medical conditions had been treated, there were many fundamental problems that had gone unnoticed.

During his life as a racing dog on the track, Lightning had been fed a raw meat diet. Dry kibble did not appeal to him, nor would his handlers have given it to him. They knew the low protein in a kibble food would never have gotten him through a race. In addition, the sudden change from a trackside cage to a large, unfamiliar, yet loving foster family was stressful. All of the medical interventions, which included anesthesia, had stressed his immune system and his psyche.

I decided that I needed to take a step back and reevaluate the needs of this particular animal after considering both his own medical history and the evolutionary history of his breed.

As a greyhound, Lightning needed a high-protein, meat-based diet. Proper nutrition and comfort are a greyhound's best defense against panic and anxiety. He needed to be supported more effectively through the transition he was making in life.

Fortunately, after a simple diet change back to raw food, some acupuncture, and herbal supplements (milk thistle, turmeric, and boswellia, for the pain and to help him detox from anesthesia), Lightning's health and attitude dramatically improved. He went from being a lethargic patient to an active family member. The rest of his life was lived comfortably, and he adorned many a couch in his retirement.

Sustained health usually involves a combined approach—something beyond an exam and a prescription. In order to be an effective healer, it is necessary to see the animal, not just the disease it presents; to build a foundation of health, not to merely eradicate one disease after the other. This is the true foundation of medicine.

Conventional Western veterinary medicine, while certainly helpful, trains us to look for the magic bullet—usually a pill or surgery. I have had greater success trying to find and access the cause of an animal's *health*. Only then can I uncover the original cause of an animal's imbalance—which may be something fundamental, such as inappropriate diet, a genetic predisposition, or a deeper systemic or hormonal or environmental issue.

A serious health imbalance can cause a cascade of symptoms. This cascade can not only disguise the root cause but also result in the animal being bombarded by treatments that may prove to be more damaging than the original problem.

---

MYTHCONCEPTION

*A dry, hot nose indicates a sick dog.*
**Not true.**
*A cold, wet, hot, or dry nose can all indicate a healthy dog.*

# RHINO AND REPRODUCTION

—— ♛ ——

I HAVE LONG ARMS THAT COME IN HANDY IN VETERINARY WORK.
Especially in rhino reproduction work.

"Can you hold this so I can use it as a guide?" Dr. Nan Schaffer asked me one day during a rhino exam.

I was elated. I was about to get hands-on experience working on a state-of-the-art, scientific effort to save rhinos from extinction.

"Of course!" I exclaimed. "Where should I stand?"

"Well, you'll have to be standing at her bum," she said as she handed me a rectal thermometer and an extraordinarily long blue exam glove.

Forty-five minutes later, my arm felt like it was made of stone, and I could barely feel my fingers. My other arm had to stop the whiplike rhino tail from painting my face with urine. I have rarely felt so important. Nan was engrossed in maneuvering her endoscopy probe into the reproductive tract and my hand was in the colon, helping her orient and measure where she was. The rhino was standing, but dreamily snoring in perfect sedation.

An often unseen but unusual feature in rhinos is their uncommonly long, twisting, tubular reproductive road to the lotuslike folds of the cervix. Dr. Schaffer was trying to work out a method for in vitro fertilization, but evidently it is nearly impossible to find your way to the eggs without a very long and slender arm in the colon showing the way, which is where I came in.

Later that day, Dr. Schaffer and I discussed the issues rhinos confront. Poaching for their horns decimated their populations, but other factors have exacerbated this sad story. If it were easy for rhinos to find each other in their fractured habitat, if their reproductive efforts had a quicker turnaround time, and if they weren't so picky about their mates, things might be just a little bit better for their species.

The female's tortuous labyrinth and the inconsistent sperm counts in semen that Dr. Schaffer collected from male rhinos made in vitro fertilization very difficult. Years later we even discussed ways to use acupuncture, as they do for human reproduction, to possibly increase sperm count. But this was early on, and I had yet to consider acupuncture in my veterinary career.

The shipping of a male rhino to mate with a potential female is a daunting undertaking. If a male can be safely shipped to the female, the pre-mating ritual itself is difficult. And after all that effort, they may not like each other.

In the wild, there is a long and often fierce battle before mating. After the male travels miles and miles to find a female, the first thing they do is fight. The female will often repeatedly attack the male, and horns and hooves fly. This is risky even in wide-open spaces of Africa, but in an enclosed space in a zoo it is downright terrifying to watch, and can even be dangerous. The male has to withstand the repeated attacks and keep the female near him by wailing and chasing after her if she tries to leave. During breeding, males have been known to toss females into the air.

After an undetermined amount of time, she may consider mating with him. Then the odd-shaped reproductive organs of each manage to sort out their differences. A rhino penis is shaped like a lightning bolt and evidently is made to navigate the twists and turns inside the female. If she gets pregnant, which doesn't always happen, she will have only one calf, and will not mate again for at least three to five years. Sadly, this taxing and involved reproductive method doesn't bode well for animals who, in some places, count their worldwide numbers in single digits.

A couple of days later, I went back to see Naivasha, the female rhino. She is one of my favorites, and the keeper and I called her name in that singsong way people do for their pets. *Naivaaaasha!* Her head popped up out of her water trough and she trotted over. All the medical tests and her exam hadn't changed her demeanor. She always seemed genuinely glad to see people. I know that most of her affection was for the carrots in our pockets and some well-deserved back and ear scratching, but I took her keen-eyed sweet look at me as rhino love. The white rhinos are more gregarious than most. What a wonderful pet she would make. If only I could live on a few hundred acres of savanna and keep her safe from poachers, while avoiding her blind mood swings.

For some species it may be impossible to duplicate the wild where they once flourished. For the rhino, they have so much at stake, and even with so many people devoted to them, their survival is still in question. We may have to rely on the extravagant powers of technology to keep the species alive. But without their habitat in place, we may never find a way to make them thrive again.

With our dogs and cats we are more fortunate. Overpopulation is a concern; extinction is not. Improving overall health is an issue. Since the needs of dogs and cats are not so complicated that we can't meet the basics to help them thrive, we really have no excuse for not doing all we can.

"How was your weekend?" my mom asked when I stopped by for a visit.

I handed her a cup of tea and said, "Well, I don't think you want to know where this hand has been."

# A DOG NAMED FLY AND
# THE GENETICS OF HEALTH

♛

*To proactively manage your pet's health issues, be
aware of breed characteristics and the potential
pitfalls of body structure.*

I HAD JUST FINISHED RE-SPLINTING A BROKEN TOE ON A SWEET poodle puppy named Sirius when I looked up to see the receptionist waving to me from across the room. She put her hand over the receiver and said, "There's a guy on the phone. He's just pulling up out front. He's not a client—he's a dog walker—but he's panicked because his client's dog may be dying and we're the closest vet."

Three vets were on duty that day, but I was handling all the ER cases. I grabbed my stethoscope and a technician and ran out to find him. He was already through the front door and we helped him carry the large dog into an open exam room.

I didn't know the man, but he was clearly traumatized. As he lifted the lifeless dog onto the table, I knew three things. I knew why the dog was dead. I knew I was probably the only person in the world who could ease this man's distress. And I knew that because the beautiful Labrador under my stethoscope was, in fact, my dog.

It is possible to be too good at something. Fly was that kind of dog. He was number one at retrieving. If you tossed a piano into the bushes, he would, I'm sure, manage to successfully drag it joyfully back to the porch. His entire body was built to be an exemplary field dog. His brain was wired for this single-minded purpose. His powerful yet gentle jaws could carry a banana soufflé over rocky terrain without disturbing it.

Over muscles rippling with health, his ebony hair coat was sleek as an otter's, appearing both wet and dry. His swimming silhouette at the surface of the water moved like the shadow of a large bird speeding overhead. For Fly, fetch was more compelling than any other activity, including eating. Bred to be the perfect retrieving machine, he was brilliant at it.

> *In reality, all dog or cat breeds are the result of years of mixing breeds to achieve certain traits.*

Fly's field trainers, stationed a few hours away, had begged to buy him from us. They'd never seen such drive and ability. But my husband and I and our children loved him; he was part of our family. Until this point all our pets were the delightful cast of characters we collected as strays and rescues, as a by-product of my profession. But Fly was offered to us by a distant relative who knew that Matt was thinking about a dog for field trial work. Fly, a purebred Labrador, had been partially trained and needed a home.

Fly was an ideal dog for our family. We all loved him immediately. Every day he met my son at the front door and they would wrestle like wild puppy-brothers. The exuberance he brought into the house was wonderful. We didn't realize that his best attribute, that of excessive energy, would ultimately prove to be his worst liability.

The trouble started when he was about eight months old. His trainers told us he was doing a typical field training run—perfectly executed, of course—when he suddenly collapsed. After a few minutes of just lying there, unable to use his legs, he collected himself, stood up, and seemed totally normal. They called immediately to let us know.

Silently outraged, I thought that somehow they had overworked our boy-genius. I even worried that they might not have fed him properly in order to increase his already overstimulated interest in retrieval. Their vet examined him and found nothing wrong, but I insisted on seeing Fly. When we picked him up, I was certain I'd have him cured and back in the field in a day or two. But of course, being a veterinarian's dog, his condition was complicated and mysterious. Ultrasounds, cardiac workup, blood tests, urinalysis, and radiographs were all performed and yielded normal results. He looked terrific. An excellent specimen, he was more handsome and more driven to retrieve than ever.

So, perhaps he had just been hungry that day? I hoped that was true, but on a hunch I sent off one final sample to a researcher in Minnesota. He was an expert on a rare condition that could explain Fly's collapse. It seemed unlikely, but I had to follow my intuition.

Still looking the picture of health, Fly went back to his trainer, with the caveat that they feed him more and work him less. Matt would come in a couple of days to work with them. They were extremely careful, but Fly collapsed again on his second day back. After another episode during a minor workout the following day, Fly had to stop training for good.

After ruling out everything else under the sun, I concluded that Fly's malady was indeed the rare condition that the Minnesota researcher had written about: Exercise Induced Collapse (EIC). There was no cure. EIC seemed to be an unmapped inability of the muscle cells to maintain their vital energy in the face of stimulation. It was typically nonfatal but would end Fly's career in fieldwork and significantly limit his ability to do the one thing he loved—play fetch.

The condition worsened whenever his enthusiasm for play became too intense. And, of course, he spent every waking hour trying to convince everyone—passersby, the mail carrier, our cat—to throw something for him. It was heartbreaking. Selective breeding had made Fly perfectly suited to do this one activity, but doing it would kill him. I wished I could have explained this sad irony to Fly.

We had good friends, Fran and Simon, with two dogs who loved Fly, so we shared ownership with them. Luckily, when Fly played with other dogs he never became overexcited enough to collapse. He could safely be allowed to romp. Even though I could tell he was severely affected by his disorder, he managed to adjust and have a good time. All of us were careful not to overtax him. We discovered we could make him relatively happy with one or two small throws, without dire consequence.

One summer weekend we were away and Fly stayed with his other family. Their dog walker, Scott, whom I had not met yet, knew how to deal with Fly's condition and took him to the park often. Fly begged to play fetch, using every language in the doggie book. He collected objects and dropped them in front of Scott, pleading with his deep, soulful eyes. Then he sat in taut readiness, hopeful and desperate at the same time. He was starved for something to retrieve. Just one toss?

Scott was a kindhearted person and chose a nice stick. But on this day, one small toss was all it took. The mysteriously faulty body chemistry shut down his muscle function, and not only did his legs stop, but his heart stopped, too.

I took my stethoscope off Fly's chest, stifled a sob, and said, "This is my dog." Scott looked stricken. "I know it's not your fault," I said. "And I know Fly died doing what he loved."

Fly's genetic mix was created using our human yardstick and human goals. His parents and grandparents were bred together because of their incredible drive to retrieve and their beautiful physiques. The result was Fly, an über-retriever. It turns out we're not as good as Mother Nature. Fly was significantly marred. His genetic makeup, resulting in his perfect retrieving body, was not determined by evolution's careful work.

> *Breeds are created using our human yardstick and human goals. It turns out we're not as good at genetic mixing as Mother Nature.*

The breeders unwittingly had bred out nature's natural defenses and lifesaving adaptations, in favor of a narrow vision for the breed. None of this was done on purpose, or with ill intent. The breeders I know are gentle, wonderful people. They are faced with choices and they make the best ones they can. But, as owners, we should recognize that our pets may have breed-specific traits that can overshadow biological functions.

Most dogs, unlike Fly, can survive well with their breed peculiarities. Some need more management. Whether it is a purebred or a mix, there are certain traits in all breeds that you can identify. These traits can cause health problems, but with proper information and action, they might be mitigated. Fortunately, a predisposition does not mean the animal will necessarily develop the medical condition. It is possible to overcome many deficiencies.

Why do so many miniature schnauzers have diabetes? The giant schnauzers—who appear to be the same breed, only biggified—have a tendency toward $B_{12}$ deficiencies. If we could identify the risks carried by each breed's genome, perhaps an ounce of prevention could mitigate the health consequences. Dogs and cats are known to have over twenty thousand genes. This is where the new field of nutrigenomics may prove useful. There are huge implications for this fascinating science in preventive medicine and functional nutrition.

*Do judge a breed by its cover. Based on our pet's physical characteristics, we can often influence our pet's health predispositions with a few ounces of prevention.*

We choose specific pets according to our personal taste. Some people don't mind a dog that drools, but others can't stand a sharp bark. For some of us, days of quiet companionship are more important than having a good mouser. Everything from the ability to frighten a burglar to being able to fit in a teacup is determined by genetics. Fly will always be remembered by our family as the dog who flew too high. His middle name was Icarus.

# BREEDS, GENES, AND HEALTH

WE SPAY AND NEUTER most dogs and cats for good reason—to decrease the number of homeless animals. Animals that are bred now do not choose each other for their fitness or even their ability to cope with the crazy food we feed them. We choose their mates for them based on looks, drive, temperament, bone structure, or other criteria.

> *Dogs and cats have not been bred for their tolerance to a kibble diet (nor should they be), or for their ability to walk on hot blacktop, to fight the effects of annual vaccinations, or to become vegetarians. At least not yet.*

It would be beneficial to recognize the essential nature of the genetic mixes we bring into our homes. When people aren't prepared for the issues that come with a specific breed, pet homelessness looms in the future. If we acknowledge each pet's biological background we will only expect it to do what it can, according to its physical, behavioral, mental, and emotional qualities. Birds gotta swim and fish gotta fly—I mean penguins and flying fish.

- 🐾 The border collie likes a job; the greyhound likes a couch.
- 🐾 A ferret will steal your wallet for the shiny money inside (it happened to me).
- 🐾 A sugar glider will not thrive alone—it takes a village of sugar gliders.
- 🐾 Though his grumblesome stubbornness and escape-artist exploits make great cocktail party stories, a Siberian husky shouldn't be expected to retrieve.
- 🐾 Terriers, miniature schnauzers, poodles, Chihuahuas, and Pekinese are known for their sharp-pitched barking. If you

## MASSAGE FOR HEALTH

Take a good look at your pet. You may not be able to see the wolf in your Dobie-basset mix, but the streamlined wild physique has been changed into squatty angulated legs, unstable vertebral discs, and long floppy ears.

Massage is one tool to help mitigate any negative health effects of these individual structural differences.

**Face**—extra skin folds? Massage in tiny circles around the face to improve lymphatic drainage and circulation and to avoid skin fold infections.

**Ears**—heavy, floppy ears? Chronic ear infections? Take the earflap and circle it like a windmill to open up the ear canal's crenulations, improving air flow and circulation. This creates a less hospitable environment for yeast and bacteria.

**Spine**—long neck/long back? Make small circles with one or two fingers on either side of the spine. Massage a circle about every 1–2 inches down the back of a long-backed dog or cat. They may be predisposed to spinal arthritis, neck instability, inflamed discs, or disc disease. Help the body clear inflammation with this massage.

**Tail**—looped over the top, low and firmly attached curl, long waving wand, sturdy whip, or not even visible? Massaging around the top part of the tail base just where the back meets the tail can improve circulation and health of tightly adhered tails, tails that curl excessively, and tails with heavy fur. Massage boosts circulation and normal nervous function to the surrounding skin, anal glands, and muscles.

Provide some gentle traction on the spine by pulling gently along the tail. This puts mild tension on the fascia around disc spaces, improving circulation and fluid flow around the spine.

**Legs**—dragging or knuckling, mild incoordination, stilted gait? Gently squeeze the feet and pull gently on each toe a few times a day (as long as your pet is amenable to this) to reestablish nerve pathways between the feet and the head. If inflammation or circulation is compromised along the spine, the brain loses its quick connection to the feet. A foot massage can rekindle neurologic pathways from the feet to the brain.

A complete massage is a great idea for any animal that has genetic conditions affecting circulation, behavior, or musculature, or an animal that is aging and suffering from arthritic changes, has scarring from trauma or recent surgery, or has circulation compromised by heart disease, cancer, or growths. Even without these factors, massage can work wonders—it'll make for a happy pet.

know your walls are thin and your neighbors are sensitive, beware of acquiring these breeds.

🐾 Cancer is prevalent in boxers. Start early with an anti-inflammatory diet.

It is possible to obtain clues from the physical structure of your pet. This will help you with their care. You will also better understand what you can and cannot reasonably expect from them.

🐾 An owner may want a dog that loves to swim, so they should know that most bulldogs sink like a stone.

🐾 German shepherds tend to be thinkers. They like complex tasks with obstacles to overcome, or they will make their own trouble.

🐾 Some breeds, such as Afghans, may like to live with one owner, whereas other breeds, such as Labradors, may prefer the chaos of family life.

🐾 A long-backed dachshund cannot be expected to enjoy having its lower back "hugged" by a toddler in the house.

🐾 Use a harness in the brachycephalic (smush-faced) breeds. Breathing can be difficult and they can have small or poorly developed tracheas. Using a harness is easier on the windpipe than a collar and leash.

🐾 Cats with a fur pattern like an Abyssinian—there are several colors, but most of the ones I treat have a slight striping on the face, warm reddish undercoat, and black ticking all over, a very distinctive look—should be considered slightly wild and in need of constant stimulation. You might consider installing a fish tank, which is fantastic cat TV, but put a lock on the top.

Traits that are normal in one breed can be entirely abnormal in another.

❧ A border collie constantly pacing the perimeter would be normal but that behavior in a basset hound might suggest he's feeling ill at ease.

> *Working breeds will probably appreciate a job to stay healthy. And toy breeds, well, they just need an allowance.*

❧ Constant respiratory noise in a pug is a given because of its smush face, but in a Labrador may be a sign of a throat condition called laryngeal paralysis.

❧ Great Danes tend to think they are lap dogs, and will curl up in surprisingly small spaces. Even though they are a giant breed, they don't require a giant house (but maybe a giant lap). On the other hand, some tiny dogs need tons of exercise and a large yard and a kingdom to rule or think they rule.

> *An animal that is a perfect fit in one home may be a disastrous fit in another.*

Are you thinking of choosing a smush-faced Persian-mix kitty? They're cute as can be, but keep in mind that the breed is predisposed to the following:

❧ nostril constriction
❧ tear duct overflow
❧ dental malocclusions
❧ polycystic kidney disease
❧ progressive retinal atrophy (PRA)
❧ upper respiratory issues
❧ cardiac disease

When I say predisposed, I don't mean those conditions will necessarily afflict your pet. The best defense is, as always, to feed the right diet. Be proactive and you may never see any severe health problems. Here are some other tips for smush-faced breeds:

- 🐾 Keep the teeth clean.
- 🐾 Keep them well hydrated by providing extra water bowls and warm water in canned or raw food.
- 🐾 Monitor air quality; avoid smoke, heavy perfumes, air fresheners, chemical cleaning agents, and off-gassing new carpets (this can also be problematic in terms of skin irritation).
- 🐾 Groom the thick hair regularly.

## GIMME SHELTER

I STRONGLY SUGGEST THAT when you want a pet, you go to a shelter and pick out an animal from the thousands that need homes. Shelter pets range from newborns to geriatrics, from slightly trained to fully trained. Some come from happy backgrounds and some have troubled pasts. Any of them will be grateful to have a home instead of a cage or worse. Those that don't find homes are often euthanized.

There are a number of breed review websites online, and hundreds of breeds. Start with your ideal pet in mind. If you are at a shelter, look for a combination of breeds that fit that ideal. There are good qualities in every breed and combination.

*A happy pet home is about managing expectations.*

Choosing which type of pet you will take into your home is important for you, but also for the pet. There is nothing worse than trying to live up to unrealistic expectations.

I serve on the board of directors of Chicago's largest no-kill shelter, PAWS Chicago. I have seen animals of many breeds go to great homes and happy lives. PAWS found a loving home for Red, a pit bull shot in the spine while protecting his owner from a burglar. Red's rear legs were paralyzed but he lives a full life in his new home in the country. He even has his own Facebook page. There are so many benefits of adopting a dog from a shelter. I recommend you find out what shelters are in your area and make a forever home for a lonely pet.

Wherever you choose to look for your pet, don't just go out and fall in love with the first cute face you see. I know sometimes it's unavoidable, but it's a good idea to ask yourself these questions in advance. You and your pet are likely to be happier in the long run.

- 🐾 Do you want a purebred or a mixed breed?
- 🐾 A dog or a cat, goat, or bunny?
- 🐾 Do you mind feeding meat to a pet?
- 🐾 A guard dog or a cuddler or both?
- 🐾 Big or little?
- 🐾 An active dog or a couch potato?
- 🐾 A shedder or a hypoallergenic type?
- 🐾 How much time can you devote to your pet's exercise?
- 🐾 A quiet dog or a barker?
- 🐾 A puppy or an older dog?
- 🐾 Long hair or no hair?
- 🐾 Two kittens instead of one?

I suggest that you always get two kittens. They don't have to be from the same litter, but they should both be under a year. Two kittens are infinitely more fun than one kitten and even more fun than a barrel of monkeys (and I'd know). They amuse each other, they still bond with their human, and they are more fun to watch than any television show.

🐾 Two puppies instead of one? Getting two older dogs is a
   lovely idea. But think twice about getting two untrained
   puppies.

I suggest only getting *one* puppy at a time, even if you separate them
by just a few months. It can make a huge difference in training, bonding,
and a lifelong attachment. Two puppies that grow up together tend to bond
to each other and think of the world as "us and them." Training two puppies at once is nearly impossible, and doing separate training for each dog
is difficult for most owners. Getting one puppy allows that puppy to have a
place in your hierarchy and an interest in learning your commands.

Several of my clients decided to get two puppies at once and were
overwhelmed by how difficult it was. In fact, several of my most famous
clients adopted shelter puppies in pairs. The complications involved in
training two dogs at once were quickly obvious to my client Billy Corgan,
even though he had an abundance of patience as well as resources. Like all
my clients, he put in a great deal of personal time and means into making it
feasible. The inter-dog bonding issue was a struggle, but he was successful
in the end.

Before choosing a pet, it's a good idea to think about your lifestyle
and where you live. Be aware that each animal is a unique personality and
you may not get exactly what you want—but you may get what you need.

MYTHCONCEPTION

*Dogs see in black and white.*
**Not true.**
*Dogs do see colors, but they have dichromatic vision,*
*which means they may find it hard to distinguish*
*the range of colors from green to red but*
*they probably see blue and yellow well.*

🐾 If you live in a very hot climate or don't have air-conditioning, you should rethink any of the smush-faced (brachycephalic) breeds we've been talking about such as bulldogs and pugs in the dog, Persian and Burmese in the cat. They don't have enough nose surface area to help cool off by panting. And the same goes for the northern breeds/Alaskan breeds and some giant breeds such as malamutes, huskies, and Saint Bernards with thick, warm coats. Remember, if you keep them thin, they can handle the heat better. Overweight animals are surrounded by a fat, insulating layer.

🐾 Even mild dehydration can skyrocket a dog's internal temperature, as their only way to diffuse their heat is through panting over a moist mouth, or sweating through their feet.

*Always keep plenty of water available for all dogs and cats on hot summer days. A cat's water requirement can increase sevenfold just to survive a very hot day. For dogs it may only be double the amount, but they need more than usual on a hot day.*

🐾 If you live in a predominantly cold climate, remember to buy a wardrobe or nice blankies for your Chihuahua, Mexican hairless, shorthair breed, or your Peterbald cat.

## THE EYES HAVE IT AND THE NOSE KNOWS

### Sight Hounds

Certain breeds of dogs, such as greyhounds, borzoi Afghans, whippets, salukis, and deerhounds, have traits that go hand in hand with their primary reliance on sight. They are visually stimulated, always looking for the flip of a rabbit's tail.

For these breeds speed is more important than endurance. Don't let them overexert themselves. They love the chase but are easily overheated and are highly reactive. Don't let them run loose, and be careful in summer.

- 🐾 Greyhounds, and the sight hounds in general, are known for their ability to relax on a comfy bed. Ironically they don't need tons of exercise. They do like a quick running romp in a fenced-in enclosure (otherwise they will run away), but it's usually over in a few minutes.
- 🐾 Greyhounds playing together often wear cage muzzles partly because they can be aggressive to each other and partly because their skin tears so easily.
- 🐾 Never leave a greyhound, or any pet, in a car in the summer. They quickly become critically ill when overheated.

### Scent Hounds

Breeds such as bassets, German shepherds, coonhounds, beagles, and Labradors are, even more than other dogs, led by their noses.

They are stimulated by the scent of their prey. They have endurance to follow a trail. They need a job and are happy to work, but their main job is to find food.

- 🐾 Good training is critical—no begging allowed. Feed only at certain times and in a certain location. Try to provide a perfect diet.

I was visiting my friend Brian's summer home when we got a lesson in scent-hound determination and food motivation. Having cooked a lovely roast, we set it on the table and went down to the waterfront to tell the other guests that dinner was ready.

When we made it back up the stairs, we saw the screen door to the kitchen was bent and almost completely off its hinges. We soon noticed that the roast was the only thing missing. The neighbor's beagle (four doors down, with adjoining yards at the back) had raced to her home with the roast in her mouth, tail wagging furiously, as if to say, "Thanks for cooking it just the way I like it!"

Seconds before the heist, the beagle burglar had been at home with her family. She suddenly sniffed the roast in the air and bolted out of the door. The neighbors weren't worried because she often visited Brian's dogs. No real harm was done, of course. The pizza was delicious.

A MIXED BREED PET may get all the best attributes of each breed, or all the worst, or a mix. I know plenty of Labradoodles that, despite their hype, still shed and have arthritis and allergy problems sometimes from an early age. I always hope for hybrid vigor and improved health in a mixed breed, but one never knows for sure if it will happen. I personally think the mystery mutt is intriguing. Some of my all-time favorite animals are of unknown ancestry.

On the other hand, it's interesting, and useful in terms of providing care, to know about your pet's particular genetic mix. It's not necessary to know the exact name of the breeds involved. You can learn much about your pet just by looking at its physical traits.

The newer DNA blood and saliva tests for breed identification to date seem to be moderately accurate at best. They can help in deciphering a lineage for many adopted pets. Breed identification is an emerging science and may improve with time. I used my own seventy-pound mutt, Henry, to see how one of these tests worked. I had no history on him because he was a stray I was fostering and decided to keep. He looks like a large fuzzy coonhound mixed with a German shepherd. His breeds came back as: 50%

Chihuahua, 25% shar-pei, 12.5% Pomeranian, and 12.5% Rottweiler. I could only believe the Rottie part.

Henry may be a Chihuahua at heart, but I don't buy him winter coats, and he doesn't bark for no reason. I do make sure he doesn't overheat in summer and I let him run and smell to his heart's content at our local beach. At 70 pounds he's awfully big for a Chihuahua. He *is* inordinately fond of Mexican food, though.

REGARDLESS OF THE THROW of the genetic dice, your pet might turn out to be the greatest on the planet. It has definitely happened to me.

Finally, I'd like to contradict myself somewhat by saying that if you fall head over heels in love with a pet, no matter what the breed or species, and are compelled to take it home, feel free to disregard some, most, or all of the advice above. You may have just found your soul mate.

MYTHCONCEPTION

*Dogs and cats from shelters are unhealthy mutts.*
**Not true.**
*Shelter pets are often there for reasons unrelated to
health or behavior. They can be purebred, mutts,
or of unknown heritage. They will all be
very grateful for a home.*

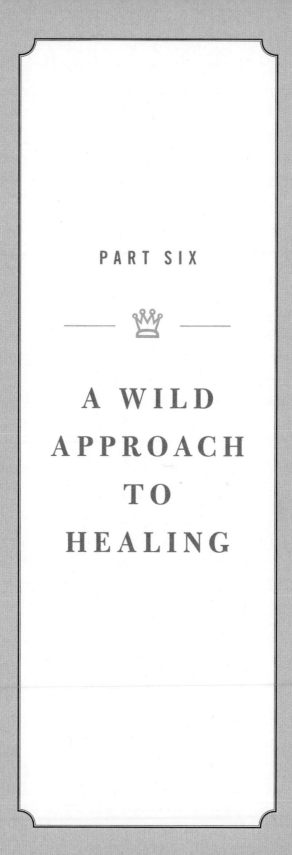

PART SIX

A WILD
APPROACH
TO
HEALING

# ACUPUNCTURE

♔

## The Point of Health

*Acupuncture is the most direct contact I have with an animal's immune system and general body flow.*

I AM AWARE THAT EVEN AS I PLACE NEEDLES INTO AN ARTHRITIC dog or an asthmatic cat, a pet owner may be skeptical. But when their pet is better, almost miraculously, they keep coming back, and the obvious improvements continue with each treatment. During treatments, some pets become very calm. Clients note that their pet looks "Zen'd out." I take this as a good sign that energy and circulation are changing.

Acupuncture is ostensibly about needles, but what the needles help is circulation, by sending a message to the body. Sharp messages such as "relax this muscle" or "a little more blood here, please" or "could you drain here" or "remember this foot?"

Using needles, I am in communication with the body. Perhaps every method of good medicine is a communication—about what the body can do, about what it needs, what works and what doesn't. I receive information and answers from the needles that assist me diagnostically. At the same time, I am treating the problem at hand. It is a gratifying practice.

I didn't always think acupuncture was a viable medical option. I had heard what I believed to be unsubstantiated rumors about patients recovering, and that some doctors found it surprisingly effective. But because I didn't understand the basis of it, I disregarded it. I always found the stories interesting, but also like fairy tales: too good to be true.

I arrived in Canada for the International Veterinary Acupuncture Society course feeling like a traitor to the training I had received in vet school. I knew that my colleagues felt that learning Chinese medicine was a step in the wrong direction and that I was wasting my time. Because they were not trained in these techniques, they did not see how they could be successfully applied to medical practice. Despite this discouragement, I still wanted to learn more. I was frustrated by the model of treating disease instead of curing it. Much of what I found when reading about acupuncture made medical sense to me. I began to think there might be some truth to those fairy tales about acupuncture and alternative healing.

The instructor began our lecture by saying: "This course is going to change your lives!" I distinctly remember thinking, "Oh, please!" At the very most, I would learn about these interesting needles and then go back to my life. I was already a doctor. Well trained and serious about medicine, I had physiology down cold. I had dissected, studied, and magnified almost every imaginable species. I knew circulation. I had traced blood vessels, nerves, and lymphatics as they branched their way through the body. If there was a pathway for the invisible "Qi" (pronounced "chee") to circulate vital life energy through the body, I had never seen it.

As we studied the ancient Chinese descriptions of disease states, the English major in me loved the dramatic and colorful imagery used to describe diagnoses: overactive liver fire acting on the weak stomach, which causes rebellious Qi (vomiting). An external wind-cold invasion through the Winds-Gate point on the upper back that is not fought off by Righteous Qi becomes an accumulation of phlegm (a cold). The acupuncture narrative was more poetic and dramatic than my other veterinary textbooks.

Then we followed case studies. There I was in class, watching, riveted, as animal after animal benefited from this ancient Chinese healing art. I saw improvements in animals with conditions such as lumbosacral arthritis, inflammatory bowel disease, and kidney disease. Diseases that I had only seen addressed in a limited way by Western medicine. There almost seemed to be a magic in it, an amazing day-to-day magic of a body healing itself. It was breathtaking.

After administering acupuncture to many species of animals, the process now makes sense to me on many levels. A neuromuscular connection is stimulated by the needles. They exhibit a measurable charge polarity that affects the tissues when they are inserted. This corresponds to chemistry—the idea of positive and negative charges that rule intercellular interactions, nerve impulses, muscular contractions, and physiologic functions.

Acupuncture needles affect body chemistry. They balance the flow of nutrients in and out of the body. Injured areas of the body have a different resistance and electrical charge than healthy areas. Needles redirect flow and impulses to deficient areas. The body is then able to facilitate the healing process. At the acupuncture points, there is an increase in nerve endings, small capillary beds, nerve fibers, and aggregations of mast cells.

## CHINESE MEDICAL DESCRIPTION

Acupuncture—Placing needles in specific points to elicit a physiologic and energetic response. These points are located on interconnected pathways, called meridians, that carry the body's Qi. The Qi, meaning vital life force or energy, responds to the needles. This response helps the body regain homeostasis and heal itself.

As a result, needled areas have a measurable physiologic change in beta-endorphin release, stimulation of circulation, and decrease in inflammation.

In pain control, experiments have shown a modification in neural impulse transmission from the spinal cord to the brain after acupuncture. There are now many studies measuring how acupuncture points affect brain oxygenation. They provide information on the physiologic responses to needles. For example, when points on the limbs that are associated with vision were stimulated with acupuncture, the optic centers of the brain increased oxygenation by 80 percent. There are more studies on acupuncture completed every year.

When I added Chinese medicine to my bag of treatments, I had not only more tools—acupuncture and herbs—but also a new way to analyze and remedy the internal and external conditions affecting an animal. Everything that goes in, on, and around an animal in his world can affect his health. This includes weather, seasons, and natural and man-made disasters.

When I feel acupuncture points and notice deficiencies, or localized heat areas, I wonder why these signposts are there for me to find. Did evolution expect acupuncturists to come along? My understanding of why we need acupuncture, chiropractic therapy, and massage is based on what animals experience in their natural environment. Their bodies are touched by the elements. They physically respond to rain, wind, snow, and everything they encounter. Their legs are scratched by grasses as they run through the prairie, or jabbed by branches as they forage in foliage.

The animal's environment itself acts as a sort of acupuncturist—stimulating circulation during a struggle through the underbrush, or a roll in the dirt and stones. The more animals are isolated from this rugged connection to the earth, the less their bodies can heal themselves in this natural way. Animal bodies expect their circulation to be stimulated by their environment—weather, wind, trees, bushes, twigs, leaves, caves, stones, water. This was one way I initially made sense of acupuncture.

Skin needs to be touched. The health of an animal depends on it. In many cases it is a medical necessity. The health of sick kittens significantly improves if they have sufficient physical contact. In the same way, the physical presence of animals has a positive influence on humans. Research shows that petting a dog or cat relieves stress and improves the health of the owners. Acupuncture is another way to touch.

A couple of weeks before I left for Canada, I had injured my shoulder lifting a large dog. It was terribly painful and I could no longer lift my arm. I had consulted with an orthopedic doctor and was told the injury was severe enough to consider a surgical repair, which would be followed by a lengthy recovery. I decided to take some time to think about my options.

The first night in the hotel, one of my acupuncture classmates offered to put some needles in my shoulder. I received a very public acupuncture treatment in the hotel lounge. After a few minutes, one of my other classmates tried to remove the needles, but they would not come out. We waited another fifteen minutes, then all the needles came out easily. My shoulder had already begun to feel better.

The needles need to stay in until they're done—which varies according to species, body part, and type of health issue. You can tell when to remove them because the needle lets go. Dogs require 5–15 minutes. Needles in cats require less than dogs: 3–8 minutes. Elephants and camels take needles for 15-plus minutes. High-energy animals, such as birds, require only 1–3 minutes—often I can just "ting" the point, which means quickly insert and take right out.

The success of acupuncture on my shoulder is pleasantly summed up in a picture of me, shortly after the course, comfortably lifting my son in the afternoon sun. Today I have no signs of that injury.

I believe that years of practicing with acupuncture have changed the way I use my hands in general. I rely on them now as a primary sense, almost as much as my eyes. When I ran the alternative wing of a veterinary specialty center, our exam rooms and offices had no windows. Everyone was worrying about Y2K—the turn of the century and the possibility that we'd have a blackout. I joked that it didn't matter to me; I could do acupuncture in the dark. The most important sense for acupuncture is touch.

Acupuncture can decrease pain and slow the progression of diseases.

Tangible physiologic changes that positively affect the health of animals often occur as a result of acupuncture. These changes can positively affect the health of an animal. Most animals I treat are relaxed during the treatment and show almost immediate signs of relief afterward.

Acupuncture's potency as a pain reliever is truly remarkable. I have treated arthritic or injured animals that regained their spunk after just one treatment. An owner reported that a patient went home and used basement stairs she had avoided for years. Another patient jumped up to a high comfy bed that would have been impossible before the acupuncture treatment. I warn owners to be alert for this potential reaction to healthier circulation. The pet's body may feel rejuvenated in one treatment, but more time is needed to restore stability and strength for improved activity. Without rebuilding muscle and reestablishing neuromuscular connections, a pet can hurt himself.

## WHAT HAPPENS DURING AN ACUPUNCTURE TREATMENT?

THE PATIENT IS CALMED as much as possible on a comfortable mat on the floor, with some water, a treat, and a rubdown. We may dim the lights, which seems to work wonders for cats. A hands-on exam determines the current points that will be used. They can be in sensitive areas that are hot or cold to the touch, depressions in the skin, scars, thickened joints, or swellings. Signs of current problems, overall condition, and other health history issues contribute to the point prescription. Points are also chosen based on the animal's tolerance and temperament. Needle size is proportional to the animal and point location. I have very tiny hand needles for very tiny animals. I use long needles specially designed for the mega-vertebrates such as elephants or camels.

The animal usually doesn't feel the needles. However, at inflamed points, the needle may feel like a sting. Stronger points may go in without any sensation, but then shortly after, a small "zing" can be felt. This is called the arrival of Qi, which is integral to the treatment. Many animals don't react to the arrival of Qi. However, some dogs are startled by the arrival of Qi, just as they are by someone knocking at the front door.

Yawning is considered a good sign during an acupuncture treatment. When an animal yawns it usually signifies a change in energy. That is the goal of the needles. If a point bleeds, it is considered a beneficial reaction. If a tiny acupuncture needle causes bleeding, the congestion in that point was released.

One of my favorite things about studying acupuncture is the vivid, poetic names for the various points.

## Some Names for Acupuncture Points

**Walks three miles.** When you think the patient is done for, put a needle in this point and they can walk another three miles.

**Surround the dragon.** Putting needles in a circle around an inflammatory skin lesion, like little tilting metal fence posts. This keeps that hot dragon skin from spreading, and cools it down.

**Kidney tiara.** Needles are put in a pretty pattern over the area on the back where the kidneys live. It does resemble a midback crown. Especially if bejeweled acupuncture needles are employed.

**Longevity point.** A point that increases longevity. How cool is that?

**A forbidden point** (CV8) is located midline in the belly button, and should never be needled. When I asked what happens if CV8 is needled, my teacher replied, "Don't ask, don't do it." But I now know it affects the immune system and overall energy flow and is a very strong point. Warming moxibustion of this point is usually the only way it is treated. Warming moxibustion is the technique of burning moxa (mugwort, *Artemisia vulgaris*) above the surface of the skin at a specific point to warm the meridians of the body. Moxa looks like a charcoal stick. One end is lit and burns like a hot coal. It is held over the area to be warmed. Moxabustion is one way to heat an area that requires increased circulation. Another way to do this is to fill a balloon or an exam glove with hot water and place it on the area. The self-made water bottle should just cover the area being treated. Large hot water bottles diffuse the heat and are not effective for this purpose.

## WHAT IS ACUPUNCTURE GOOD FOR?

Developed over thousands of years, the medical system of acupuncture can ameliorate almost all medical conditions, including:

- 🐾 Arthritis, disc disease, post-op orthopedic surgery, and many musculoskeletal conditions
- 🐾 Seizure disorders
- 🐾 Anxiety, behavior problems, and other neurologic conditions
- 🐾 Allergies, autoimmune diseases, inflammatory intestinal conditions, immune system disorders
- 🐾 Asthma, kidney, liver, and heart disease, and other systemic diseases
- 🐾 Cancers—to boost the immune system and to mitigate side effects of chemo
- 🐾 Dermatitis, lick granulomas, hot spots
- 🐾 Incontinence, bladder stones and chronic infections, urologic diseases

Methods:

- 🐾 Dry needles—just the needles
- 🐾 Aquapuncture—injection of substance into acupuncture

points to stimulate them instead of needles. Can be vitamin B$_{12}$, saline, Traumeel, or other substances.

🐾 Electroacupuncture—wiring the needles to a stimulation that looks like cruel torture but is sublimely effective at decreasing pain, decreasing inflammation, and improving circulation in cervical disc diseases

🐾 Laser acupuncture—I use a class 3B cold laser to stimulate points instead of needles.

🐾 Acupressure—massage-like small circular finger pressure to improve circulation. I teach owners to do this for certain conditions. See below.

🐾 Moxabustion—heating points using a lit charcoal made of mugwort warms and increases circulation.

🐾 Gold bead implants—surgical procedure to implant gold beads in acupuncture points, typically used around joints, especially the hips

Acupressure points I teach my clients to use for pets, for the following conditions:

🐾 Seizures—the midpoint of the ear, between the eyes
🐾 Nausea—inside the forearm above the wrists
🐾 Anxiety—the midline on the head, at the top of the head on the crest of the skull
🐾 Hip arthritis—three points above the head of the femur-like cap on the hip joints
🐾 Kidney disease—a circle of points that cross the spine, behind the ribs

I treated Affie, an African elephant, with acupuncture for her arthritic front legs. I couldn't use many points because of logistics. Acu-points on her bladder meridian would have involved me climbing on her back, and she was not an elephant who tolerated passengers. I would have used points on the inside and back of her rear legs if it hadn't been life-threatening. I chose accessible points, and she let me put needles in a number of very effective spots.

Affie was never chained or restrained. If we called her and she didn't come, we didn't force her to come, we just held off the treatment that day. Every interaction between us was aimed at strengthening our bond.

As with all animals that are closer to their wild side, Affie took her time to get to know me. Then we started the dance. I moved deliberately and continuously, placing needles in the leg she presented to me. Most of the points are put in by feel, so it was easy for me to watch her as she watched me.

I stopped when I saw the whites of her eyes. Eye movement is one indicator of an elephant's emotional state. When Affie was calm, I could see the dark color of her iris, and the pupil, but very little of the outer white part of her eye was visible. As with a human, when an elephant is worried, surprised, or shocked, her lids open in a different way and you can see the whites of their eyes. If she seemed anxious, I offered her a treat and said something reassuring. I was also vigilant about my escape route.

We were all careful not to drop a bucket, trip on a cord, or make a sudden move. Elephants never forget and a wrong move could frighten her and make her wary of me. Fortunately, she became increasingly comfortable as time went on. She tolerated not only the acupuncture, but cold laser acupuncture as well.

Cold laser, also called low-level laser light treatment, is a painless method to decrease inflammation and improve circulation in an area. Stimulating the body's own response on a cellular level, the laser, measured by joules of energy on the machine, penetrates the cells and enhances anti-inflammatory mediators to increase circulation. Despite an elephant's thick skin, the energy penetration is still effective. Once she was comfortable with the machine and its beeping, Affie was not bothered by the treatment.

Putting in the needles can be challenging. I use what's called an insertion tube: a small tube that surrounds the needle. If you tap several times with the tube before you push the needle through, the skin is fooled into

## FAGIN

A feisty fifteen-year-old Labrador was brought to me because he was having trouble with his rear legs and couldn't go up stairs or jump anymore. He had severe lumbosacral arthritis (spinal arthritis where the spine joins the hips). I treated him successfully with acupuncture and the underwater treadmill. For over a year he was doing very well but then all of a sudden, he couldn't walk at all. I added electrostimulation to his regimen of weekly acupuncture. After just two treatments he was back to his favorite stroll in his garden. These two modalities, which have no side effects, kept him going strong in his golden years.

ignoring the needle. According to traditional Chinese medicine, acupuncture needles actually have a sharp but rounded tip. They feel different than hypodermic needles. According to this ancient medical lore, they push aside the cells rather than cut through them.

Every animal, breed, and species has its own reaction to acupuncture. It is a very individualized treatment. Some breeds, like Weimaraners or whippets, are more skin-sensitive than others. Other breeds, like terriers, take longer to respond to acupuncture because, I believe, they are contentious by nature. Labradors will seem to benefit from the needles right away. Cats are surprisingly complacent about acupuncture. I think this is because they are accustomed to sharp claws and teeth. I love treating cats because their response is rapid and dramatic.

You can tell by feel alone when the needles are done working. When they are inserted it feels as if I'm pushing through tight gravel. The needle is being grabbed by the fascia and tissue as it goes in. When the body is done with the needle, it lets go of it. Then the needle, which up until that second couldn't be pulled out easily, comes out as if out of butter. I've heard an acupuncturist for humans say, "Leave that needle in until it falls out." I've also heard that humans are slow boats when it comes to the length a needle has to stay in for treatment.

## GETTING STONE ROLLING

IMAGINE A LONG, THIN, completely hairless cat, with a sweet temperament and constantly in motion. His skin felt like the shortest velvet, smooth and cool. Stone was a Peterbald cat with a history of more than two years of constipation and megacolon (which sounds like what it is, a distended large intestine). He was a moving target when it came time to insert the needles. We changed him to a high-protein diet with increased fiber and supplements (pumpkin, psyllium, and aloe) and gave him a wonderful herbal cascara combination that I order from Natural Path Herb Company. After four weeks of treatment he was having much more normal stools. We weaned him off the stool-regulating pharmaceutical meds and continued his acupuncture treatments, after which he would usually go right home and poop. He took herbal supplements and was fed his new diet. He continued to do well. Eventually, we decreased the herbs and continued acupuncture, though less frequently. If we went too long between acupuncture appointments he had a flare-up, but those became fewer and farther between. Now Stone comes in once every six months for a tune-up. The only treatment he requires these days is a great diet and supplements based on his stool output—which is now normal.

I HAVE SEVERAL CLIENTS who bring me more than one dog to treat at a time. The dogs don't mind having acupuncture with each other, and it is fun to see how they interact. With the needles in, most dogs will Zen out and relax together.

Bella, nearly thirteen, and Jake, almost ten, come together for their arthritis treatment. Jake is a gentleman. He is a German shepherd mix and acupuncture makes him feel wild. Bella is a beautiful and opinionated husky. She's not averse to biting if she's not pleased with something. I've been lucky and have managed, with her permission, to treat her for many months. She is one of my favorites because she is spunky, and she responded immediately to treatments. Using acupuncture and their new diet, we improved this elderly couple's overall health, reduced their pain, and improved spinal circulation and rear foot placement. Underwater treadmill sessions helped them both regain their muscle strength. Both dogs were stiff and slow, but now they roughhouse and act silly again, like puppies.

Sharky (Lhasa apso) and Rick (schnauzer) come together for maintenance treatments every three to four months. They both are excited to come and vie for my attention even if it means accepting acupuncture needles. I treat Rick for arthritis and to improve his immune system after he had malignant melanoma surgery. Sharky has disc disease. Their owner notices that their treatments have made them significantly healthier and pain-free.

Amadeus is a German shepherd whom we treated for his kidney disease. We combined our acupuncture treatments with the treatments of the local kidney specialist. He had been treated for months before we started. We did not recommend a low-protein diet. Amadeus had a high-protein diet and thrived on it. We used points that improved circulation to the kidneys, supported his circulation, and boosted his immune system. His kidney values improved and then plateaued over the months of his treatments. He did not have the precipitous decline in kidney function that was originally a concern for him. He also worked out in the underwater treadmill for his overall health.

Sometimes, even though a patient comes to me for acupuncture, I may recommend some other treatment. Pippa is a young long-haired dachshund who came to me with disc disease. She had been healthy until two days before, when she came in from the yard and started falling over. The veterinarians at the ER didn't do a radiograph because she was a dachshund with obvious signs of disc disease, including poor sensation in her rears, walking drunkenly, and pain in her spine. They started steroids and sent her back to the vet the next day. The vet was concerned when the steroids didn't seem to be working, so she sent the dog to me for acupuncture.

It didn't make sense. I wanted radiographs. I was as shocked as the owner when the radiographs showed a broken back. Rather than treating her with acupuncture, I sent her for back surgery to stabilize her back.

There had been a windstorm the day she was injured. Several tree branches in the yard had fallen, and one must have hit her.

After surgical repair of the fractured spine, she came for acupuncture, as well as underwater treadmill treatments to help her recover. She is healthy and active and walks and runs quite well now.

One day, I was heading over to work a double ER shift when I began to get a migraine. I called my internist for advice. I told him I couldn't take migraine drugs before an ER shift.

"What about acupuncture?" he said.

"What?" I said.

"You're taking that acupuncture course, aren't you? Do you have any needles? Aren't you supposed to practice on yourself?"

"They didn't teach me points for migraines. I don't think animals get migraines."

"Try it," he said. "You've got nothing to lose."

I worked out my Chinese diagnosis and placed the needles in my forehead, ears, hands, and elbows. Thirty seconds with needles in and my migraine was gone.

# GETTING THE MOST
# OUT OF YOUR VET VISITS

A VETERINARIAN IS THE INTERMEDIARY BETWEEN YOU AND YOUR pet. He or she is the much-needed translator who interprets the signs you are noticing, assesses their significance and seriousness, and determines the best course of action. In my experience, pet owners are not only looking for solutions; they are also looking for reassurance and a plan, even if the prognosis might be poor.

## What Clients Want from a Veterinarian

- Confidence and competence
- Advocacy for their pets
- Love for their pets
- Well-informed, sensible options
- For things to be easier rather than harder
- Kindness
- For their pet to be evaluated within the context of their lives and to develop a plan for health

*Nothing medical should be so complicated that you can't understand it on a basic level.*

Visiting the vet can be stressful. Animals are keenly attuned to fear, worry, anxiety, pain, and illness of other animals. Most pets take their emotional cues directly from their owners. So a *relaxed* owner can calm down the whole vet visit. When we take blood pressures on dogs and cats, we routinely subtract about 15 percent or more from the values because of the "white coat factor."

Many clients bring their complicated or "hopeless" cases to me. It is understandable that they are stressed before they walk in. Don't hesitate to let your vet know you are anxious. My colleagues in veterinary medicine are some of the most dedicated and kindest people I know. They may be able to quickly alleviate some of your anxiety.

Years ago a keeper brought a cotton-top tamarin monkey to the zoo hospital because of an intestinal problem. Several options were discussed. We were finally settling on a surgical solution when the keeper burst into tears. The young tamarin immediately began to struggle and panic.

We had assumed that because the keeper was a professional and had dealt with medical procedures daily, she would be fine with the idea of surgery for the little one she had raised. But the emotional attachment between an animal and a person cannot be underestimated—even among professionals.

In this case, it was essential to alleviate the fears of both primates, the human and the little tamarin. We explained to the keeper that the procedure had been successful on a number of tamarins and that we didn't anticipate any issues. As she calmed down and dried her tears, the monkey calmed down as well.

During stressful situations, the adrenal glands begin to fire. Adrenals produce either adrenaline, glucocorticoids, or mineralicorticoids. Systemic effects of these hormones can hinder healing. Alleviating stress can prevent the onslaught of these volatile hormones. This can improve the chances of unblocking an animal's own immune response. In addition, therapeutic treatments, anesthesia, and blood tests are more accurate, and negative reactions, as well as side effects, are decreased.

A little attention to detail and a calm explanation make clients and their pets less stressed. As busy vets, we can be focused on clinical details and miss the signs of distress. Don't be reticent about telling your vet your concerns.

## Questions I Discuss with Owners About the Care of Their Pets

🐾  What would you like to do, what can you do, or what are you willing to do, to restore the wild health of your pet?

🐾  Other than being a chauffeur to the vet, do you feel you can be an effective advocate for the health of your pet?

🐾  What have you tried, or what have you been told to try, but cannot?

🐾  From food choices to pharmaceuticals, do you feel you are overwhelmed by options or out of options?

🐾  Does your pet's condition make you sad, stressed, or fatigued?

---

ROYAL TREATMENT TIP

*Bring your dog to the vet office for random visits—without having an appointment—so he can just be there with you and greet everyone. This way he will have a good association with the vet instead of tension about medical procedures. Be sure to give him a treat there.*

---

## Exam Room Etiquette

🐾  Animals should typically be examined in the presence of the owner. But there are exceptions to this. If the exam needs to be done in a different room, ask why that is the case. Logistics or restraint issues may be the reasons. Or it may be necessary in order to do multiple procedures quickly— this can save time and decrease stress to the animal. Or it may be warranted because the pet does better without the owner.

🐾 If your trusted vet feels strongly that your pet needs an exam without you there, defer to his or her judgment.

🐾 Blood drawing and other invasive procedures are often best accomplished in a different room than the exam room. This ensures that the exam room remains a happy, calm place for communication and examination, and, in my practice, a comfortable place for acupuncture. A calm animal benefits more from acupuncture and other treatments than a stressed one.

🐾 Where possible, have your vet draw routine blood work from the jugular vein in a dog or cat. It may seem barbaric, but it is just the opposite—a much less painful and easy-to-heal area for venipuncture. If, in the future, an IV catheter needs to be put in a leg vein, it won't be as scarred from multiple vein sticks over the years.

🐾 Radiographs must be taken without the owners present because of radiation exposure and adherence to the rules specified by the Occupational Safety and Health Administration.

*Make sure that the tests make sense to you, and that the results will not only provide information, but also directly affect a course of action and treatment.*

# STANDARD OF CARE

"STANDARD OF CARE" IS what would be considered cautious, reasonable, and prudent for any diagnostics procedures or treatments used in veterinary medicine. While a generally accepted measure of any doctor's basic plan of treatment, standard of care is not a specific set of guidelines. It is only a subjective and changeable checklist that comes into play when a treatment is questioned between veterinarians or in a legal action. This measure is a way to make sure that veterinary care maintains a level consistent with the current standards of excellence. But it can also be a deterrent to innovation, as it may encourage practitioners to blindly follow accepted protocols, even when the outcomes continue to be negative. If everyone is doing it, it must be correct (and vets are safe from lawsuits). Standard of care helps define tests and procedures that most vets in the same circumstances would perform.

> *If you can't understand your vet, or they can't explain the process, the action, or reason for testing, think twice.*

When there is no better plan in place, a test or procedure may be the only action a vet can take. There are times when it is better to avoid a false step and more information is needed before proceeding. But it is always reasonable to ask how any diagnostic test might affect the overall treatment plan.

Ask Your Vet:

🐾 Is the test painful or stressful, or does it pose other risks such as bleeding or infection?

*If you have a small animal, your vet should minimize the blood taken for testing. Tiny animals do not have large volumes of blood and can't spare much for testing.*

🐾   Is there a less invasive way to find this information?

🐾   Does the benefit of the test outweigh the risks of the test?

🐾   Is the test itself more of a risk than the possible disease?

🐾   Will the test yield a treatable result?

🐾   Will the test results prove the obvious or are the results predictable without the test?

🐾   Will the test results change the treatment plan or the outcome?

🐾   Is the test looking for something highly unlikely?

🐾   Is the test exorbitantly expensive?

🐾   Will the test results be reliable, specific, and sensitive?

And then ask yourself:

🐾   Does the test make sense to you?

*Tests themselves may cause a problem that didn't exist before.*

Tests and procedures should be governed by efficacy. Of course, an animal can't choose for itself, and we, as advocates for our pets, are responsible for developing a medical plan that makes sense. Choose tests and procedures that will improve the prognosis and/or quality of life, and make sure the chosen tests are the best way to provide answers. Sometimes a test may be needed for a vet to rule out a hunch or follow a thin lead. As long as you can see some logic, trust your vet.

Because they have the technology to do them, veterinarians increasingly rely on diagnostic tools. However, test results do not always provide information that leads to a correct diagnosis. A thorough physical exam can sometimes preclude invasive tests. I was taught in vet school to obtain as much information as I can prior to testing, and then move into clinical diagnostics.

One of the many advantages of integrative medicine is that I can treat an animal without relying solely on a "Western diagnosis." I can treat animals using holistic protocols that heighten an animal's own response to disease in general. These protocols include alternative methods such as acupuncture, massage, supplements to support the immune system, improving diet, decreasing debilitating medications, and improving emotional conditions, as they impact the patient's specific condition and needs.

## THE ECHIDNA

Small, spiny, and prehistoric-looking, the echidna is one of the few egg-laying animals that are mammals. It weighs between four and eight pounds.

Long ago, researchers in England seemed to have proved that captive echidnas develop anemia over time. Monthly blood draws showed this to be true. But other conclusions can be posited: 1) Researchers may have drawn so much blood from the tiny animal that it could not compensate for the blood loss and therefore became anemic. 2) Echidnas may regenerate blood loss at a slower rate than other species. 3) The stress of the testing suppressed the echidna's red blood cell regenerative process. And I'm sure there are others.

## When Should the Vet Take a Rectal Temperature?

A rectal temperature may be unduly stressful to an animal. Some pets tolerate it with no problem; others will fight it valiantly. This can exacerbate other conditions and take valuable energy away from their healing process.

A vet must ascertain whether a fever is a real concern. If it is not, the rectal thermometer can be put away. I may forgo taking the temperature in view of the totality of the situation, resorting to taking the temp later or using a less accurate ear thermometer.

## Are X-rays Safe?

Radiographs (X-rays) are useful diagnostic tools. While no amount of radiation can be considered unequivocally safe, radiation from the newer radiograph (X-ray) machines is minimal. To put things in perspective, the veterinary X-ray machine in my practice will give 0.05 mSv of radiation—significantly less than just one transcontinental airline flight.

If a radiograph is required for treatment or diagnosis, I don't hesitate to take one. It is possible to take great X-rays without anesthesia. In my practice, it is a rare case that requires sedation for an X-ray. If your vet requires anesthesia for all X-rays, I would ask why. Sedation may be required if you have a pet who rolls like a croc and stings like a bee; needs X-rays of sinuses, head, or teeth; or is in too much pain to hold the correct position for an X-ray. However, the trend to routinely sedate all animals to take X-rays should be reconsidered.

## Blood Test Ranges May Not Always Be Correct

Another common issue that may confuse pet owners is a pet's BUN (blood urea nitrogen) level. If you are feeding an appropriately high-protein diet, your pet's BUN may be higher than some laboratories' normal ranges. When an animal eats more protein, the body will have more protein by-product (blood urea protein) in the bloodstream. In fact, there are several laboratories that have increased their normal value range to accommodate the expansion of BUN values in normal animals. Even though some of my patients have BUN levels slightly above the normal range, it is not due to any kidney malfunction. Their kidneys prove to be healthy. The increase may be a normal number for an animal eating appropriate protein.

Many reference ranges were originally determined using laboratory animals, often beagles, eating a "normal" diet of kibble. But the typical kibble foods were much lower than 30 percent protein. It is possible that most normal BUN ranges in laboratories may be set too low.

## WHERE THE WILD THINGS ARE HEALED

FEELING APPREHENSIVE IN A place that is designated for healing is counterproductive. Here are five reasons to keep patients and clients relaxed.

1. Physiologic reactions to stress release hormones and chemicals that make the body ready for flight, rather than mobilizing forces for healing. This makes healing a more difficult task.

> *A calm animal has better results from acupuncture and other treatments than a stressed one.*

2. Animals and humans who are stressed present a side of themselves that may not be typical, a side that could mask an illness or lameness. When an animal is stressed it overcompensates, attempting to appear healthy. Not wanting to be an easy target, its primary concern becomes escape.

3. When stressed, the brain does not readily absorb or retain detailed information. A pet's health depends on the owner's understanding and implementation of a plan outlined by their vet. Stressed owners aren't as likely to follow through fully on the health plan.

4. The nervous system of a stressed animal may not respond readily to acupuncture needles, and the beneficial neurological effect could be lessened.

5. It is far healthier for a regular patient to be excited about coming to the vet than to be dragged in with blood pressure soaring and heart racing in fear—and that goes for the owner, too.

Owners are often reluctant to mention supplements and herbals they have gotten over the counter, for fear of ridicule. Therefore, they don't always tell the full story to their doctor. I often hear new clients say, "I've never told my vet, but I have been giving . . ." or "I found these things online, but I was afraid to tell my vet I've been giving them . . ." or "I love feeding from the table, but my vet disapproves, so I don't mention it" or "Please don't tell my veterinarian I told you this . . ." Owners may feel their concerns are either too frivolous or in conflict with "real medicine."

I have designed my practice to have a soothing atmosphere, conducive for healing. I believe it is a place where both the pet and the owner can feel comfortable. When a new client comes to me, I encourage them to provide a complete picture of their pet's life.

My clinic has pinewood walls, high ceilings, superior ventilation, large windows, and an abundance of natural lighting. The waiting areas have individual barnlike stalls designed specifically to decrease the stress of animals having to interact with other animals. The walls between the stalls are three feet high. This protects pets from other pets while allowing owners to be able to talk to each other. My exam rooms have Dutch doors that can be fully closed or open halfway to decrease the feeling of isolation for both client and patient. The upper door has a window in it, letting in natural light. Rooms are equipped with a dimmer switch to lower the lighting when it is needed to calm a patient.

The textured, blue-painted concrete flooring in my clinic provides good footing. For most animals, the exam and treatments take place on a large athletic mat on the floor. A massage pillow is on the client chair.

Make sure your pet knows you feel comfortable at your vet's office. This alone can make a big difference.

### Elements of a Great Vet Visit

- Your common sense
- Treats for your dog, maybe for your cat, too
- List of questions/concerns
- Be ready to describe your pet's health issues—write them down beforehand
- Complete list of food, treats, medications, supplements, and ingredient lists
- Ask your vet to put these lists in your pet's record
- A muzzle, if your pet needs it
- A favorite brush for your pet
- A book for yourself. If possible, just focus on your animal and the issues at hand. This may not be the time to multi-task.
- A comfortable distance between you and your pet—If your pet wants to be near you, move your chair closer. If you prefer to sit on the floor with your pet, ask for a towel or a blanket if there is no mat.
- Ask first—Avoid misconceptions about how to appropriately pay for your vet's time and expertise.
- Enough time—There are important health decisions to be made, so try to schedule enough time. If time runs out and

you have more questions, make sure to ask the best way to get them answered—either by phone message, email, or another appointment.

I tell my clients that our first appointment will last at least an hour. I like to have time to listen to my clients, and I have a lot of opinions.

## FINANCES AND YOUR PET

DISCUSSING FINANCES IS STRESSFUL for many clients. I make a point of talking about the cost of treatments, or diagnostics. If finances are causing clients to lose sleep at night, I want to know about it. Treatments, diagnostics, foods, supplements, and medications have to be affordable to be sustainable. There are times when an owner has to make difficult decisions based on cost. Ideally, a vet should be able to help find alternative ways to proceed in a financially feasible way.

One of my clients instituted a treatment fund for animals in need. We now keep a log of services and items that people donate to help other clients in need. This has made a difference in many cases.

## INDIVIDUALITY AND YOUR PET

IT CAN BE USEFUL to categorize dogs and cats by general personality traits and constitutions to get better results in handling and treatments. Letting the veterinarian know your dog's tendencies is not a bad idea.

In traditional Chinese medicine, the Five Element Theory describes five constitutional types that relate to the animal's overall genetic and emotional type. They correspond to an increased susceptibility to specific health conditions. Determining which constitutional type your pet is can aid diagnosis, treatment, and preventive medicine. It is also an enjoyable exercise to see how well these descriptions may fit your pet.

# The Five Constitutions:
# Fire, Earth, Metal, Water, Wood

Here are descriptions of the five Chinese constitutional categories as they relate to pets (based on a combination of my experience and Cheryl Schwartz's book *Four Paws, Five Directions*).

## *Fire Constitution*

Example: The Yorkie or small cat that is hyperactive, superhappy, overaffectionate, and, at times, anxious to the point of frantic behavior when they are left without their owner in a strange place. They overheat easily, and dream actively—appearing restless and paddling through their dreams. They may be so happy to see their owner reappear that they pee nervously. This pet would be subject to conditions, such as cardiac disease and metabolic disorders, relating to the heart and small intestine.

## *Earth Constitution*

Example: The chocolate Labrador or fat cat type that is food-motivated, willing to please, gently friendly, or an overweight couch potato. She would sleep late and improve in energy as the day progresses, but can have low stamina and be a worrier. Her health issues could be related to the spleen/pancreas and stomach and she may show possible signs of periodic GI upset or arthritis or possible lipomas or tumors.

## *Metal Constitution*

The schnauzer or Siamese cat that is tough, somewhat aloof, and clever. He bonds strongly and has trouble recovering from loss of a fellow pet or a human. He may have issues with the lung or large intestine. He could have a constantly runny nose, congested sinuses or asthma, or loose stool, and may have problems with the sense of smell.

## Water Constitution

A tabby cat or a Dalmatian that is terrified of strangers, noises, the vacuum cleaner, anything new. She is slow to rise from a prone position and is chronically thirsty, and craves salty foods. She may have medical problems associated with her kidneys and urinary bladder such as chronic urinary infections, and urination issues, which worsen in the winter and cold weather.

## Wood Constitution

A calico cat that frequently picks fights or a terrier mix that barks at visitors. The type of animal that is suddenly testy when being petted. Possessive over food and is small but powerful. She has health issues that relate to the liver and gallbladder. These relate in Chinese medicine to the skin and to eyes. She would often have red eyes that may have a discharge, a strong-smelling allergic skin, and possibly skin allergies. Because of the connection to the digestion through the gallbladder and liver, she could have loose stools with blood in them.

IN REAL LIFE, ANIMALS rarely have just one of these types. Most animals have a predominant characteristic constitution, and then one or more subtypes.

## Some Basic Dog Personality Types

Knowing each personality type can make a difference in how the pet is handled in the clinic, and how they respond to treatment.

1. *A nervous shadow.* Standoffish, somewhat protective or shy, may be head-shy. Difficult to keep engaged, or to bring out from under a chair. Synced into owner's emotions and movements.

2. *Territorial teenager.* Appears benign, but doesn't hide from confrontational circumstances. Can be provoked to bite apologetically and usually won't break the skin.

3. *Equal-opportunity saliva-sharer.* Overly friendly, hyper, jumping, aggressive licking, and nervous urination. Ask vet to bring in a towel. Would never bite anyone.

4. *Everybody's best friend.* Relaxed and friendly, moves comfortably between humans, involved, happy to please, looking to owner for cues. Happy tail-wagging causes colorful shin bruises.

5. *Mr. Chill.* Everything is fine; not all that interested in human activity and will tolerate almost anything. Has a vibrant inner life.

6. *Everyone is a postman; everyone should be bitten.* Aggressive/protective of space, may lunge, bite, or snarl. May even consider biting owner.

Aggressive dogs (number 6) require some serious consideration and handling. A dog like this may be protective of their space. At the vet, this means they may feel compelled to guard the exam room. If you have an aggressive dog, the vet should not enter the exam room where you and your dog are waiting. It is wiser to have the vet go in the room first. It can be tricky logistically, but well worth it in terms of safety for all.

## Aggressive Dogs Take It Down a Notch Tips

❧ Ask if you can enter the room when the vet is already there. This means you need to be told when the vet is ready to come to your exam room.

- When the vet is outside the door, immediately leave the room with your dog and have the vet go into the empty room.
- Wait a few seconds and return to the room with the vet already there. With the vet claiming the space, your dog will not guard the room when he and you return to the exam room.
- Inform your vet if your dog resents being looked directly into the eyes, as some aggressive dogs do, or is head-shy, or hates the color red.
- Do not be offended if a muzzle is used. Many aggressive animals are less stressed and less aggressive if their mouth, their major aggressive feature, is under control. When muzzled, they are forced to relax. Never underestimate the stress level in a room where there is an aggressive, unmuzzled dog. Once a muzzle is on, staff, vets, and even the pet's own family members are more relaxed. The calm is contagious. Consequently, your dog will receive better care.
- Bring a favorite toy such as a tennis ball or laser light, or bring a treat. Let the vet offer it to develop a rapport.
- Divert the dog's attention. I have been known to take the leash and walk the dog out of the exam room. I have even escorted the dog outside for a full change of venue. This shows the dog that I am allowed to be in charge. Distracted by the walk, they are less worked up when we get back. If need be, I can even do the exam outside.

## CATS IN THE EXAM ROOM

*The best way to keep cats from becoming fractious is to not let them get out of control in the first place.*

## FIBBER

Fibber was a Rottweiler who hated acupuncture. He had already bitten several acupuncturists. It was the owners' last shot at alleviating Fibber's severe hip arthritis pain. I asked his owners what distracted him, and they told me, after a lot of thought, that the only thing he was transfixed by was a cat in a storefront near their home. I put our clinic's cat, Chainsaw, in a carrier in front of Fibber during his acupuncture sessions. It was amazing how well it worked. Fibber stood motionless staring at the cat. Needles were totally ignored. Chainsaw didn't mind; he was used to dogs. Eventually I was able to do acupuncture by just showing Fibber a carrier with a stuffed toy in it, then just the carrier, and finally nothing at all. We became great friends and he tolerated his acupuncture treatments well.

WHAT WILL CALM YOUR NERVOUS CAT? Nothing. Cats are always thinking, "I must get home." Cats, unlike people-oriented dogs, are place-oriented. Their home is often the only place they are comfortable. Cats are less interested in who is with them than where they are. Unlike dogs, who generally feel better if their owner is with them, cats are not impressed by anyone pretending to help or be sympathetic. Some cats will not be happy until they return to the comfort of their windowsill. Don't expect cuddling to fool them. Exam, testing, and treatment for a cat should be relaxed, yet speedy.

That being said, a vet should still take a little time to relax them. They sometimes do respond to face rubbing. This is similar to being licked by their mom when they were a kitten. They often can be more easily examined on the doctor's lap on a thick towel.

> *If you know your cat likes a good ear rub, or has another favorite place to be scratched, don't hesitate to tell your vet this useful information.*

## How to Tell If Your Cat Is Stressed

❧ Dilation of the pupil (black part of eye) indicates stress level. A stressed cat tends to dilate her pupils—leaving a black-looking eye, with a very small strip of color around the edge.

❧ A panicked cat may simply freeze or may turn into a wild thing.

❧ Cats may flatten their ears and fluff out their fur and tail when threatened.

## How to Alleviate Stress in Cats

❧ Rub around the face in smooth strokes, starting from behind the head and quickly moving around the eyes, until the iris (color part of eye) responds by widening and the cat is not dilating her pupils as much. This is a more relaxed condition for healing.

❧ Let them hide their head under a towel or under your arm if they're on your lap.

❧ Full-body-wrap them in a towel or give a mild pressure with open hands on the shoulders—this can simulate a "hug" feeling that calms some cats.

I find that cats can usually be managed with a combination of gentle, slow intention and efficient, speedy exams. They respond well to firm but gentle restraint. I usually do my cat exams with the cat sitting on a towel in my lap. I can easily feel when they tense their leg muscles for a spring, or shift their heads before turning to bite. It also makes my legs a human force plate to help diagnose musculoskeletal problems.

Not all cats are calmed by being wrapped in a towel and so they manage to crocodile-roll out of it, regardless of any restraint. Those cats can do better wearing a firm Elizabethan collar or a pointy conelike plastic mask. It is impossible for them to turn and bite as long as this stays on. Nails trimmed before the appointment improves the chances of a bloodless interaction with the vet.

## Leave Your Vet Visit With:

- A healthier pet
- Fewer treats
- Your questions answered or at least addressed
- A plan for the short term, and maybe the long term
- Peace of mind

# THE LOST ART
# OF THE PHYSICAL EXAM

♛

*I have seen too many exceptions to*
*always expect the rule.*

ONE OF THE MOST POWERFUL LESSONS I HAVE LEARNED FROM animals is to pay attention to details. During a fifteen-minute physical exam, I am able to assess many things. These initial minutes allow me to become familiar with the totality of the animal.

Taking the time to look and touch, I have found conditions that were not readily discernible. I have also often surprised myself and the owner by coming to a different diagnosis than the one we had all expected.

Before I even begin the hands-on exam, I have already formed an impression about the overall condition of the pet based on energy, interest, ambulation or gait, weight, hygiene, and eye contact. Dogs and cats are some of the few species that truly look *into* your eyes. Neck and back posture, tail action, respiratory rate, and muscle tone also tell me much about the animal before I begin to physically examine them. I might be thinking "oh my, what a lot of energy," or "great condition," or "oh dear, how sad," or "an obvious problem," or "this is a tangle that needs unraveling," or "none of this makes any sense."

What do I know at a glance? Here's what goes on in my brain (enter at your own risk):

**Coat.** A coat should have some luster to it, and some shedding is okay. Any shaved areas should show regrowth—unless it was recently shaved—or it may be an endocrine or nutritional issue. Dull, thin, poor hair coat could be caused by a recent bad haircut or playing in a dust bowl or secondary to an underlying systemic condition (endocrine, nutrition, organ function, mange/immune). Visible dandruff? Why is it there? Generally it means poor circulation to the skin. I may have to follow up with blood work or other diagnostics.

## GREYHOUND CORNS

Unique to greyhound breeds are the painful corns that are thickened, keratinized areas of the pads that can cause severe lameness. Often the corn is discovered in a limping dog after many X-rays and other diagnostics have come up with nothing. Corn pain improves when walking on softer surfaces, or if the foot is in a bootie.

When examining greyhounds, check the feet first! Corns are subtle, hidden in the keratin of the pad. They are circular, flat, much firmer, and may protrude slightly. Corns are easier to see if the pad is wet.

Curing them can involve anything from periodically soaking and curetting them away, having the pet wear a boot for several weeks, or even just sticking a small cutout of duct tape over the lesion. When you remove it some of the tissue comes off. This is repeated every few days until it is gone. Check with your vet for the most effective treatment for your pet.

**Gait.** The way the legs move provides valuable information about the whole animal. Dogs and cats come equipped with three legs and a spare. Even mild irritations can make them choose to avoid a leg, and over time cause muscle atrophy and secondary back pain.

Watching how an animal walks gives clues as to what, where, and how bad the pain is, anywhere in the body.

Animals that walk hunched up and as if they are on eggshells could have limb pain or arthritis. Or this kind of tentative walk could mean a sick or injured core, or serious disk or neck injury. They could also have meningitis, or a central nervous system disease such as syringomyelia. Even a kidney or liver infection, or a painful spleen from a tumor or injury could be present. The animal may be walking slowly because they don't know where they're going. Typically with a cognitive (brain) issue or blindness, they will high-step, or look like they are goose-stepping.

**Eye Contact.** Interest in surroundings, hydration status, fear, aggression, pain, anxiety, friendliness, hunger, and blindness are all visible in the eyes.

I teach all my interns to look at the retina. The retina is a thin screen at the back of the eyeball that detects light impulses and sends them to the brain. Cats and dogs have a beautiful, reflective, iridescent area called the *tapetum lucidum*, which can be seen with an ophthalmic lens. It can be gold, blue, green, or variations thereof. It sits behind the photoreceptors of the retina and magnifies the available light. This is how pets can see so well in the dark. If the retina becomes detached, the *tapetum lucidum* is no longer visible.

I learned the eye component of the physical exam from my veterinary ophthalmologist friend Elaine. When we were in vet school, her enthusiasm about looking at retinas was contagious. We each bought the fancy, expensive lens so that we could look at retinas. In order to see the retina, the pupil needs to be dilated. Medical dilation is not necessary for felines, however, because most cats will naturally dilate their pupils out of fear of

## NO-JUMP MISTY AND THE BLIND
## LEADING THE TEST

Misty was a cat with arthritis in her hips. She was sixteen years old, very active, and had always been a jumper. She could jump onto her owner's shoulders in one leap. One day, she suddenly stopped jumping, but everything else seemed fine. A quick visit to the vet and some radiographs confirmed that her hip arthritis had worsened in the last three years. The owners wanted to pursue acupuncture rather than anti-inflammatory meds that could affect her kidneys. I did my typical physical exam on her. She was in pretty good shape but needed some diet adjustment. Her heart rate was a bit fast and she was so scared, her eyes were fully dilated. Cats don't generally do gait exams well. They resist walking, and if they do walk, it always looks crouched. She was no exception. I moved on. She did seem stiff in her hips on palpation. But it didn't make sense to me that she had stopped jumping so suddenly. So I took out my ophthalmic lens.

Misty's retinas looked like parachutes billowing in a slow wind. Misty was blind. High blood pressure had blown the retinas off the back of her eyes. The good news for Misty was that her blindness wasn't permanent. Within two weeks, a combination of acupuncture (even one treatment can transiently lower blood pressure), medication, and supplements, Misty was able to leap to her owner's shoulder. Her hips had never been the problem.

vets. Fear-dilation can work as well as dilating eyedrops, and doesn't last as long. A quick look at the retina, even when normal, can divulge secrets that other parts of a physical exam won't. Retinal clues have helped me to diagnose Lyme disease, brain tumors, and congenital problems.

## THE BODY SCAN BY HAND

AFTER MY FIRST IMPRESSION is made, I move on to the manual exam. Nothing is more illuminating than getting my hands on an animal. I can sense much of what is going wrong. While I am impressed by the fine detail in digital radiology and the accuracy of genetic testing, I have to get my hands on the animal before I feel truly confident about any diagnosis. The physical exam is the lens through which I read every diagnostic test.

Technology should not replace the power of our hands. Instruments are, of course, an extension of our hands. They allow us to go places and do things we couldn't do otherwise. I have worked with many tools including MRIs, endoscopy, surgery, and others. But I never underestimate the value of a good old-fashioned physical exam.

> *When you have an extra minute,*
> *do a hands-on body scan of your furry friend.*

I don't expect you to be an expert on physically examining your pet. But a good place to start for most pet owners is the simple hand scan. Your hands give you information about the health of your pet through his or her skin. Heat, cold, discharge, swelling, and/or sensitivity are important signs.

Move your hands over your pet's body from nose to tail, down each leg, under the belly, and around the tail. A body scan will make you an authority on what is normal for your particular pet. If your pet is amenable, let that scan include a quick trip around the teeth and a gander inside the mouth. Take a good sniff of the mouth and ears. Become familiar with your pet's normal odor. Changes in an animal's odors can be the first sign of trouble.

A body scan will also tell you if your animal is overweight. You should be able to feel his or her ribs without too much pressure. When you are aware of what is normal for your pet, you can better assess weight loss and gain.

If your pet turns his head to look at you every time you move your hand over a part of his body, that is where a painful area could be. This is called guarding. Animals, like people, can be ticklish. Over time you'll get to know the difference between feeling a ticklish area and a painful, guarded area. Don't forget to examine less visible places, such as under the collar or between the legs.

A cat was brought to me because she couldn't walk well. She was in a perpetual crouch and was barely moving at home. Her family hadn't noticed that the fur was so matted between her legs that it restricted her stride. It was basically a little fur straitjacket. We shaved the cat's matted hair and watched her leap around the examining room.

The salutation is the first part of my physical exam. I rub and scratch around the neck. This is calming for most animals. Other comforting moves include circles around the ears, between the eyes and down the nose, or around the neck, and rubbing on the forehead. The exam will be better tolerated if the animal is relaxed.

A dance of getting to know each other takes place during the physical exam. If an animal seems resistant during this initial phase, I do not drag them over to me. Instead. I will offer something appealing, such as a terrific meat treat. Often they take the treat and retreat to a corner of the room or under a chair. But usually they will come right back when I call them because of the possibility of another treat. They will now be more comfortable because it is our "second date." This time I won't let them go until the exam is over.

Odor is an important part of the exam. If there are any unusual odors from the ears, mouth, or anywhere else, I take note. Infections or pH problems have a distinct smell.

Many mouths have normal black pigmentation. To check the mucous membrane color, I pull up the lips to find an unpigmented pink spot. The coloring there can be various shades of pink, I press on the gum or cheek, turning it white. I count the seconds to measure how quickly the pinkish color returns. All this tells me about circulatory health.

I look at the tongue for color, size, and coating. These qualities of the tongue are an integral part of Chinese diagnoses.

The eyes should be moist and clear and the left and right pupil size should be uniform. I note any discharge and its color. The part of the eyeball above the iris should be mainly white with just a few pink vessels in it. If this upper part looks very vascular (not white but pink or red), the eye is irritated. Causes can range from allergies to infections to corneal ulcers to just "I'm hot and excited because I've been straining on a leash." If the leash is the suspected reason, I'll recheck at the end of the exam. It is normal if the lower part of the lid, when pulled down, looks vascular. I also check the eyelid margins for any growths, and nostrils for discharge.

Next I palpate the whole body for lumps or bumps. I check for lymph nodes under the jaw, on the front of the shoulder, in the armpits, behind the knees, and in the inguinal area.

After this, I palpate the abdomen, feeling for any lumps or bumps. For a cat, I will lift up the front legs to make the kidneys more accessible. Nothing I do when I palpate the abdomen should be painful. I will back off if I feel the pet tightening abdominal muscles or "guarding" any part of the abdomen. An area might need further investigation, and I will probably repeat that palpation later in the exam.

I look under the tail, checking the anus to make sure the anal glands don't look swollen or have any masses or discharge. In girls, I'll check the vulva and surrounding area to see if there is discharge or saliva staining red. In boys, I'll extrude the penis and look at the sheath to make sure everything is normal.

I conduct a range-of-motion exam for all joints on all legs, checking for flexibility, strength, heat, and arthritis.

I check the spine for motility and comfort. Enticing with a treat, I make the head move in all directions. While I'm doing this, my hand is on the animal's neck so I can feel any spasms or tension. I rub the sides of the spine with a light pressure of my fingers—not to elicit pain, but to feel the subtlety of muscle tension, heat, or cold over an area. I don't need to make them scream to find a problem area.

We must be respectfully cautious of technology. This includes tools. When I get out the tools, everything changes for a skittish or recalcitrant

### FINNEGAN

Finnegan, a twelve-year-old overweight Labrador with severe joint and spinal arthritis, was afraid to use stairs. He had had several bad falls because his rear legs were weak. He avoided stairs and wouldn't use his painful rear legs. His weight was shifted forward off his rear legs when he walked—about 75% of his weight was on the front legs and 25% on the rears when it should be about 60% front and 40% rear. His atrophied muscles made the rear legs even more unstable. His owner brought him to me for therapy. First we had to alleviate the pain and inflammation. Acupuncture, weight loss, and a new diet worked wonders. The underwater treadmill helped him regain his muscle strength. Finally, we had to convince him to use the stairs again. This proved difficult until we hit upon the idea of putting treats on every step. It worked like a charm.

animal. One good way to ruin the friendly relationship I've built is to take out a tool. I have to be surreptitious about it. Once they see me about to use even a harmless stethoscope, the animal often acts as if I am an alien. (I guess they don't remember our first two dates.) I may place the treat on the tool and let them come over and sniff it. From then on, I must act with efficiency and speed. I use an ophthalmic lens and a light to look in the eyes and see the retina, searching for anything abnormal. I inspect the ear canal all the way to the tympanic membrane, looking for any ectoparasites, infections, discharge, or growths.

Finally, I take out my old friend, the one piece of equipment that goes with me everywhere, the stethoscope. As I place it on the chest, I feel the inside of the thigh where the femoral pulse is palpable. I assess the pulse with each beat of the heart, looking for three things: force, depth, and width. This is part of a Chinese diagnosis. I am also looking for pulse deficits. I listen to the heart for murmurs or odd beats. I auscultate the lungs and along the trachea to discern any respiratory noises. If I'm concerned about the GI tract, I put the scope on the four quadrants of the abdomen, listening for borborygmus (one of my favorite words), meaning the rumbly tummy noise heard in the digestive tract.

If there is an orthopedic problem, I'll take the animal into a bigger space for a comprehensive assessment of their gait.

People like to say that "numbers don't lie." But numbers can be skewed for many reasons. Without a framework, the tests and numbers can be misleading. The physical exam is a reliable framework for my integrative practice.

## LAMENESS

LAMENESS IN YOUR DOG is more obvious than lameness in a cat.

Most lameness is easiest for owners to see when an animal is walking. An animal can often hide lamenesses better when running.

## NALA

A client came to me in a panic. The family had moved, and he had taken his Weimaraner, Nala, to the local vet, who had found extremely high blood pressure (over 200 mm Hg systolic). I had already been treating Nala after knee surgery and the owner still drove to me for post-op therapy sessions. We discussed the blood pressure results. I remembered when I had first seen her three months before: She had been so terrified that she had to be carried into the exam room. She was shaking uncontrollably. I asked if that was her normal behavior or was exhibited only at the vet. The owner told me that Nala shook when she went into any building other than the houses she knew. She was a rescued pet and no one knew her history. Over the course of therapy, she had become so relaxed with us that she would run into my clinic. Her physical exams had been great and she was doing well. It didn't make sense to me that she would suddenly develop high blood pressure. I suspected that she had been terrified at the new vet, just as she had been when she had first met me. The owner confirmed that she had been seized by a full-on terror with the new vet. We recommended having her blood pressure taken at home. It turned out to be normal.

Use common sense and double-check a result if it seems unlikely. Paying more attention to the numbers than the patient can be dangerous. Giving Nala the recommended blood pressure medication could have been harmful to her.

## Head Bobbing

This means a front leg is most likely the issue. "Head down on sound" means that an animal's head will be down while stepping on the leg that is the "sound" leg. In other words, it is not the painful leg. The head will be lifted to decrease pressure as they put their weight on the painful leg.

## Shortened Stride

The leg that is lame is kept off the ground longer, letting the other legs do the walking.

## Knuckling

Walking on the knuckles is a sign of slowed reflexes through the spinal cord, usually from disc disease. Occasionally it can be caused by significant weakness in a leg, joint inflammation, or a neurologic disease.

Check for soft tissue injury if arthritic animals are suddenly lame on a rear leg. Long-standing arthritis does not typically cause sudden-onset lameness.

MYTHCONCEPTION

*A limping dog may just be trying to get attention.*
**Not true.**
*Lameness, in most cases, is caused by a physiological problem.*

# GOING DENTAL

♔

M ANY YEARS AGO, WHILE WORKING AT THE ZOO, I MET THOR, the polar bear. He was anesthetized on the table awaiting a root canal. He had huge teeth, claws like rakes, and a massive athletic body. He was 100 percent carnivorous. For his species, any living thing is prey. This instinct is strong, even in captive polar bears.

> *If people have tried to befriend polar bears, they have not lived long enough to write about it.*

Thor had been drooling and pawing at one side of his mouth for a week. The probable cause of Thor's colossal toothache was the olive bread and marshmallows he was being given as treats. This hadn't occurred to me at the time. I don't remember any discussion about the cause of Thor's impending root canal. He was suffering and we were there to help him—business as usual.

## DON'T BITE THE HAND THAT CLEANS YOU

A GNAWING CONCERN FOR owners is when their pets have bad breath or trouble chewing. There is a correlation between these conditions and significant health risks.

Dental disease can contribute to heart and lung disease, diabetes, gastrointestinal problems, kidney disease, leukemia, cancers, abscesses, and gum disease. It is not just about a pretty smile or a clean bite. Dental care reflects systemic health.

> *It is possible to clean teeth—without anesthesia—in a friendly, tolerant animal.*

Many pet owners are nervous about their pet receiving a dental cleaning because of the risks associated with anesthesia. While this is a valid concern, many animals require full anesthetic to properly clean the teeth under the gums, treat cavities, take dental radiographs, or do extractions. If an animal is properly assessed and has a good temperament, it can also be possible to chip off tartar and to scale and polish teeth without using anesthesia. If the main dental problem is just tartar, improving breath, dental condition, and overall health can be done without anesthesia. For animals that cannot tolerate anesthesia, cleaning the teeth this way can be a useful alternative.

At my practice, we schedule an hour long cleaning appointment and have extra staff available to help calm the animal and hold the lips up. With calm pets, we often get all the teeth done in one appointment. If an animal needs a break, we schedule several shorter visits.

After chipping off tartar, there is the possibility of finding a more sinister issue below. I make sure clients are aware that this could require anesthesia to repair or remove.

## TARTAR

WHAT IS THE SOURCE of that troublesome bacteria? The answer, my friend, is blowin' in the wind—literally. Fresh air, not saliva, is one of the significant causes of tartar buildup. Saliva has enzymes to help keep the mouth clean after a meal. Many veterinarians have noticed that "mouth breathers" (chronically nervous/panting dogs, brachycephalic dogs) have more trouble with tartar buildup. As the oral cavity dries out, tartar, which is sticky, builds up more quickly from breathing through the mouth rather than the nose.

## TEETH BRUSHING

ONCE TEETH ARE CLEAN, you can keep them that way by brushing them— even if you do it only a few times a week. Tartar takes two to three days to fully set. Brushing a pet's teeth every day is difficult for most people, including me. Use dog, not human, toothpastes—the fluoride in human toothpaste is too strong for them. Avoid dog toothpastes that have sugars or artificial sugars in them. Or use a paste of baking soda and water. Add a little ground fennel or peppermint oil (a few drops) for breath issues. Once tartar is solidly on the tooth, it usually won't come off with just brushing. Don't fall back into the "dry food will chip that tartar off the teeth" mentality. It is a fallacy.

Dental disease is also affected by genetics, chewing behavior, nutrition, systemic disease, breed, treats, and even stress. Not every dog is born with a perfect set of teeth or an even bite. Many dogs are born with a tendency to harbor bacteria that produce tartar.

## CROOKED OR BROKEN TEETH

A TOOTH THAT IS cracked or broken doesn't always present a health risk. If there is no pulp (nerve and blood vessels) exposure, and the animal isn't obviously in pain, a veterinary dentist can try a conservative approach. If there are signs of an abscess or pain, prompt action may have to be taken. Signs include a dog avoiding chewing, pawing at its mouth, foul odor from the mouth, and excessive drooling. Injured teeth can be extracted, or you can opt for a root canal or other restorative solution. I often refer patients to veterinary dental specialists.

## DENTAL CHEWS AND BONES

CHEWING ON CERTAIN TYPES of bones and rawhides can help reduce tartar and keep the gums healthy. Every dog chews a bone differently. Some are gulpers. They swallow large pieces of the bone. Gulpers generally don't improve their teeth and don't do well with bones/rawhides. But calm chewers can benefit from a good American-made plain rawhide, bully stick, yak milk bone, ostrich tendon, or other animal-parts chew. Raw bones can be great, although a little messy. (My dogs chew them outside.)

*Never offer cooked bones* since they splinter off in dangerously sharp pieces that are serious trouble for a dog if swallowed. It's best to keep a close watch on an animal while it is chewing any bone, to avoid problems. And consider throwing out the bone before it becomes small enough to swallow whole.

I do not recommend offering compressed vegetable/wheat bones since these add wheat or soy to a dog's diet. There are better ways to keep a dog's teeth clean and keep a dog healthy, including good moist food, brushing, and animal-product chew treats.

## HALITOSIS

BAD BREATH IN A dog can signal health problems such as gastrointestinal issues, systemic disease, dental trouble, or gum disease. It is surprising how many owners view their dog's progressive bad breath as an unavoidable part of pet ownership. Discuss halitosis with your vet and rule out these treatable problems.

QUESTIONS TO ASK YOURSELF AND YOUR VET
ABOUT DENTAL CLEANING

1.  Does your pet have the temperament that would allow someone's hands in their mouth and not bite the hand that cleans them?
2.  Will your pet think the dental procedure is terrifying? If your pet is going to be so stressed by being held still, it may be better to use an anesthetic.
3.  If your pet does stress easily, are there any other significant health issues stress or struggling could worsen (heart conditions, disc disease, etc.)?
4.  Do any teeth need to be extracted or radiographed?
5.  Are there oral diseases such as masses, gum disease, severe gingival recession, or fractured teeth that should be addressed with an anesthetic procedure?
6.  Are there any other reasons you might want to have an anesthetic procedure anyway, such as a mass removal or a neuter? Could both be done safely at the same time?
7.  How expert is the person doing the dental?
8.  Is a vet there if needed?
9.  What will be involved in the dental procedure?

In Thor's case, everything about his root canal procedure was a success. And he definitely needed anesthesia for the procedure. We were all happy he didn't wake up in the middle and eat us for a snack. He went pain-free back to the Bear Line, the enclosure where the bears are housed, and I moved on to vet school. It was many years later when I saw Thor again. I was at the zoo with my son, Sean. The keepers gave us a personal tour. They also let him feed Thor his favorite treat—olive bread.

# PART SEVEN

# WILD
# NATURE

# CHAT ABOUT THE CAT

THE RULE ABOUT CATS IS THAT THERE IS NO RULE ABOUT CATS.

# FERAL CATS, SNOW LEOPARD
# TAILS, AND BABY TIGERS

I LOVE CATCHING FOOTBALLS AND JUGGLING PINS. I GUESS IN RET-
rospect, I should have realized the fractious cat would have landed fine,
as cats do. But when she leaped into the air, my first instinct was to catch
her, and she landed in my hands, fangs first.

I called my doctor and he recommended I get to a hospital. I cleaned,
bandaged, and put ice on my aching, bleeding hand. I opted not to go to
the hospital right away. I took a gamble the hand would be all right. My
first priority was to get home in time to watch the final episode of *The West
Wing*, my only TV addiction. After the show, I unwrapped my hand. It
had swollen to the size of a baseball.

I ended up in the hospital with IV medication and a new motto: "Step
away from the flying cat." This illustrates that allopathic medicines are
often necessary. It also confirms that doctors are the world's worst patients. And television is bad for you. The hand healed perfectly, despite the
warnings from the ER doc that I might lose some function. I also took the
homeopathic medicines arnica and Traumeel, which I believe helped the
healing process considerably.

> *A cat bite is a dire medical emergency. The bacteria in a*
> *feline's mouth can cause serious infections in a human.*

I began to learn big things about big cats years ago, when I worked at the Lincoln Park Zoo. I frequently stopped at their outside habitat before starting my workday. I was privileged to help care for a litter of adorable baby cheetahs there. Felines large and small are to me the cat's meow. They truly are a force of nature. At times quiet couch potatoes, they have an underlying playfulness, speed, and power that they unpredictably display.

Lying in his enclosure, in a lazy, legs-akimbo position, the tiger was clearly sound asleep. Or so it seemed to an unobservant pigeon tiptoeing by. In a split second the pigeon was in the tiger's mouth. The tiger's paws moved so quickly, I barely saw it happen. I imagine the pigeon was equally surprised. I was stunned by the tiger as he then executed a standing jump up a sheer fifteen-foot wall, landing comfortably on a narrow ledge that would have better served as a perch for a housecat. His utterly athletic moves, dignified habits, and vivid stripes really were the definition of cool.

In Chinese culture the tiger symbolizes the balanced forces of yin and yang. I like that dynamic idea. I can identify with the tiger. One minute I am cozily surrounded by my pets and family, thinking I would be happy to sit there forever, and later that day I find myself leaping from a taxi, late for a flight to Cuba to give a lecture.

Zoo medicine teaches a lot in a rarefied, reactive atmosphere—it concentrates, distills, and magnifies all issues pertaining to the creatures there. They are captives and we control their environment, unlike in the wild, where nature plays a much bigger and more random role. When I started zoo work, scientific evidence about zoo animal medicine, surgery, and husbandry was in short supply. In a huge percentage of the cases, we had to extrapolate from empirical evidence—and find a way to resolve an animal's issues quickly. It was a matter of life or death. The microcosm of the zoo taught me to see the intricacies in healing—the complex interactions that can occur to create a breaking point in health or disease.

One fall day, in the center of the zoo's Big Cat house, two anesthetized felines—a tiger named Spot and a snow leopard named Kabul—were stretched out as if sleeping amid a hubbub of vets, techs, volunteers, media, and zoo personnel. As I walked by the snow leopard, I ran my hand down the length of his gorgeous tail. I appreciated how Mother Nature had given leopards this long, thick tail to protect them from frigid mountain climates. With a tail like that I would even brave Chicago winters.

> *Snow leopards' tails are so thick and long they are able to wrap them around their face past the chin, making their own warm scarf.*

There was no problem finding a vein on this feline. I recorded, "blood collection completed." I felt for his femoral pulse inside the rear leg. Even through the thick fur you could feel the intensity of the life force in his pulse. The annual "house call" was in full swing. All the cats were getting their full examinations—blood draws, dental care, radiographs, and nose-to-tail examinations. It was essential care for the big cats and it was an exciting media event at the zoo.

These cats were generally healthy, but the tiger Spot had shown some lameness, and sure enough, her paws had light ulcers on the pads. The keepers thought the new cement on the floor of the outer enclosure might be too tough on Spot's feet. The roughest areas of flooring were taken out and regular footbath trays of diluted Betadine were put in strategic locations for her to walk through to ward off infection and toughen the skin on the pads of her feet. Diluted Betadine is not only a good antiseptic, but also frequently used to strengthen injured footpads.

After the vet finished Spot's exam, she was returned to the recovery area. An hour later, I accompanied the vet to do a final check on her, this time in her enclosure. As we neared, she rushed the bars, letting out a terrifying roar. My instinct to throw myself down on the floor and sink into the brickwork shocked me. This was primal fear, and also, just another day at the office.

> *Housecats' tails are highly expressive—a seemingly innocuous flick of it can be an aggressive warning to another feline.*

When a dog wags its tail it is usually, though not always, friendly. When a cat wags its tail, it could mean the cat is swearing. Even though she may be sitting in my lap and tolerating my exam, her whipping tail is telling another story.

To avoid being bitten by a cat, be alert to these signs: a whipping tail, flat ears (I call them the Chinese hat of irritation), raised fur, raised spine (Halloweenesque), growl, hissing, lying on her back and looking at you with dilated pupils (or flying through the air with teeth bared).

Most feline health issues, such as urinary tract infection, diarrhea, asthma, and vomiting, can be a response to stress. If the stress trigger can be isolated, the cat can often be cured. If the trigger can't be found, the stress will continue to exacerbate the conditions.

## MYTHCONCEPTION

*Cats don't like water.*
**Not true.**
*Some cats love water.*

❧ Turkish van, Bengal, and Egyptian cats like water so much they will jump in the bath with you.

❧ Cats at my clinic don't mind walking on the underwater treadmill. They definitely prefer not to be *thrown* into water, but in the treadmill, the warm water comes up gradually while they walk on the treadmill, and most felines feel comfortable.

## FOLLOWING THE GOLDEN THREAD

I DIDN'T HAVE ANY clue that after becoming a conventional veterinarian, I would become an acupuncturist and then veer into alternative medicine. My trajectory has been as exotic as the animals I have cared for.

My astrological sign is Pisces, so watery Seattle suited me well the summer I was a zoo intern, in my final year of vet school. With the constant rain, the ocean to the west, and the lake on the east, Seattle gave me an island feel. My small apartment had a white welcome mat that quickly became dun-colored from me tromping in and out with my mud-caked zoo work boots.

My second week at the zoo, Dr. Collins told me a baby Sumatran tiger had been born the night before. I don't think there is anything cuter than a tiny Sumatran tiger. The minute I saw the furry baby, named Songkit, meaning "woven with a golden thread," I was overcome with love and concern. Evidently the tiger mother was not nursing the baby very often and was overcleaning the enclosure—clearing away the bedding and every shred of warmth-giving substrate that the keepers put on the floor. This cute little gal was getting too cold. The zookeepers had to warm Songkit, add extra bedding, and return her to her mother. This unfortunate scenario was repeated for a few days.

Eventually Songkit had to be removed from her mother's care because she was not gaining weight. It is possible that Songkit's mother had never learned the right way to care for a baby, because she was an orphan.

The hospital staff took over Songkit's feeding. They worked out an appropriate formula and we all took turns. Until I had my own children and heard their cooing noises, Songkit's little *fuff-fuff-fuff* noise was my favorite sound on earth. Baby tigers only use that noise when their moms arrive—perhaps it translates into "I love you, I want your attention, and I'm hungry." I was in love with a baby tiger.

A week later, Dr. Collins said there was a situation he needed to discuss with me. With me? I was just an intern. Was I in trouble? I sat down in his office and he outlined the problem. Apparently a holiday weekend was coming up and construction needed to be done at the zoo. The issue was that the baby tiger needed to be cared for, but many zookeepers would be out of town. Could I take the tiger home with me for the long weekend?

In my head, I went into high-gear mommy mode and imagined the minuscule striped carnivore tucked in a blanket in my arms, in my garden apartment, fuff-fuffing. I pictured myself hand-feeding her with a bottle.

Dr. Collins interrupted my reverie. "The feeding protocol is extremely complicated," he said, "but we'll give you formula and detailed instructions about everything you need to do. I have to warn you, though, even with that, there will be some trial and error involved."

"Yes, well, I'm a trial-and-error kind of gal," I said.

"Great," said Dr. Collins. "We'll put everything together for you. And by the way, Barbara," he said, "Songkit is one of only five hundred Sumatran tigers left in the whole world, so be sure to return her to us alive." I tried to smile, but I was panicked that he was entrusting me with this priceless living being.

And so it was that a tiny tiger came to stay at my apartment. Matt, my wildlife biologist boyfriend, had traveled to Seattle for the long Fourth of July weekend. Needless to say, we didn't go to any fireworks display, and soon Matt was as much in love with Songkit as I was. We all roughhoused and acted like a tiger family. Matt, Songkit, and I slept on the floor. It seemed more natural for her to cuddle up and sleep next to us, and we didn't want her to fall off the bed or to leave her alone in the crate. I only wished someone had phoned me in the middle of the night. Then I could have said, "Hang on a sec, my baby tiger just fell asleep on my arm."

Songkit loved to romp on the carpet and cuddle on the couch for her meals. She was a kitten but her body felt like a small bear. She had fuzzy, big floppy feet; a chunky torso; velvety ears; sharp teeth; dull claws she rarely used; and a long, soft tail.

The tricky part was her diet. Obviously, her mother's tiger milk would have been ideal, but we had to make do. We battled Songkit's diarrhea, distended abdomen, and discomfort. The formula recipe was mostly protein with an equal amount of fat and carbohydrate and a small amount of vitamins and minerals. According to Songkit's response, we adjusted the ingredients. Dr. Collins and Harmony, the head tech, provided excellent advice. This is an excerpt from my records just before Independence Day weekend.

REASON PULLED: maternal care, but infant temp 96.0 and low weight with decreasing weights over 3 days. Dehydrated.

FORMULA: Modified San Diego "Dr. Nelson Tiger Diet"

        4 TBLS Casec powder

        70ml Enfamil

        20 ml corn oil

        190 ml pedialyte

mixed above 1:1 with esbilac (one can)

add 5 drops per quart milk of lactaid.

(Nelson diet had H2O and KMR. No lactaid.)

Currently, d/t diarrhea, mix with 1:3 with Pedialyte

Schedule for feeding: 7am 10am 1pm 4pm 7pm 10pm 1am

AMOUNTS: 40ml per bottle—30ml pedialyte. 10ml Formula

PLAN: Once able to handle a change will EITHER increase volume or concentration. At 1 month of age—29 June—should be able to go to 6 feedings a day.

After the intense and wonderful weekend, I brought Songkit back to the zoo. I continued being one of her "moms," and I enjoyed watching her grow. Soon she became too big for me to safely go into the cage with her, even though I was a foster mom. Tigers establish territory by fighting with their mom, much like a teenage girl. Whoever wins gets to stay, and the other moves on. I knew which one I would be.

After bottle-feeding Songkit, I took a greater interest in the subtle and intricate life of big cats. Back in Chicago, I spent time watching the tigers. One tail flick can mean, "Don't walk by me. I am holding this space sacred for the moment." An hour later, an ear twitch can mean, "Come on over and let's wrestle a bit." This kind of conversation between cats is critically important in the housecat. If you have multiple cats, you may not understand what is really going on between them. They may look calm and relaxed lying in the same room, near the single litter box. But little twitches and tail flicks are saying things like:

"Why can't I go to the litter box?"

"If you do, I'll attack you."

"But I really have to go."

"Too bad, I will let you move when I feel like it. And don't try to get to the water bowl either."

Often the cat who does the pouncing is not the one who is actually in charge. An in-charge cat may not need to pounce. The underdog cat ("undercat") may need to pounce to try to gain some respect. Trying to understand felines in human terms doesn't work.

The saying that cats have nine lives seems true to me. They have an uncanny ability to heal themselves. I once treated a four-week-old stray kitten that was brought to us critically ill with a profound anemia. Her packed cell volume (PCV), which measures red blood cell amounts, was 4%, which is not a number compatible with life. Normal values are 25–45%. I examined the cold, almost lifeless little fuzzball. Her heartbeat was barely audible, her eyes tightly closed. The techs and receptionists stood nearby, blinking, holding their breaths. Everyone was emotionally involved.

There was something in the firmly shut little eyes that made me feel this petite thing was still fighting for her life. Her only chance would be a blood transfusion, warmth, and love. We certainly had lots of love in that room. I desperately hoped she could heal herself of whatever had dropped her blood cell count so low.

The other vet on duty and I both knew it seemed futile. But we agreed to work on her together. With lots of luck and a cheering section, I managed to get an IV catheter into the thread of a vein. After that, she did it all. We warmed her, gave her the blood transfusion and medications, cuddled her, and stroked her. Many vets, including me, believe human touch will markedly improve a kitten's recovery. When she finally opened

### FACTS ABOUT CATS

A cat's nose has ridges like a human fingerprint and each nose print is unique to each cat.

Because of the shiny *tapetum lucidum* that reflects and amplifies light at the back of their retinas, they can see with only one-sixth of the light humans need to be able to see.

They can run up to 30 miles per hour.

A cat's own purring can be medicinal to them because of the frequency it gives off to the cells nearby. Humans can also benefit from the healing power of a purring cat sitting in the lap. It is believed that cats use their own purring to make themselves feel better when they are sick.

A cat's body is perfectly designed for stealth and hunting. Sharp claws and teeth, a Velcro tongue, flexible spine, muscles that can spring their bodies seven times their height, fabulous night vision, and a fourteen times stronger sense of smell than we have.

her determined eyes later that day, we could see she was going to make it. I believe she used up a couple of her nine lives to survive, but she's going strong and still has a few left.

Cats are sensitive to medications and anesthetics. I think twice about giving strong meds such as chemo and certain sedatives to a cat. I am also careful about more common medications such as anti-inflammatories. A cat liver doesn't metabolize medications well. If doses aren't carefully monitored, medications accumulate in their bloodstream and can reach toxic levels.

Integrative medicine is ideal for cats because of their delicate systems. A healthy diet can decrease the need for medication. But when intervention is needed, I opt for treatments with minimal side effects.

The biggest problem with oral meds is how to get a cat to take the prescription. One great solution has been to use homeopathy for cats. The doses are small, easy to administer, and go undetected by the acutely sensitive nose of the feline.

Another fabulous modality for cats is acupuncture. Initially, I wondered if acupuncture for cats would be as effective as acupuncture for dogs. But I have found that cats respond rapidly and strongly to acupuncture. Just a few needles can work wonders.

Yin, a Siamese cat, was brought to me because she would vomit several times a day and was wasting away. With a minor diet change and her first acupuncture treatment, she went from being at death's door to being a feisty, normal cat again.

Yin is doing well now, and I rarely need to treat her. Occasionally, I give her an acupuncture treatment and her periodic flare-ups subside. When I come into the exam room, she is dramatic. She complains bitterly, hissing and growling, but she calms down quickly once the needles are in. It seems as if her protestations are an act, to appear as tough as a tiger.

# HOUSECATS ARE WILDER
# THAN YOU THINK

♔

CATS ARE THE NUMBER-ONE PET IN AMERICA, AND WE SPEND more annually on cat food than we do on baby food. Aloof, cuddly, sensitive, selfish, sweet, tough, complicated, playful, silly, elegant, unpredictable, and incredibly resilient, cats are highly entertaining. An astonishingly powerful design, beautifully packaged into sweet softness. They are unique and specialized, and cat ladies and gentlemen who understand this will raise cats with distinct health benefits.

Multiple-cat households need to be set up to deal with the cat psyche. One of my clients has eleven cats and they function well as a group. She has twelve litter boxes, separate food and water areas, and has even built several tall but accessible caged-in areas for the cats to be outside. Most likely there is still some inter-cat strife, but it doesn't seem to affect their health.

Medical problems that I routinely see in cats include obesity, inappropriate urination, diabetes, inflammatory bowel disease, kidney and liver disease, dental disease, hyperesthesia (itchy skin), allergies, thyroid disease, asthma, and behavior issues. All of these conditions can be negatively affected by the body's response to stress. In addition, nutrition requirements for cats are quite specific. For example, without the amino acid taurine in their diet, they become blind and develop heart disease.

Many commercial cat foods may not provide enough fiber. In the wild, the feathers, beaks, nails, and fur would clean up the intestines and help maintain their health. But for our purposes, other fibers can do the job of intestinal scrubbing. I recommend adding a bit of pumpkin (a teaspoon of unsweetened canned pumpkin per day will do), or psyllium (¼ tsp mixed in wet food per day), or ⅛ teaspoon of guar gum to the meal. This regulates their stool—making it neither too hard nor too firm—and thus keeps intestines healthy. Cooling aloe juice (about ⅛ tsp) is also a good intestinal supplement for most cats.

As kittens, cats learn what food is edible and what isn't. There are commercial raw foods that are a great option for a cat. Once cats come to trust a specific type of food, it can be difficult to incorporate other foods into their diet. There is a window of learning about foods that closes once the cat becomes an adult. The cat that has only eaten dry food all of his life may never be able to change to canned food, and vice versa. A cat unaccustomed to eating steak may starve to death rather than eat it. Cats do not like unfamiliar food. They have evolved to be very finicky about what they put in their mouths. This indicates that choosing suitable food, from an evolutionary standpoint, is vital for the survival of the cat species.

If you are considering making your own raw cat food, the website catinfo.org has great information. It is written by Dr. Lisa A. Pierson, who is a vet. Anytime you change diets, be sure the cat will eat the new food and that it agrees with her. Slow changes are best—over 10 to 14 days. Offer the new food first thing in the morning or when she's hungry, just as a meal is due. If the cat doesn't eat it, feed another food that she will eat. They must eat every day to stay healthy. It's no use trying to "force" a cat to eat the food. Cats typically won't eat what they don't want. Calm and gradual coaxing is often the only effective method.

# CAT WALKS

EXERCISE IN THE FORM of walking a feline can be challenging. "Walking" on a leash for many cats ends up being "dragging" on a leash, providing more exercise for you than the cat. If you are one of the lucky ones who can walk your cat on a leash, it's a great idea. If your cat is treat-motivated, you can throw a treat down a hallway or staircase and he will run and retrieve it. When he feels like it!

Cats walk in my underwater treadmill at my clinic (yes they can!). These cats are rehabilitating from injury, arthritis, or other musculoskeletal problems. Water therapy ameliorates specific conditions as well as contributing to overall body health.

Felines are not pack animals, but they do enjoy a few BFFs. There is a delicate social balance among cats that may be invisible to the untrained human eye. It can be useful to know whether a cat is top, bottom, or in between in the family hierarchy. High stress levels in cats can wreak havoc on their health and immune system. A cat sitting on a window ledge can be harboring many stressors but showing few signs of it.

A serious territory war may only be seen in that slight tail flick, or a slow change in posture. These subtle stressors can increase adrenal gland activity, blood glucose levels, muscle tension, or gastrointestinal transit time—all very useful physiologic changes for a short war, but not useful for daily life in close quarters. And certainly not helpful for long-term health.

### Keep a Cool Cat

- 🐾 Owners with multi-cat households should be aware of each singular cat's nature and provide safe havens for troubled or troublemaking cats.
- 🐾 Procure the right number of litter boxes. The solution for this is to have a box for each cat and then add one more. Four cats, five litter boxes.

- Choose a few quiet places for the boxes that are easy to access.

- Clean the litter box daily. Cats have a superior olfactory sense. Use a chemical-free litter.

- Don't use an uncomfortable mat, or sharp plastic grass in front of the box.

- If you have multiple cats, maintain multiple food and water stations to decrease stress. Are these bowls easy to access? Cats are desert animals, and by the time they feel thirsty, they may already be dehydrated. If they are feeling intimidated, it may add to a health problem. If your cat is fighting kidney or urinary tract issues or diabetes, plentiful water is a must.

- Feed your cat a "Catkins" diet—a low-carb diet. Feeding a cat a high-carb diet is a disaster in many ways. Carb-heavy diets increase the incidence of obesity and are associated with diabetes, inflammatory bowel problems, and allergies. Without the carbs, cats with these conditions improve and lose weight. If your cat is underweight, have your vet

### COOL TIPS

Butter your cat's feet or fur to distract them during inter-cat stress situations or introductions. They prefer to groom it off (and enjoy the butter) rather than fight or stress out.

Use lemon peels or spray lemon juice to keep cats away from the couch—or anywhere they shouldn't be going—or use tinfoil, plastic wrap, or double-sided tape.

rule out all possible underlying issues, such as parasites, hyperthyroidism, and kidney disease, and then feed more of a high-quality food.

🐾 Most pills can be crushed into tuna juice or meat baby food. If the cat won't eat it, you can syringe-feed from the side of the mouth.

🐾 Coat pills with butter and place at the back of the tongue—it will go down easily.

🐾 Compounding pharmacies can make most meds into a tasty liquid.

🐾 Minimize contact, where possible, with plastic bowls. They exacerbate chin acne and allergies.

🐾 Make sure there is low stress associated with the food bowl, litter box, and living situation.

🐾 The high moisture content of canned or frozen raw foods is more suited to a cat—an animal that would rarely drink water in the wild.

## ACCIDENTS DON'T HAVE TO HAPPEN

WHY ISN'T YOUR CAT using the litter box? There are myriad medical reasons why cats avoid using the litter box: UTI, crystals, stones, painful urination or defecation, growths in the bladder. And logistical issues—unclean litter box, too few litter boxes, doorway mat not comfortable (plastic grasses, etc.), litter box location or box size (for example: too small)—may upset your cat. Litter box avoidance can also be caused by a urinary tract infection. The cat thinks, "The last time I went in there and peed, it hurt, so I'm not going back." There can be other behavioral causes. The cat may not like the new kind of litter, or, as already mentioned, the social pressure of a more dominant cat forms a blockade to the litter box.

Cats may urinate on any rug with a rubber or nonstick backing, such as a bath mat. They also like to urinate on dog beds that contain granular or beanlike filling, and on bean bag chairs. Perhaps it is the odor of the bath mat or the texture of the dog bed and chair that attracts them.

For cats with urinary issues, a low-carb, canned-food, or raw-food diet should be seriously considered. The increased water content and higher protein will help maintain the urine pH and the cat will stay healthier naturally. Dry food only dehydrates a cat further. If they drink water after eating kibble, it will be used mostly to digest the dry food. Even when healthy, cats are not big water drinkers, so add warm water to a favorite food to increase hydration when needed.

Because some feline urinary issues can be life-threatening, it is always best to consult a veterinarian and have a urine sample checked when faced with a rogue cat urinating out of the box.

CATS ARE UNIQUE CREATURES, exquisitely sensitive yet still little tigers at heart. A cat needs to experience its catlike essence. There are cats that simply aren't happy as indoor cats and need to be allowed to go outside, if possible. This can relieve a significant amount of tension. I recommend putting a bell or two on the collar to keep the cat from killing unsuspecting birds or wildlife. Or if you're lucky your cat might tolerate a harness or go on walks with you without one. My neighbors watch incredulously as I parade by with my dogs on leashes and my cat accompanying us, leashless, indicating our direction with a flick of his tail.

> *I am not a cat man, but a dog man, and all felines can tell this at a glance—a sharp, vindictive glance.*
> —JAMES THURBER

# WHAT'S TRUE, PUSSYCAT?

🐾 **Q:** *How do I get my cats to stop wildly playing at night? I can't get any sleep! If my feet move under the covers, they jump on them, and they push things, like my keys and water glass, off the table. If I close the bedroom door they throw themselves at it and bang on it till I open it again. Are they crazy? Do they need drugs? Do I?*

**A:** Cats are, I'll have to admit, crazy. At least my cats have always been. Your cat problem is not unique. It probably has to do with the age of your cats and the fact that cats are nocturnal. I assume that they are young, and are still getting used to your crazy (according to them) diurnal schedule of sleeping during normal midnight activity time. There are several things you might try, short of taking something strong to help you sleep at night. Try to encourage lots of play in the early evening and before bed. Then they may at least start the night with a good long nap. They also will have a postprandial dormancy, which means they get sleepy after a meal. So feed the largest meal in the late evening. If you keep food unavailable in the afternoon and then offer it at about 8 P.M., they are more likely to eat it.

Make sure they are not eating too much carbohydrate (check their treats as well), which can add to their craziness. If they are used to milk, you could try a warm milk nightcap to calm them down as well.

Cats can be trained to sleep at night. Make them cozy spots away from your room. Try melatonin or valerian supplement to calm them. Ask your vet for the correct dosing.

# CAT LITTER

♔

## Thinking Inside the Box

O THER THAN WHAT MOTHER NATURE PUT ALL OVER THE EARTH, I don't think that there's a perfect cat litter out there. But here is my list of pros and cons for the different types of litter that my clients use. My top two "picks of the litter" are recycled walnut shell litter and recycled-wood litter. I like a clumping litter. However, I don't want to support strip mining for bentonite clay, which is used in most clumping litters. I also want it to be easy to scoop, to avoid corn and wheat, and to have moderate odor control. Recycled walnut shell or recycled-wood natural clumping litter makes the most sense to me. I do not recommend composting any cat litter, as there are potential pathogens in cat waste that most compost piles do not get hot enough to destroy.

### Clay Litter

PROS

Effectively absorbs moisture
Effectively absorbs odor
Easily found in most stores
Inexpensive
Has other uses, such as traction for icy driveways

CONS

Very dusty

Has been known to cause permanent respiratory problems in cats
and humans

Not biodegradable

Is obtained through strip mining

Needs to be replaced often to avoid ammonia-like smell

## Clumping (Scoopable) Clay Litter

PROS

Dust-free

Clumps eliminate odor buildup

Easy to scoop

Works well for multi-cat households

CONS

Not biodegradable

Not flushable

Has been suggested that this litter can cause intestinal blockages
in cats who ingest it

Obtained through strip-mining

More expensive than regular clay litter

## Clumping Recycled Walnut Shells

PROS

Made from recycled walnut shells

Good texture

Good odor control

Low tracking/dust

Okay for multi-cat households

Environmentally friendly

Great for cats with allergies

CONS

Hard to find in stores

Dark color makes pee and poop hard to find to be scooped

Caution for humans with nut allergies

Urine clumping is not perfect

## Clumping Recycled Wood/Green Tea

PROS

Made from recycled wood

Good texture

Low tracking

Easy to scoop

One bag lasts a long time

Okay for multi-cat household

Environmentally friendly/biodegradable

Nice odor

CONS

Dusty when poured

Hard to find in stores

## Corn Litter

PROS

Soft texture

Very little tracking

Biodegradable

Flushable

Clumps for easy scooping

CONS

Expensive

Not all cats like the texture/smell

Very dusty

When they lick their feet, they may ingest it and have corn-related allergy, GI, and health issues. Perhaps corncob litter (not the corn kernel itself, but the cobs only) might be better, as it contains more fiber. Some consumers express concerns about genetically modified (GMO) corn affecting the cats, and about aflatoxins, a deadly mold that grows in corn products with a high moisture content. This mold could conceivably flourish in the wet atmosphere of a litter box. I have not seen any substantiation to the worries about aflatoxins, but it is serious enough to consider.

## Crystal Litter

PROS

Very absorbent

Unlikely to grow mold/bacteria

Dust-free

Owners will use less crystal litter compared to traditional clay

CONS

Some cats do not like the feel of crystals on their paws

Must be stirred daily to keep urine from pooling in the litter box

Some controversy on whether chemicals in it are safe if ingested

## Paper Litter

PROS

Made from recycled newspaper

Biodegradable

Safe for septic systems

Dust- and scent-free

Safe for kittens and cats after surgery/declawing

Very absorbent

CONS

Some cats do not like the feel or texture of litter

Can be more difficult to scoop, leaving behind soiled clumps of paper

Not easily found in stores

## Pine Litter

PROS

Biodegradable

Recycled product

Safe flushing

CONS

Some cats do not like the scent

Scent can aggravate asthma/allergies in cats

Not easy to scoop

## Sand Litter

PROS

Natural

CONS

Dust can aggravate allergies in humans

Dusty

Easily tracks through the house

Messy in general

Does not clump well

## Wheat Litter

PROS
Biodegradable

CONS
Does not clump well
Minimal odor control
Dusty
Can aggravate allergies/asthma, and can be a problem if ingested
by licking paws. The same possible issues with GMO and af-
latoxins as with corn litter.

---

MYTHCONCEPTION

*Cats pee out of the litter box because they're angry.*
**Not true.**
*Usually there is a medical reason for inappropriate
urination.*

PART EIGHT

# MEDICINE GONE WILD

# CANCER DOESN'T
# COME FROM NOWHERE

—— ♛ ——

WHEN I WORKED AT THE ZOO HOSPITAL, THE BEAR LINE BUILD-ing was outside our gate. I loved to watch the spectacled bears climb. (They are appropriately named. They do look as if they are wearing yellow spectacles.)

One year, the zoo recycled Christmas trees by putting them in the bears' enclosure for behavior enrichment. The bears liked them very much. One of these studious-looking bears managed to stack up several tree trunks and climb right out of his enclosure.

Several zoo visitors saw him meandering along in a public area, checking out the contents of garbage cans. Eventually a zookeeper spotted him outside the aviary. Spectacled bears are the most herbivorous, calm, and amiable of bears, so luring him back into his enclosure with a loaf of bread was easy.

The female spectacled bear, Lena, had watched the whole adventure, but she had stayed put inside their enclosure. About eight years later, Lena developed mammary cancer and I was called as a surgical consultant to do a mastectomy on her. It had been a while since any of the zoo vets had done this procedure, so they asked me. Tumors in bears behave similarly to tumors in dogs. While locally aggressive, they are not likely to metastasize elsewhere.

This spectacled bear was a favorite, and twenty people came to watch the surgery. I have had a few onlookers, students, techs, or other vets watch me in surgery, but never this many people, all of whom considered the patient to be part of their family. It was rather unnerving.

Having large blood vessels, and vasculature along their mammary chain, bears bleed a lot. The first few minutes looked like a bloodbath, and the crowd gasped every time I moved my scalpel. But as Lena's vessels were ligated and the bleeding stopped, the crowd cheered. I was relieved that the rest of the tumor removal was relatively straightforward.

The closure was intricate. No catgut, nylon, or typical sutures for this girl. The zoo vets had recommended that I use thin, flexible, stainless steel sutures for the entire length of the site. They are strong, inert, and don't cause any tissue reaction, and Lena would be less likely to be bothered by them. Any other suture would have been ripped apart by her strong nails in a matter of a few minutes. Closing the incision with wire took twice as long as the entire surgery. The doctors were right; she recovered well and left the incision alone.

At the time, I remember asking if mammary tumors were common in spectacled bears in the wild. I was told they were not. My only thought was, "That's interesting." I was still strictly a conventional veterinarian.

It is clear to me now that something went wrong to cause Lena to have cancer. Why would an otherwise healthy bear develop cancer? Does it follow that since dogs and humans suffer from mammary cancers, spectacled bears should as well? Shouldn't the discussion go deeper? Unalterable circumstances of her city zoo life, a well-meant, yet imperfect diet, and annual anesthetic procedures could all have adversely affected her health. Zookeepers are aware that even a plastic toy, a chemical cleaner, or a carcinogen in a treat can pose a problem to an exotic zoo animal. These details are more likely to be examined with zoo animals and wildlife than with our own pets. Conventional veterinary medicine doesn't teach vets to consider the significance of the day-to-day environment, but it should. Vet school had trained me to remove the cancer and move on, which I did for Lena, the spectacled bear.

Strawberry was a little carp with a cancerous growth on her eye. Like Lena, she was a favorite with the keepers, and they all came to watch as I performed surgery on her. She could only be sedated for eleven minutes or else the anesthetic agent might overwhelm her system. In front of an audience, I had to speed-remove the tumorous eye from an orange goldfish half-floating in a bowl. Fear-induced adrenaline made me intensely efficient, and I successfully completed the procedure in under eight minutes. Strawberry was free of the tumor and lived a long life.

Cancer is everywhere—even in fish. After removing the growth from the little carpfish, Strawberry, I was invited to be part of the surgical team called in to the Shedd Aquarium to excise the cancer from the head of a two-hundred-pound grouper. This room-sized fish had been carried from his tank in a sling and put in a small holding tank, which was the surgical suite. We used hoses to blow an anesthesia/water mixture across his gills. As with the carp, there is a time limit for how long a grouper, or any animal, can be under sedation.

Anesthesia for fish can be dangerous and we worked furiously. All of a sudden, the oxygenated spray of the anesthesia machine under the water began foaming. It was like a Mr. Bubble commercial. We were having trouble keeping the bubbles from obstructing our view of the surgical site. At first I had no idea why we had to scoop the frothy handfuls out of our way. Then I heard muffled laughter from several male aquarists. One of them said, with raised eyebrows, "He's really enjoying the surgery!" In response to the anesthesia, the huge grouper had ejaculated sperm in a protein-rich fluid causing the bubbles and much hilarity.

After the surgery was completed, we discussed how little evidence there was of tumors in wild groupers. We rationalized this grouper's malady by saying he was relatively old. Cancer in zoo and aquarium animals is often considered unavoidable. But there is plenty of research to the contrary. Many cancers in humans and pets are linked to diet and environmental conditions. There is a study that states that 85 percent of cancers in people are caused by a combination of poor diet and lifestyle choices. Genetics is not always the predominant cause of cancer, thus many types of cancer can be avoided.

In fact, cancer rates in people have increased over 25 percent since 1950. That number is much larger if you include cancer caused by smoking. There are similar trends in pets. Cancer is increasing in zoo animals as well. There is also mounting evidence that pollutants and toxins are causing an increase in wild animal cancers.

## ROYAL TREATMENT
## CANCER TIPS

**A reevaluation of diet is the most urgent action necessary.** Feed your pet the most biologically appropriate food—that way the body has the correct tools to fight cancer cells.

**Do not feed your pet known carcinogens.** None of us would want to do this, but we may unwittingly feed our pets carcinogens. As already mentioned, many foods contain dangerous ingredients that are not listed on the label.

**Processing methods can create carcinogens in food.** There is a risk of creating carcinogens when meat is cooked using high heat. Heating a meat to above 212 degrees can cause the formation of compounds called *heterocyclic amines*, which are believed to be carcinogenic. If a product contains oils and carbohydrate starches, such as corn or potatoes, high heat can create *acrylamide*, which is also considered carcinogenic in animals. Neither of these compounds will be listed on the ingredients. They are by-products of the high-heat extrusion process that forms many dry kibbles.

Canned food does not contain these high-heat chemicals, and does, as I have mentioned, tend to have more meat, and no preservatives. But canned foods have a drawback, too. To increase shelf life and keep the contents from reacting to the metal or sticking to the sides, many can linings have *bisphenol A*, a plastic component that is considered a carcinogen. There is a movement to stop this practice and many companies are claiming to not use it in their cans.

At present the FDA does not regulate the quantity or presence of BPA in can linings. Therefore, there is no penalty for pet food companies misrepresenting their cans as BPA-free. However, if they are to be believed, there are many companies not using BPAs in their cans. Small aluminum cans tend to be BPA-free. Large steel cans are likely to have a BPA lining.

Although there is some new concern about BPA now being put on all flip-top lids, the trend to keep small cans BPA-free is promising. My website, www.royaltreatmentveterinarycenter.com, periodically compiles a list of companies that claim their cans are BPA-free. Call or write your pet food company. If you would like a prepared letter to send your pet food company requesting information on a number of topics of concern, you can download it from my website.

A pre-prepared commercial raw food is a great option as an anticancer diet. I have many patients on commercially available raw foods. But if your pet is undergoing chemotherapy for the cancer treatment, you can fully cook the raw patties. Check the food for any larger fragments of bone that might splinter when cooked. Different manufacturers have different sieve mesh for sifting out bone fragments. Cooking the food destroys any bacteria and pathogens that might assault a chemo-weakened immune system.

Freeze-dried raw foods can be fed as is, or can be rehydrated. With the freeze-drying process, the food remains nutrient-dense but pathogen-free. There are complete diets or freeze-dried supplements. This is another option for a cancer patient. Freeze-dried foods tend to be expensive, but they are easy to feed, light, and portable.

Home-prepared food is a great option, if you can spare the time and effort. Again, if there is raw meat involved and your pet is on chemo, cook the raw meat before serving. If you prepare your dog's food at home, be sure to use a recipe in which the calcium and phosphorus ratios are correct. Having the proper balance of vitamins and minerals supports the body's fight against cancer.

**Consider having your water tested by a certified laboratory.** You may find that improving water quality could help the whole family. Increasingly, we find chemicals in our water that shouldn't be there and are not good for anyone. There may be a link between high amounts of fluoride in our water and an increased risk for *osteosarcoma* (bone cancer) in large breed dogs. Water processing makes our water clean of parasites and bacteria, but the chemicals used to do this and their by-products may be more insidious. Water doesn't have to be shipped from a mountain spring in Tibet, but you can buy a water filter to improve the water quality for your pet. Hydration is essential for healthy cells. In addition, do not add medicines to a pet's water bowl. Pets tend to drink less water if it doesn't taste normal to them. Call the Safe Drinking Water hotline at 800-426-4791 or visit www.epa.gov/safewater/labs.

**Avoid using plastic bowls for pet food and water.** Even small amounts of plastic or BPA leaching into the water or food are a cancer risk. Eliminating as many carcinogens as possible in your pet's life is a sensible health decision. Our world is full of carcinogens, even from the sun, and we are fighting cancerous cells every day. As pet owners, let's improve the odds where we can.

**Minimize the use of vaccines where possible.** Cats can develop vaccine-associated sarcomas (tumors) at the sites of vaccines. It starts as an inflammation that turns into a cancer if it goes unnoticed and unchecked. Administering vaccines to cats is not a purely benign procedure. New protocols were developed in light of these tumors. Cat vaccines are not given in the neck area anymore. They are placed farther down the leg, so that owners can check for lumps at the vaccine site. If a cancer is found there, the leg can be amputated.

This seemingly reasonable and gruesome solution is based on misguided medical reasoning. Why are we willing to regularly inject a substance that could cause a leg to be amputated? The statistics show that one in every thousand vaccinated cats will develop a vaccine-associated sarcoma. How can this be good medicine? Better vaccines must be created. In addition, studies proving that many vaccines last much longer than a few years should give rise to even safer vaccine protocols.

A sweet eighteen-year-old black cat named Topaz was brought to me a couple of years ago for arthritis treatment. She had gorgeous yellow-green eyes. She was an outside cat for much of her life, so her annual vaccinations included rabies, feline leukemia, and distemper, which were often given in her hind end. For eighteen years she had come in at night and slept in bed with her owners. All of a sudden she had stopped jumping up on the bed, and would cry when landing on any surface. She lost interest in going outside.

The owners took Topaz to the ER. After an exam, the doctors said they could do X-rays, but it was not necessary. It was obvious that she was old and arthritic. They gave her an anti-inflammatory and recommended a follow-up with their regular vet.

The regular vet concurred with the ER doctors that Topaz's arthritis was getting worse because of her age. The owners continued giving her anti-inflammatory meds and were told to add joint supplement injections for her stiff rear end. But the crying became even more frequent. She also whimpered when being picked up.

When the owners came to me for acupuncture for Topaz's arthritis, I felt the diagnosis didn't make sense. Animals with arthritis generally don't cry out in pain—at least not chronically. They may cry out as they take a wrong step or after an injury to a stiff joint. But crying with everyday movements was unusual. In the wild, broadcasting feebleness or pain is not an evolutionary advantage because predators will quickly attack.

Topaz's neurologic status was normal. She did not appear to be senile. I believed this cry came from something so unbearable it could not be kept quiet. I could feel heat emanating from her stiffened and thickened lumbar spine. I recommended getting X-rays.

The cancer had enveloped and eroded the bone in her lower spine and extended around part of her hip. It looked terribly painful. It was a *fibrosarcoma*, a locally aggressive tumor most likely caused by vaccination. There was very little we could do for her at that point. Her owners were heartbroken.

It is not yet fully proven how these sarcomas develop. They could be reactions to the vaccine agent or something in the surrounding fluid, or just an overreaction to the injection. The evidence is building. While vaccination may be lifesaving, overvaccination is not in anyone's best interest. The American Association of Feline Practitioners (AAFP) recommends that distemper vaccines not be given more frequently than every three years.

The blood test to check the duration of immunity after a vaccination is called a vaccine titer. In my practice, I have found that most cats show good immunity years after the three-year mark without a booster vaccine. Many doctors interpret the AAFP guidelines as saying the vaccine should be given every three years, but I have found that for most cats, we can go much longer.

Veterinarians may be vaccinating based on old or incorrectly interpreted information. Reeducating veterinarians and encouraging owners to ask for better vaccine options is critically important in the treatment of cats.

In dogs, vaccine reactions can include local inflammation, hair loss, and lesions at vaccine sites, but they rarely turn into vaccine-associated sarcomas.

Building immunity against a life-threatening disease is a good idea.

But vaccination where immunity already exists makes no sense. Immunity, like any fighting force, must choose its battles. When immune cells are overstimulated it is often at the expense of other immune functions, and so there can be a greater risk of imbalance and disease.

**Avoid chemicals, medications, and toxins where you can.** Minimize medications like flea and tick products—except where the risk of tick-borne disease is great. Use heartworm prevention only during mosquito season, and one month after.

**Beware of too much sun exposure if your pet is white or "color-dilute" or has no fur either genetically or because of being shaved.** I recommend protective clothing gear rather than sunscreen. Do not use sunscreen for cats, as they metabolize the *salicylates* (an ingredient in some sunscreens) into *salicylic acid* (aspirin metabolite), which is toxic to them.

**Cat litter should be as pure as possible.** Avoid fragrances, chemicals, and other toxins that might be in litter.

I AM GRATIFIED TO know that when I have to treat a patient with cancer, I have tools to help improve their health without causing distressing side effects. In many cases, the cancers in my patients have been stalled—often way past the predicted prognosis. I am aware that this could mean the prognosis might have been inaccurate, but I can't argue with the results we have seen at the Royal Treatment Veterinary Center. I believe protocols for diet and immune system support have contributed to restored and prolonged health in our cancer patients.

With a comprehensive exam, a determination can be made as to what other deficiencies have contributed to the existence of many cancers such as sarcomas, lymphomas, osteosarcomas, and mast cell tumors. The successes I see in my patients fighting cancer are not due to a single pill, supplement, or food. They are due to a combined approach that includes diet, supplements, nutraceuticals, and healthy lifestyles.

I tailor supplements individually for each pet. According to the animal's issues and responses, I prescribe different dosages and combinations. Body constitution, type of cancer, and general health condition, as well as the potency of immune response, determine which, how much, how often, and for how long I will use any supplement. Some supplements can't be given to patients undergoing chemo, while some can, and many can help support animals during chemo.

## Royal Treatment Supplements Used to Help Fight Cancer

- Hoxsey-like formula and Essiac tea. Hoxsey and Essiac are two elegant combinations of herbs known to herbalists as anticancer and anti-inflammatory combinations.
- Artemisinin (given five days a week with one complete week off a month)—an herb used to fight cancer by affecting iron uptake
- Vitamins A, C, and E—antioxidant properties and support for killer T cells to induce cancer cell destruction
- Omega-3 fatty acids—antioxidants for overall health
- Maitake and reishi mushroom combos—anti-inflammatory and anticancer properties
- Astragalus—immune support, circulatory health
- Ashwaganda—immune support adaptogen
- Milk thistle—liver support
- Turmeric—well-researched anti-inflammatory and anticancer properties
- Green tea extract—antioxidant properties
- Transfer factor—reported to enhance the ability of the natural killer cells to fight cancer cells.
- Beta-glucans—polysaccharides from mushrooms and other

sources. Considered "biological response modifiers" because they help activate the immune system.
- 🐾 Probiotics—support healthy GI tract, repopulate good bacteria in the GI tract
- 🐾 Coenzyme Q10—vascular support for healthy vessels and circulation.

> *Green tripe is a fabulous supplement food to help soothe the GI tract and promote GI health. The beneficial bacteria, digestible protein, high fat content, minerals, and beneficial bacteria are medicinal. The smell is foul for owners, but heaven for a dog or cat. It helps animals with chronic diseases or cancer that may affect appetite or GI health.*

By the time it is diagnosed, most oncologists agree that a bone cancer such as an osteosarcoma has already spread throughout the body. Chemotherapy is typically recommended to rid the body of those cells. There are instances in which chemotherapy is indicated and can be a cure. However, I have serious reservations about any approach that does not build on the foundation of health while combating disease. This is where I work with the oncologist and the owners to formulate an effective integrative plan for health. I am fortunate to work with wonderful oncologists in Chicago. When I collaborate with my colleagues, I am encouraged about the integrative future of veterinary medicine regarding cancer treatments and other conditions.

Many of my clients with pets diagnosed with osteosarcoma decide to avoid the toxicity of chemotherapy. They opt for amputation to relieve the pain, and then no further allopathic medication. When they come to me, I help these patients maintain vibrant health, with the hope of letting the animal's body destroy its own cancer cells. We have had great success with proper diet, acupuncture, supplements, and exercise to support the innate health of cancer patients. I treat many amputee osteosarcoma patients who have been in remission for many years, and have not been through chemotherapy.

With a three-legged loping gait, Isabelle, the adorable shepherd mix, races into my clinic. It's been two years since osteosarcoma was the reason that her leg had to be amputated. She knows treats and water-walking are in her immediate future. Excited by the social side of her visit, she says hello to the staff. After a treat or two, she starts her workout, without risk of falling or slipping, in the underwater treadmill. Her owner watches as Isabelle's muscles and gait improve. Because of therapy, she will have fewer falls on land and will have more stamina for play. She never had chemo. She is healthy and active, and when she runs on the beach, she doesn't look handicapped at all. Or thirteen years old, for that matter.

Isabelle's success is not an anomaly. It is a testament to what can be done with a dedicated owner, an excellent diet, regular acupuncture, anti-cancer supplements, and a great exercise program.

Lymphoma, caused by a faulty, overacting immune system, is one of the common cancers I see in pets. It is often responsive to chemo. I work with owners to mitigate the side effects of the toxic drugs by using acupuncture, homeopathic remedies, diet, and supplements.

Mast cell tumors, an immune cell disease, are another relatively common cancer. Normal mast cells are reactive immune cells that arrive when the skin is inflamed. The mast cells can also create a hot, inflamed tumor. In addition to specific supplements based on my exam, the skin-cooling power of aloe juice—about ½ teaspoon for every 30 pounds of animal—can improve skin health.

I treat animals with many types of cancer these days, but I am comforted to know that I have tools to help improve health and decrease some of the deeper causes of their disease. Many things have to go wrong for cancer cells to grow. Our job is to minimize the possibility of things going wrong. I can't say we have found a cure for cancer yet, but we find we can stall its progress in many ways—often way past what the prognosis predicted. I believe that the Royal Treatment integrative protocols for diet and immune system support in cancer cases can restore and prolong the health of our patients.

I wish I could report that wild animals are still relatively unscathed by cancers, which used to be the case twenty years ago. But as toxins and chemicals have increased in the world, they are affecting wildlife, too. There is a great deal of information that shows direct connection between cancers in wildlife and human-made toxins in their environment.

# VACCINATIONS

*I am not **against** vaccination;*
*I am **for** a healthy immune system.*

P ETS ARE OVERVACCINATED IN THIS COUNTRY—OFTEN TO THEIR
detriment. However, the judicious use of vaccines can be beneficial
and lifesaving. I believe river otters in Illinois benefited from vaccinations.
During my junior year in vet school, I was part of the otter release team
that inoculated them.

Rivers in Illinois were so polluted that river otters had become extinct.
But there had been great strides in cleaning up the rivers. My professor,
Dr. Laura Hungerford, was working with several other states to vaccinate
and then reintroduce otters to Illinois waterways. I remember worrying
about possible side effects from the vaccines. However, otters can contract
distemper or parvovirus from dogs, foxes, raccoons, and skunks. They
would have to contend with these deadly viruses after being released back
into nature, and they could increase the spread of these diseases as well.
Therefore, the benefits of vaccination outweighed the risks.

Were I to be reincarnated, I would hope to be an otter. There are
thirteen different types of otters and they all play with vigor, eat with
gusto, sleep like babies, and seem to live every moment to the fullest.
Adorable fuzzballs as babies, clever and ingenious as adults, they float,
swim, play tag, use tools, and seem to be bursting with a joie de vivre.

I have seen them in ocean kelp forests, and frolicking in the rocks and pools of a winding river. Even in zoos and aquariums they are active and entertaining.

The first otters we were to release were from Louisiana. They were animals that had been trapped and were slated to be killed as vermin. This would be my first experience up close with one of my favorite species. I recall the first group of otters arriving in the back of a pickup truck. Once the engine stopped, I could hear the hissing and grumbling of the caged otters. Their combined voices whirred like a Vespa. When I looked inside, I saw that the state of their health varied. Our job was to do an exam, suture, fix, clean, medicate, vaccinate, tag, and release them into the Little Wabash River. Several groups were to be released over the next year for a total of 346 founding otters to start the population.

My friend Jane and I transported the first batch to our makeshift hut/clinic by the river. It was disheartening to see the injuries they had sustained from being captured. They had broken, lacerated, or swollen feet from traps, and various cuts and bruises. They were not thrilled to be in cages. The hissing and irritated chatter was constant. They were more adorable and wilder than I imagined.

We worked quickly, handing each other instruments and recording each procedure. The hut smelled of their musk. We had to allow ample time for them to fully recover from anesthesia before releasing them early the next day. We set them up in warm cages for the night. The worst vaccine reactions typically happen within the first twenty minutes of the shot, so we watched them carefully. Thankfully, none of the otters had a reaction.

The next morning, we went to a site we'd chosen as the most likely to be hospitable to a group of wild otters. The wire cages were cold, unwieldy, and hard to unlock. I struggled with the door to one of my favorite otters. He had lighter fur on his head and had lost a toe in a trap. I had sewn up the wound with purple suture. I named him RipTide. Even though he tried to bite me, I loved him anyway.

The agitated otters were ready to go after a big breakfast of sardines and canned cat food. A few more hisses, and we had released them all. No fanfare, no instructions about how to hunt or eat in their new river home. They seemed ecstatic to be released, and we were thrilled to release them. Each in turn, when released from their carrier, slid quietly into the river and never looked back. There are now thousands of river otters in Illinois.

Because we only had a day with these wild animals, we had no choice but to do all our treatments and vaccines at one time. We wanted them protected from the diseases, and we also didn't want them to become vectors for spreading disease. In regard to pets, we do have options. We can choose when and how often we vaccinate. And we have ways to limit exposure to disease until immunity is complete. A vaccination schedule should be individualized and carefully considered for each pet.

IMMUNE SYSTEMS ARE AFFECTED by many factors—diet, stress, exercise, circulation, toxins, disease, and vaccinations. Where possible, I choose to minimize the use of vaccines, employing them only after they are proved both safe and effective.

### WEIGHING THE RISKS

1. Is the vaccine safe (few life-threatening reactions)?
2. Is the vaccine required by law?
3. Is the timing appropriate? (Is there still immunity? Is there a longer-lasting vaccine?)
4. Is the pet healthy enough to mount an immune response?
5. Is there a reason *not* to give the vaccine (possible signs of illness or upcoming stressors)?
6. Is there really a risk of this disease for this pet?
7. Is the disease serious enough to require protection via vaccination?

8. What is required for kenneling/grooming/boarding or by the city or dog parks?

Currently, the vaccination for leptospirosis (a dangerous bacterial infection that can lead to liver and kidney failure and is spread by rats, cows, and several other vectors) is being encouraged by veterinarians. I am not convinced it is a good idea. One of many reasons I feel this way is that two types (serovars) of leptospirosis have been a part of the annual vaccination combo for twenty years and many adverse reactions to the combo vaccine in the past were considered to be due to the leptospirosis portion of it. Currently there is a newer, "cleaner" vaccine on the market that includes four serovars of lepto. It allegedly causes fewer adverse reactions. I am thrilled that pharmaceutical companies are trying to make these universally used vaccines safer. Despite this, I have seen severe adverse reactions to the new formulations. Just because they say it is safer, doesn't mean it is safe enough.

A client brought their twelve-year-old German shepherd, Bank, in for rehab following surgery to remove a brain tumor. The tumor had caused seizures and made him unable to walk. After integrative treatments that included a diet change, acupuncture, and underwater treadmill therapy, Bank regained his mobility. Although he looked a little drunk when he walked, he recovered well enough to be able to go up and down stairs, and play outside. His seizures had stopped since the surgery.

Two years later, Bank seemed to be maintaining a healthy life. At that point, his regular vet, concerned about a recent increase in the number of lepto cases in the city, recommended giving him the new lepto vaccine. The owner called me for my opinion and I strongly recommended against it. I was concerned about the seizure side effects associated with that particular vaccine. I advised him that lepto, while life-threatening, can often be treated and cured with antibiotics. I also pointed out that the vaccine provides immunity only for about nine months. The owner, however, was very concerned about Bank contracting lepto and decided to allow him to be inoculated with the vaccine.

Within two days, Bank presented with serious cluster seizures and was hospitalized at an ER specialty clinic. Thankfully, the neurologist managed to stop the seizures by treating him for this vaccine reaction. Bank returned to my clinic for integrative detox and rehab therapy. He improved over time and regained much of his mental and muscular functions. However, he never fully returned to his happy pre-vaccine state. He stared into corners much more frequently and was more anxious than he had previously been.

Everyone involved in Bank's case was motivated by concern for his well-being. What troubles me is the default acceptance of pharmaceuticals as the only safe treatment of choice, regardless of circumstances.

Many people have a blind faith in pharmaceutical medicine. TV shows have taught us to expect miracle cures from high-tech procedures and medications. Dedicated doctor, plus brilliant diagnosis, plus last-minute pharmaceutical/surgical intervention equals a happy ending.

Pharma is a gargantuan business motivated by gargantuan profits. They have much to lose if doctors, vets, and patients examine other, non-pharma options. But I am concerned about the health of animals. A reevaluation of all annual vaccines is warranted, especially the ones associated with higher risk.

Subcutaneous and intravenous injections bypass the body's security systems. The gamble is that the antigens will strengthen the immunity of the animal to win against the disease. However, any time you inject an agent into an animal, there are risks. It is a veterinarian's job to make those medical judgments. Don't hesitate to ask your vet about the rationale and risks of any injection.

If you do opt for a vaccination, keep in mind that a vaccine is not protective the moment you give it. In fact, most vaccines cause an immune suppression for about ten days after administration. Therefore, it's best to keep a newly vaccinated animal in a restricted environment for the days immediately after the vaccination.

The law places limits on the recommendations a veterinarian can provide. Rabies vaccination protocols, for example, are established by law, so veterinarians are only allowed to recommend state requirements. In some states that means yearly vaccines; in others a three-year rabies vaccine is accepted. Owners can sign a waiver declining rabies vaccination for their pets. In those cases, I always recommend running a rabies titer test to check for immunity.

Research has shown that the one-year rabies vaccine does, in fact, last much longer than one year, after the administration of the second dose. As a result, you may have the option to give your pet the three-year vaccine, unless it is a puppy. In Illinois, I recommend the three-year vaccine rather than the one-year for all adult pets to avoid stressing the immune system unnecessarily.

## THE SEVEN-YEAR FIX

WE HOPE TO HAVE proof soon that the three-year rabies vaccine actually provides immunity for five to seven years. When that study is FDA-approved, I will recommend the five- or seven-year rabies vaccine.

Be aware that the one-year rabies vaccine must be given to puppies or to pets without a known treatment history. One year later, they can be given the three-year rabies vaccine as a booster. Separate vaccines to avoid overstressing the immune system. For example, give the distemper combo at one vet visit, then the rabies vaccine about three weeks later.

I obtain much of my information about vaccines from the brilliant and dedicated Dr. Jean Dodds in California. Her work has furthered the discussion about safe, effective vaccination. She and Dr. Ronald Schultz are on the front lines of the movement to prove that the rabies vaccine does last five to seven years. You can read more about her research and donate to the Rabies Challenge Fund by going to www.rabieschallengefund.org or www.hemopet.org.

Here are Dr. Dodd's vaccine protocols for dogs and cats.

| CANINE VACCINATION PROTOCOL—2011 *Minimal Vaccine Use* | |
|---|---|
| **Note:** The following vaccine protocol is offered for those animals where minimal vaccinations are advisable or desirable. The schedule is one I recommend and should not be interpreted to mean that other protocols recommended by a veterinarian would be less satisfactory. It's a matter of professional judgment and choice. | |
| **AGE OF PUPS** | **VACCINE TYPE** |
| 9–10 weeks | Distemper + Parvovirus, MLV (e.g., Intervet Progard Puppy DPV) |
| 14 weeks | Same as above |
| 16–18 weeks (*optional*) | Same as above (*optional*) |
| 20 weeks or older, if allowable by law | Rabies |
| 1 year | Distemper + Parvovirus, MLV |
| 1 year | Rabies, killed virus, 3-year product (give 3–4 weeks *apart* from distemper/parvovirus booster) |

Perform vaccine antibody titers for distemper and parvovirus every three years thereafter, or more often, if desired. Vaccinate for rabies virus according to the law, except where circumstances indicate that a written waiver needs to be obtained from the primary care veterinarian. In that case, a rabies antibody titer can also be performed to accompany the waiver request.

| FELINE VACCINATION PROTOCOL—2011 *Minimal Vaccine Use* | |
|---|---|
| **Note:** The following vaccine protocol is offered for those animals where minimal vaccinations are advisable or desirable. The schedule is one I recommend and should not be interpreted to mean that other protocols recommended by a veterinarian would be less satisfactory. It's a matter of professional judgment and choice. | |
| **AGE OF KITTENS** | **VACCINE TYPE** |
| 8–9 weeks | Panleukopenia, calicivirus, rhinopneumonitis virus (FVRCP) |

| 12–13 weeks | Same as above |
| --- | --- |
| 24 weeks or older, if required by law | Rabies (e.g., Merial Purevax, recombinant) |
| 1 year | FVRCP booster |
| 1 year | Rabies, same as above but separated by 2–3 weeks from FVRCP |

Perform vaccine antibody titers (a blood test) for panleukopenia virus every three years thereafter, or more often, if desired. Vaccinate for rabies virus according to the law.

LIKE MY VETERINARY COLLEAGUES, I struggle with worries about adverse effects of vaccinations, while recognizing vaccines' necessity. Adverse vaccine reactions include allergic reactions, skin lesions, hair loss, swelling, epilepsy, chronic allergies, autoimmune diseases, cancer, anaphylaxis, and death.

The Lyme vaccine has been implicated in causing some of the signs of Lyme disease, including joint pain, arthritis, swelling, and fevers. These vaccine-induced signs do not respond to the antibiotic treatment one would use on the actual Lyme disease. In other words, if you contract Lyme disease *from the vaccine*, antibiotics will not cure it. That is why I do not recommend the Lyme vaccine. A safe, effective human vaccine for Lyme disease doesn't exist, despite the fact that Lyme disease is a troubling health issue on the east coast of the United States.

Bordetella vaccines can also cause the signs of the disease being vaccinated against, which is a honking cough and an upper respiratory infection. This vaccine is required by kennels and does have some protective ability as well. When it is given as nasal drops, rather than as an injection, I see fewer adverse reactions. Bordetella vaccine is given to animals at high risk for bordetella exposure in such places as boarding facilities, groomers, day care, and kennels where ventilation between animals is limited.

# MEDICINE CHEST

♕

————  ————

*There is a wealth of healing treasures,*
*from allopathy to homeopathy.*

B ECAUSE OF THE MANY MODALITIES I ROUTINELY EMPLOY, I
can treat an animal effectively even if I don't have a diagnosis. The
final arbiter of health and disease is not whether a group of symptoms
has a name. From the standpoint of proper treatment, uncovering the
onset of the disease is as important as making a diagnosis. Tracing the
cascade of contributing factors and events can determine an effective
plan of action.

Every animal preserves *homeostasis,* which is the maintenance of a
dynamic, physiological equilibrium. Signs of disease are actually feed-
back provided by the healthy part of an organism in response to detrimental factors. When these factors reach a critical mass, the animal
will exhibit signs of disease. The severity of signs will determine which
changes must be made.

**Does pain medication only suppress symptoms?** No, is my answer. While painful areas in a pet alert us to an unhealthy condition, pain
must be managed or it can further debilitate the animal. My goal is to relieve severe pain before an animal leaves my clinic. Pain meds are the first
step on the road to healing. Extreme or chronic pain is debilitating and requires energy that would be better used for healing. Only when inflamma-

tion, nerve pain, and severe or chronic pain is addressed can the immune system instigate the body's own healing mechanism.

> *Medications must be reevaluated as*
> *the animal gets better.*

It makes sense to adjust the dosages of a medication as the animal comes into balance and begins healing. Be sure to ask your vet how long you should continue giving a medication before deciding if it is working or not. For instance, if a cat with an upper respiratory infection is not feeling better after weeks on a medication, the medication should be reevaluated. Or if your poodle is no longer itching, discuss weaning off steroids with your vet.

> *Starting new medications?*
> *Pay attention to your pet's reactions.*

Don't go out of town, if possible, when your pet starts new medication or food. If you must leave your pet, please give detailed instructions to the pet sitter about possible side effects or negative reactions.

Finally, cortisone (steroids) as well as herbal combinations have a place on the healing curve. Sometimes serious medication is needed to alleviate inflammation or limit tissue damage.

| HERBAL OPTIONS AND SUGGESTED USES | |
| --- | --- |
| **ALLERGIES** | |
| Omega-3 | free-radical scavenging |
| Aloe vera | cooling for skin and GI |
| Vitamin E | vitamin for skin function |
| Red clover | soothing skin support |

| HERBAL OPTIONS AND SUGGESTED USES | |
|---|---|
| Nettles | antipruritic (anti-itch) |
| Plantain | antipruritic, soothing |
| Garlic | antiparasitic/bacterial |
| Skullcap | decreases swelling |
| **ARTHRITIS** | |
| Boswellia | anti-inflammatory |
| Turmeric | anti-inflammatory |
| Pennywort | anti-inflammatory |
| Feverfew | anti-inflammatory |
| Celery seed | anti-inflammatory |
| Apple cider vinegar | pH regulation |
| Arnica | blood mover/decreases bruising |
| **ANXIETY** | |
| Valerian | sedative effects |
| Chamomile | sedative effects |
| Lyme blossom | calms the mind |
| Skullcap | calms the mind |
| Kava kava | sedative effects |
| **CARDIAC DISEASE** | |
| Coenzyme Q10 | vascular integrity |
| Hawthorneberry | improves overall cardiac function |
| Omega-3 | free-radical scavenging |
| **CONSTIPATION/MEGACOLON** | |
| Cascara | colon motility stimulant |
| Ginger | GI motility stimulant |
| Kelp | minerals and laxative |
| Slippery elm | fiber and soothing |
| Licorice | antispasmodic |
| **DENTAL** | |
| Peppermint | odor relief/antibacterial |
| Blackberry | antibacterial |
| Echinacea | immune enhancing |
| Burdock root | anti-inflammatory |

| HERBAL OPTIONS AND SUGGESTED USES ||
|---|---|
| Licorice | odor relief/anti-inflammatory |
| **DIABETES** ||
| Gymnema | blood glucose regulation |
| Corn silk | blood glucose regulation |
| Uva ursi | blood glucose regulation |
| **DIARRHEA** ||
| Pumpkin | GI regulation/fiber |
| Slippery elm | fiber |
| Psyllium | fiber |
| Wild yam | GI regulation/fiber |
| Blackberry | tones GI lining |
| Peppermint | antispasmodic |
| **FLATULENCE/BELCHING** ||
| Chamomile | GI soother |
| Licorice | antispasmodic |
| Slippery elm | fiber/GI mover |
| Fennel | antigas |
| Kelp | GI soother |
| Peppermint | carminative |
| Ginger | antinausea |
| **GASTROINTESTINAL** ||
| Peppermint | carminative |
| Cinnamon | GI warmer |
| Ginger | antinausea |
| Parsley | carminative |
| Wild yam | GI soother |
| Fennel | antigas |
| Slippery elm | fiber/soothing |
| **GERIATRIC** ||
| Omega-3 | free-radical scavenging |
| Milk thistle | liver protectant/tonic |
| Ginseng | cognitive support |
| Arnica | blood mover |

| HERBAL OPTIONS AND SUGGESTED USES | |
|---|---|
| Boneset | joint support |
| **IMMUNE SYSTEM** | |
| Ashwaganda | enhances immunity |
| Shiitake mushroom | enhances immunity |
| Licorice | enhances immunity |
| Echinacea | enhances immunity |
| Astragalus | improves healing |
| Bupleurum | enhances immunity |
| **INFECTION** | |
| Oregon grape | antibiotic properties |
| Oregano | antibiotic properties |
| Barberry | antibiotic properties |
| Garlic | antibiotic/antifungal/antiviral |
| Peppermint | antibiotic properties |
| **KIDNEY/BLADDER TONIC** | |
| Dandelion | diuretic |
| Cranberry | pH regulation |
| Stone root | bladder stone dissolution |
| Gravel root | diuretic |
| Hydrangea | antispasmodic for bladder |
| Corn silk | diuretic/anti-inflammatory |
| Uva ursi | antiseptic/anti-inflammatory |
| **LIVER** | |
| Milk thistle | liver protectant/tonic |
| Omega-3 | free-radical scavenger |
| Vitamin C | free-radical scavenger |
| Dandelion | improves fluid balance |
| SAM-e (denosyl) | normalizes liver function |
| **NEOPLASIA** | |
| Vitamin A | induces apoptosis |
| Vitamin C | free-radical scavenging |
| Turmeric | anti-inflammatory |
| Mushrooms | enhance immunity |

| HERBAL OPTIONS AND SUGGESTED USES | |
|---|---|
| Green tea | anti-inflammatory |
| Hoxsey formula | anticancer combo |
| Maitake mushroom | immune boost |
| Omega-3 | free-radical scavenging |
| Milk thistle | liver protectant/tonic |
| OCULAR | |
| Bilberry | ocular vascular support |
| Eyebright | ocular tonic |

## GENERAL DOSING FOR HERBAL PREPARATIONS

UNDER THE SUPERVISION OF a vet, begin giving an herbal dose at or below the minimum dose. Try it for a few days, then increase to a mid-range dose.

| | TINCTURE | GRANULE/ POWDERED |
|---|---|---|
| **CANINE** 1–15 LBS | ¼–½ ml | ⅛–¼ tsp |
| 15–30 LBS | 1–2½ ml | ¼–¾ tsp |
| 30–60 LBS | 2½–4 ml | ¾–1 tsp |
| 60LBS–GIANT | 4–7 ml | 1–1½ tsp |
| **FELINE** | 4 drops–½ ml | ⅛–¼ tsp |

You can also dose tinctures 1 drop per pound of body weight per day. The daily dose can be divided.

## MARBLE THE RABBIT

I had never before been asked to treat a pasteurella sinus infection in a rabbit without antibiotics, but when I was, the request made sense. Pasteurella infections in rabbits are all too common and can be life-threatening, causing abscesses anywhere, including the brain. Pasteurella is managed, but usually not cured, by repeated courses of antibiotic treatment. The owners of Marble the rabbit were concerned about the effect of antibiotics on his delicate digestive system. Antibiotics can upset the stomach and the intestinal flora and pose serious health risks. Colic and GI upset in rabbits (as well as in horses) can quickly become life-threatening.

Marble's owners were hoping for another way to treat his infection and upper respiratory signs. We devised a plan that would boost his immune system. I did insist that they take home a "just in case" course of antibiotics—which they still have, unused—but this integrative plan worked well.

Once a week this soft, sweet rabbit allowed me to place tiny needles around his face, ears, and body to stimulate circulation in the sinuses and to support his immune system. I also gave him periodic injections of vitamin $B_{12}$. His herbs included echinacea, goldenseal, nettles, red clover, elecampane, oregano, and Oregon grape. Being a rabbit, Marble ate them with gusto. We also gave him vitamin C, cranberry, a good probiotic (Bene-Bac), and a ho-

I often recommend these combination products:

- **Serenity** (Gaia) is a calming herb mix for anxious dogs or cats.
- **Dog Gone Pain** (DGP) (Harmony Company) is an herbal anti-inflammatory combo for dogs.
- **Cholodin** (MVP Laboratories) enhances cognitive function in dogs and cats. It combines choline, lecithin, vitamins, minerals, and brain function enhancers. This is especially indicated for animals that walk into a room and seem to have forgotten why they are there.
- **Si Miao San** (Natural Path) is a versatile Chinese combination for inflammation, arthritis, and allergies.
- **Hoxsey** (Natural Path) is an elegant combination of anticancer/anti-inflammatory herbs.
- **Traumeel** (Boiron) is a homeopathic combo for trauma, inflammation, and pain.
- **Cascara Combo** (Natural Path) is a tincture combining herbs for constipation and poor GI motility in the colon.

meopathic remedy for cough and upper respiratory signs (spongia tosta).

Armed with a healthy diet of fresh greens, timothy hay, vegetables, and our supplements, we gave his body the chance to fight back.

Over a year later, Marble hadn't relapsed into any significant pasteurella episode. And he'd never had an upset stomach.

- **Discus Compositum** (Boiron) is a homeopathic remedy for disc disease.
- **D-Mannose** is used to decrease incidence of chronic urinary tract infections.
- **Minor bupleurum** is a Chinese herbal combo used often for hind end weakness.

## Other Supplements

- **Probiotics**—*Bacillus coagulans* modulates GI microflora as well as GI immune responses.
- **Honey** is used topically for wounds and orally for allergies.
- **Adequan,** an injectable nutraceutical glycosaminoglycan, is used for arthritis or joint injury. It is a precursor for healthy joint fluid. Injected subcutaneously rather than in the muscle.

## Home-Care Remedies and Tips
(Yes, you can try these at home.)

- Skunk odor remover recipe: 1–2 tbsp of dish detergent (I use Dawn), ¼ cup baking soda, 4 cups of hydrogen peroxide. Don't close mixture in a bottle—it will explode!
- Administer topical flea medication if needed, spreading it sideways, high up on the neck, from left to right, rather than trying to part the hair down the middle.
- Peanut butter or olive oil to dissolve sap/gum.
- Place steeped, but cooled tea bags on hot wounds/lick granuloma/swelling/irritated eyelids.
- Daily coconut oil can help with gastric reflux—1 tsp per meal for a 50-pound dog.
- Use Murphy's Oil Soap (yes, the same soap used for wood

floors!) as a shampoo, to soothe itchy, scaly skin. It's a gentle vegetable-based soap, and it has the proper pH.

❧ Apply silver sulfadiazine, an ointment used to treat second- and third-degree burns, topically on hot spots/wounds.

❧ Nail bleeding after a trim or being broken? Don't have quick-stop powder? Apply cornstarch, soap shavings, tea bag, cotton gauze, and apply pressure while you elevate the limb. Do not use water or rub.

My good friend and colleague Dr. Richard Palmquist, a well-known integrative veterinarian in Los Angeles, is an expert practitioner of, among many other things, homeopathy. The basic principle of homeopathy is the idea that "like cures like." This area of medicine uses small amounts of agents whose toxic symptoms match the symptoms and signs that are exhibited by the patient to cure them. Below is a homeopathic first-aid kit Dr. Palmquist recommends pet owners keep on hand.

| A HOMEOPATHIC FIRST AID KIT FOR PETS | |
|---|---|
| MAIN SIGN | HOMEOPATHIC AGENT |
| *Insect sting:* red, hot, and swollen | *Apis mellifica* |
| *Insect sting:* painful, swollen, and bruised | *Arnica montana* |
| *Insect sting:* inflamed and blistered | Cantharis |
| *Foxtails and other foreign bodies* | Silicea, *Myristica sebifera* |
| *Hot spots:* sudden red and hot | Belladonna |
| *Hot spots:* yellow, oozing discharges | Graphites |
| *Hot spots:* red with swelling, hive-like | *Apis mellifica* |
| *Vomiting:* small amounts of stool, angry | Nux vomica |
| *Cough:* after wet weather | Drosera |
| *Early stages of illness with fever and fear* | *Aconitum napellus* |
| *Shock/trauma* | Traumeel, *Aconitum napellus* |
| *Bleeding/bruising and resulting shock* | *Arnica montana* |

Homeopathics I Use in My Practice

---

*Ruta graveolens*—for tendon circulation

*Rhus toxicodendron*—rusty gate syndrome, stiff when first moving

*Spongia tosta*—for dry cough

*Aconitum napellus*—for colds or flu

*Asclepias tuberosa*—for cough

*Symphytum/comfrey*—to "knit bone" for fractures

*Arnica*—for bruising, strokes, and blood congestion; it moves blood

Dosing for homeopathic pellets usually works out to be about one pellet per 10 pounds, up to three times a day.

## IS THERE EVIDENCE FOR HOMEOPATHY?

POSITIVE RESEARCH EXISTS FOR homeopathy in both animals and people. A recent German trial showed that the homotoxicology agent Zeel worked as well as the nonsteroidal anti-inflammatory medication carprofen for arthritis of the knee. Both treatment regimens were well tolerated, with the three treatment-related adverse events all in the carprofen group.

A very important aspect of my work is encouraging veterinary research and scholarship in integrative medicine. Not surprisingly, big pharmaceutical companies do not support alternative research. As a board member of the American Holistic Veterinary Medical Association Foundation, I am proud to say that research and scholarships in integrative medicine are now being funded on a larger scale than ever before. Donations to this nonprofit organization have been used to support much-needed integrative medical research and veterinary student scholarships. A portion of my book sales will be donated to this organization. (To donate, visit the website: www.foundation.ahvma.org.)

# EMERGENCY CARE

♛

I T'S ALWAYS A SHOCK WHEN A PET SUDDENLY BEGINS TO EXHIBIT signs of serious illness. Without warning, you are confronted with an emergency. Usually at two in the morning. On a holiday weekend when your vet is closed.

Sometimes it is obvious that an animal needs immediate medical attention—in a case of acute pain, for example. But more often, pet owners are confused about whether their pet's condition warrants a trip to the emergency room. That indecisiveness can be dangerous—even potentially fatal to their pet.

If you phone the ER before going in, you may be able to obtain information. But there are many problems that can't be assessed without an exam. Emergencies depend on both the animal's condition and the owner's ability to deal with the problem. Although a bleeding toenail may not be life threatening, if an owner can't stop the bleeding it could be something that requires immediate attention at an ER.

Keep the phone numbers for your vet, the closest animal emergency center, and the ASPCA's Animal Poison Control Center (888-426-4435) in a place that's easy to find. Also, take a drive by the nearest animal ER during daylight hours to be sure you can find it in an emergency, when you may be fighting panic.

Allopathic medicine (conventional medicine that uses pharmacologically active agents or physical interventions to treat or suppress symptoms or diseases) shines in a real emergency. After the emergency is over, however, consider alternative methods, dietary changes, and supplements to avert future issues and support the overall health of your pet.

## THE ER—TO GO OR NOT TO GO

**Bloat** is a life-threatening condition most commonly exhibited by dogs when the stomach is overfilled with air or gas and is possibly twisting.

### Signs of Bloat

- Obvious discomfort
- Pacing
- Hypersalivating (drooling)
- Extreme nausea accompanied by retching
- Abdomen may appear distended
- Gums may be pale
- Collapse

### Action

- Go to the ER as soon as possible.
- Bloat is a real emergency where minutes count. It can become life-threatening very quickly.
- In mild cases, you can try to get the dog to burp by standing them on their rear legs, as if you were dancing. Don't waste time if it doesn't work immediately.

**Urinary blockage in cats** is a serious condition where male cats strain to urinate indicating an obstruction from stones, crystals, swelling, or infection in the urinary tract that blocks the flow of urine.

## Signs of Urinary Blockage

- Frequent visits to the litter box with no urine production
- Pacing and crying, sometimes near the litter box
- Small amounts of urine, sometimes bloody, in inappropriate places
- Loss of appetite
- Listlessness
- Vomiting

## Action

- Go to the ER.
- Urinary blockage is a real emergency where time is of the essence.

**Difficulty breathing** can be caused by a number of illnesses, including lung disease, pneumonia, asthma, tumors, pulmonary fluid, heart disease, pain, airway obstruction, laryngeal paralysis, fungal infection, parasites, and trauma.

The X-ray machine is a much more effective tool than the stethoscope for diagnosing lung disease.

## Signs of Trouble Breathing

- Increased respiratory rate
- Increased abdominal effort to breathe—belly moving dramatically with each breath

- 🐾 Increased respiratory noise
- 🐾 Shallow breathing
- 🐾 Pale gums or any shade of blue, rather than pink

May be combined with an inability to lie down or lying in a prone (sphinx-like) position.

### Action

- 🐾 Trouble breathing is always considered an emergency. Go straight to the ER.

### Bleeding

- 🐾 Any kind of bleeding could be an emergency or just a temporary response to trauma—just as in humans.
- 🐾 Pay attention to how much and how quickly the blood is coming.
- 🐾 Ears, tongues, feet, and tails bleed profusely and often justify an ER visit.
- 🐾 Blood in the urine may look terrifyingly dramatic because it is diluted in the urine. This needs to be treated, but may not be an emergency if there is no straining. Consult with a vet.
- 🐾 Although it is alarming and can indicate a severe problem, many dogs develop diarrhea with blood as a reaction to gastrointestinal irritants A trip to the ER may be necessary.

### Action

- 🐾 Use common sense.
- 🐾 Cuts will bleed but usually can be stopped with pressure or a bandage where possible.

- Try to elevate the bleeding body part above the heart and apply pressure to the bleeding area for several minutes.
- Excessive bleeding that doesn't stop is an emergency.
- Bleeding toenails stop bleeding when you apply a quick-stop powder, styptic pencil, bar-soap shavings, cornstarch, or tea leaves from a used tea bag, with firm pressure to the bleeding nail. It should stop after a minute or two.
- Whether to go straight to the ER because of bleeding is a judgment call. You might ignore a mild cut and go back to sleep, but if blood can't be stopped you may need to race to the ER in your pajamas.

## Trauma from Being Hit by a Car

- Go to the ER. Have the pet checked by a vet as soon as possible.
- Even if animals appear fine after being hit by a car, they need to be assessed by a vet.
- Internal injuries—bruising to the heart muscle, contusions on the lungs, and small hairline fractures—can be missed by the untrained eye.

## Prolonged Vomiting (for More Than a Day)

- Animals that have not been able to keep food or water down for more than a day will probably need a visit to the ER.
- Note what is being vomited up.
- If it is early-morning vomiting on an empty stomach, with yellowish fluid (bile), and the pet still has a good appetite, it is likely to be less of an emergency and more a chronic diet/acidity issue.
- If it includes pieces of fabric or a toy and you're concerned there might be more, that is more of an emergency.

Some dogs seem to be thinking, "I'll eat this and if it isn't good for me, I'll vomit it up." If they act normal after vomiting and their appetite returns, this is probably not an emergency, unless a toxin is involved.

Note: Don't keep giving food to a vomiting animal. If they are also vomiting water, withhold that too, and call a vet or your ER.

## Lethargic Puppies or Kittens

- There can be many causes, but often this indicates hypoglycemia and the pet needs ER care.
- Put honey or syrup on the gums, but then get to the vet or ER.

**Heatstroke** can occur if the animal is exposed to high temperatures over 85 degrees without water or shade, or even less, depending on their health and age. Ambient temperature may be as low as 70 degrees but the temperature in a car—even with windows open—can climb to over 100 very quickly. Within minutes! Be careful about leaving animals in cars! A greyhound arrived for a routine rehab with a temperature of 104.5 just because her owner's car air-conditioning wasn't working for the ten-minute drive to my clinic.

## Signs of Heatstroke

- Panting
- Restlessness
- Vomiting/diarrhea
- Excessive salivation (thick, ropey saliva)
- Stumbling gait
- Seizures
- Collapse

## Action

- If you take a rectal temperature in a heat-stressed animal and it's over 104, go to the ER.
- Cool animal down by using coolish (not ice-cold) water all over, especially in groin area, on the feet and head, and go to the vet.
- *Do not use alcohol.* It can be absorbed through the skin and may be toxic to the animal.
- A veterinarian may need to give IV fluids and other treatments to stabilize the pet.
- Heatstroke can become life-threatening very quickly, especially for greyhounds, brachycephalic breeds, and cats.

**Choking** is a known or unknown obstruction or foreign body blocking the airway.

## Signs of Choking

- Sudden collapse from no oxygen, depending on the cause and severity of the obstruction
- If airways are partially obstructed, the pet may paw at his face or mouth, trying to vomit.
- Lying down in odd positions
- Running around with the neck stretched out
- Salivating excessively

## Action

- Choking can be a real emergency.
- Try clearing the airway before going to the ER. This is an emergency where seconds, not minutes, count.

🐾 If an animal has an object stuck in its mouth or throat,
try to remove it if it is visible but avoid getting bitten. Put
something in the mouth to hold it open for you, such as a
cloth or a roll of thick tape.

🐾 Administer the Heimlich maneuver—apply quick pressure
just under the ribs. Use a two-handed fist, one hand
covering the other, and aim up and in toward the head.
Attempt this several times. At times, the obstruction may
be dislodged, but the dog won't start breathing unless
artificial respiration or CPR is performed. That type of
action is beyond the scope of this chapter, but animal CPR
courses are available.

Usually from chewing on electric cords, **electric shock** can result in
anything from no injury to a mild oral trauma at the base of the teeth, to
severe life-threatening injuries, which can include fluid in lungs. Signs can
be difficult to assess without the help of an exam and radiograph.

## Signs of Electrical Shock

🐾 panting
🐾 high-pitched screaming
🐾 trouble breathing
🐾 dizziness
🐾 walking oddly
🐾 visible burns on mouth/skin
🐾 lesions in the mouth
🐾 chewed electrical cord

## Action

🐾 After an electrical shock, you need a veterinarian to assess the damage and pain issues with an exam and possibly a radiograph.

❧ Go to your vet or an ER.

**Lameness** is when an animal is not using a leg properly.

## Signs of Lameness

❧ A lame animal that can bear some weight on the leg and is otherwise acting normally does not usually need a visit to the ER and may wait for a regular vet appointment.

❧ When an animal is not using a leg (or legs) at all, or can't get up on its own power, or if there is bleeding or any significant swelling or pain in a limb, it's time to get to the ER, especially in breeds prone to disc disease (long-backed animals).

## Signs of Eye Issues

❧ Squinting/shying away from light, significant eye swelling, bleeding from the eye, or animal showing significant pain is an emergency.

❧ In most cases, tearing, moderate discharge, and mild reddening can wait for a regular vet visit.

## Action

❧ Go to the ER for severe signs. For milder eye issues, see your regular vet.

**Seizures** are involuntary twitching/convulsing, sometimes accompanied by involuntary urination or defecation.

- Twitching can be local, like snapping motions with just the muzzle or jaw, or it can involve the whole body—paddling and shaking.
- The animal usually is not in pain during a seizure and is most likely not aware of the seizure.
- If the episode lasts more than one or two minutes or returns immediately, or they come in clusters, it is an emergency.
- First-time seizures are in the emergency category because the cause may be determined to be something treatable—for example, toxin or illness—if caught early enough.

## Action

- Generally, it is best to see a vet or go to the ER immediately if your animal has a seizure for the first time and it's undiagnosed.
- Don't worry about them "swallowing their tongue." They won't—you'll only get bitten if you put your hand in the pet's mouth.
- Try to keep them from falling or injuring themselves, and keep them cool—prolonged seizures can dramatically increase body temperatures.
- Go to a vet if the seizures are prolonged or are in clusters, or the animal's temperature starts to rise due to the seizure.
- If it is possible, apply gentle pressure on closed eyelids to help decrease the heart rate and calm a seizure. If there is a lot of shaking, uncontrolled poking at the eyes can cause damage, so just get to the ER.

## Anorexic Cats

- Any cat that has not eaten anything in over twenty-four hours should be seen by a vet.
- Not eating is a life-threatening situation for a cat, especially for an overweight cat. They can quickly develop fatty liver from mobilizing too much body fat for energy because food was not available. Fatty liver is a serious condition.
- Try offering foods that are warm, that have extra warm water added, or that have a new flavor to tempt them.
- Sometimes assist-feeding with a dropper in the side of the mouth can jump-start cats to eat again.

## High Fevers

- Normal temperatures in dogs and cats are about 101–102.5 degrees.
- Anything above 103.5 degrees should be assessed. Over 104 degrees, go to ER.

## Dog or Animal Bites

- If your dog tussles with another dog, try to detect any areas that seem unusually hot. Bite punctures may not bleed much or be immediately apparent. If you don't feel heat, wait an hour and then check again. Any painful areas may need medical attention, and bite wounds usually require oral or topical antibiotics.

## Assist Feeding

- See page 116 for assist feeding instructions.

## Toxins

- 🐾 Dark chocolate and baking chocolate are the worst.
- 🐾 One ounce per pound of body weight of milk chocolate is a toxic dose. For a 30-pound dog, eating about 2 pounds of milk chocolate could be toxic. Smaller amounts cause diarrhea and possible vomiting.
- 🐾 One ounce per three pounds of body weight of semisweet chocolate is a toxic dose.
- 🐾 For the same 30-pound dog, eating a little over half a pound of semisweet chocolate may be toxic.
- 🐾 1 ounce per 9 pounds of body weight of baker's chocolate is a toxic dose.
- 🐾 If a chocoholic 30-pound dog ate just three ounces of baker's chocolate—a typical candy-bar-size amount—it would be toxic.

## Other Common Toxic Substances to Avoid

alcohol

antifreeze (1 tsp can be toxic to a 7-pound dog or cat)

cleaning agents (some are more toxic than others)

grapes

lily plants (very toxic to cats)

marijuana (paper/remains of burnt marijuana are all toxic to dogs and cats)

onions

raisins

rodenticides, insecticides

toads (eating or licking toads or frogs can be toxic depending on the species, and, I suppose, the amount of licking . . . )

wild mushrooms (especially amanita)

xylitol sugar-free sweetener (can be very toxic even in small doses)

There are many other toxins that, because of space, we can't list here.

## Action

- Call your veterinarian or the ASPCA Animal Poison Control Center immediately.
- Provide information about the type of animal you have: its weight and as much information about what the pet has ingested as possible: the label, the packaging type, when it was eaten and exactly how much.
- Do *not* induce vomiting without consulting a veterinarian first. Some toxins or other substances can do more damage on the way back up than they do on the way down.
- *When advised to induce vomiting,* you can do so by giving fresh hydrogen peroxide orally—about one ml per pound of dog—which is about ⅛ cup for a 30-pound dog and ¼ cup for a 60-pound dog. If there is no vomiting in 10 minutes, repeat dose. Hydrogen peroxide works best if it's fresh—less than six months old.

Over the holidays pets are exposed to many toxic or dangerous seasonal items. Even one or two mistletoe berries can be extremely toxic for a pet. On the other hand, poinsettias are only irritating to the mouth and, although they may cause vomiting, are not as toxic as people believe. Decorations, electrical cords, tree ornaments, and tinsel are all possible dangers to pets. Holiday candy that is toxic for pets includes chocolates, and sugar-free candies with xylitol. Easter lilies are toxic to cats. Don't leave wrapped gifts that are food/candy under the Christmas tree or in an accessible area. Animals may try to drink the water for a Christmas tree, so don't put in chemicals. An abundance of leftovers can be too rich for a pet's GI tract. Your holidays will be less stressful for you and your pets without a trip to the ER. However, if something does go wrong with your pet, don't hesitate to seek emergency care.

# ALLERGIC PETS

AN ITCHY PET MAY not be a medical emergency, but it is often a mental emergency.

Allergies are a big issue in veterinary medicine. Although a sneeze can be an initial sign of allergy, a more common sign of allergy is itching. Itchy dogs and cats chew at their skin and feet, scratching, licking, irritating, and even ulcerating skin. Itching is distressing for both pets and owners. It's hard to live or sleep with a pet that can't stop scratching. The irritated pet can really weigh on the mind. Not to mention the extreme discomfort the pet is going through.

Not only are people allergic to animals, but animals are allergic to our world, too. I use the analogy of a cup overfilling when I explain allergies to my clients. As long as the cup isn't brimming over with allergens and immune problems, the animal won't show any signs of irritation. However, when the cup runneth over, the itchy signs maketh themselves known.

Note: Some of my clients have been told that their pet is allergic to meat. I believe it is highly unlikely that a carnivore is allergic to a meat. Although I know it can be true, it should be the exception, not the rule. More commonly, the culprit is the chemicals in processed meats or poor-quality meats, or the grains and chemicals in the processed food irritate an animal's GI tract, making the intestines a poor border protector. An unhealthy GI tract may allow more antigens into the bloodstream. When a food change alleviates allergies, it is more likely because the food improves the health of the GI tract by providing a good protein content, and fewer grains or chemicals. A healthy GI tract makes all the difference in resolving allergies.

## Relieve Allergies

🐾 **The most important change:** feed the pet an anti-inflammatory diet, which is one that excludes corn, wheat, soy, white potato, and peanut butter

- ☙ alleviate the effects of itching and inflammation (meds, herbs, baths, topicals)
- ☙ uncover possible allergens
- ☙ discover ways to empty the cup of those allergens
- ☙ strengthen the immune system
- ☙ support the overall health of the pet
- ☙ sustain the pet's comfort level by monitoring allergens and keeping them at a minimum
- ☙ Moisturize and safely clean hair coat and skin with a mild, natural shampoo and rinse or Murphy's Oil Soap.
- ☙ Herbal remedies

The main concept behind herbal remedies is to support overall health, circulation, and lymphatic drainage, while also regulating the immune system, which is overreacting to the allergen.

Western herbs and supplements for allergies include:

ashwaganda—adaptogen and immune regulation
nettles—blood cleanser, relieves itching and hives, and can be used in gout.
quercitin—supports and regulates histamine levels
bromelain—anti-inflammatory effect
aloe vera—cooling for the skin
coconut oil—soothing and nutritive for skin

Chinese herbal formulas can also be very effective for an allergic animal, and can be prescribed based on the animal's particular condition. The herb Si Miao San is particularly versatile. I advise using Chinese herbs only when prescribed by a practitioner. I also use laser therapy on skin lesions caused by allergies. It can help calm down the inflammation.

## Medical Conditions/Tests to Consider in an Allergic Pet

- 🐾 Thyroid status
- 🐾 Cortisol (adrenal function)
- 🐾 Anal glands (full or impacted anals can cause generalized itching)
- 🐾 Mites
- 🐾 Resistant bacterial infections
- 🐾 Skin cancers
- 🐾 Overbathing or not rinsing well enough
- 🐾 Overperfuming

## Allergens to Avoid

- 🐾 Plastic feeding bowls
- 🐾 Wool blankets/carpets/toys
- 🐾 Dust mites (check ductwork and keep floors extra clean)
- 🐾 Cat litter with wheat or corn
- 🐾 Secondhand smoke
- 🐾 Plastic chew toys

## Skin Growths and Cancer

- 🐾 If actively bleeding and not manageable at home, skin growths can be an emergency.
- 🐾 Cauliflower-like growths that suddenly appear on lips, tongue, gums, or feet are generally benign viral papillomas and are not an emergency. They can indicate a compromised immune system and are usually seen in puppies. Based on physical exam, homeopathic and herbal supplements can be recommended.
- 🐾 Masses on the toes or in and around the mouth may be

infections, abscesses, melanomas, squamous cell carcinomas, or other malignant or benign tumors. On the toes and around the mouth, cancers can be aggressive. It may not require an ER visit, but make a vet appointment soon.

❧ Pigment changes on the nose can be hormonal or thyroid related—not an emergency.

❧ Animals that have unrelenting itching may be suffering from mange, allergies, fungal infections, or other conditions. Though not life-threatening, this is debilitating and needs serious, prompt attention.

❧ Eyelid growths are not an emergency unless the mass is actively bleeding or the cornea is affected. Signs of cornea involvement include squinting, pawing at the eye, redness, and discharge.

❧ Ear infections are usually not an emergency unless the animal is in extreme pain.

❧ Ticks can look like growths and vice versa. Look carefully and remove the tick promptly. They are more likely to transmit disease the longer they are embedded in the pet.

## PET FIRST AID KIT

HERE IS A LIST of things that come in handy when you're dealing with a pet problem at home or getting veterinary advice over the phone.

Use a portable container with compartments for easy storage. I found a tackle box works well.

1. Digital thermometer and lubricating jelly for thermometer
2. Quick-stop powder to stop bleeding—nails and other areas
3. Vet wrap or Ace bandages
4. Tweezers or hemostats
5. Emergency blanket

6. Instant cold packs

7. Eyewash/saline/artificial tears

8. Activated charcoal (buy the veterinary formula)

9. Arnica gel—bruises/trauma

10. Calming herbal formula like Serenity by Gaia—about ¼ of the capsule orally for a cat, and 1–2 capsules for a 50-pound dog up to every 8 hours

11. Calendula cream or tincture (disinfects/cleans)

12. Silver Shield gel (disinfects, supports immune system, great for burns)

13. Arsenicum—for allergies

14. Traumeel tablets (homeopathic, safe anti-inflammatory for pain/trauma/arthritis)

15. Aloe gel—cooling and supportive for the skin for burns/rashes

16. Peppermint—oral oil very diluted or even some of those little red and white pinwheel candies can work to calm the stomach (carminative)

17. Betadine—antiseptic cleaner, can be diluted with cool water for skin lesions

18. Triple antibiotic ointment and cortisone cream for topical use when directed

19. Benadryl liquid (small pets) or tablets (over 25 lbs)—works for allergic reactions, hives, muzzle-swelling reactions. The dose is 1 mg per pound or 25 mg for a 25-pound dog; 75-pound dog would take 75 mg (that seems like a lot but is okay).

20. Hydrogen peroxide (fresh bottle every 6–12 months)—antiseptic and can be used to make an animal vomit (1 teaspoon per every 5–10 pounds) but only if directed. Some things are worse coming back up than continuing through.

21. Cotton balls—for everything, but don't let your dog eat them, especially after cleaning the ears (they love to eat them then)

22. Animal ear cleaner for after swimming/irritation/infection

23. Pet shampoo (not human shampoo) or something soothing such as Murphy's Oil Soap
24. Latex exam gloves (for gross things)
25. Bulb syringe (to help clean out wounds)
26. Feeding syringe
27. Muzzle (animals in pain may try to bite)
28. Doggy life preserver—for boating, and to help lift injured dog or help them up the stairs
29. Carrier if appropriate

## EQUALLY IMPORTANT WHEN DEALING WITH GASTROINTESTINAL PROBLEMS

1. White rice
2. Chicken broth or jars of meat baby food (chicken, lamb, without onion powder) to help give pills, use as bland diet, assist feed or rehydrate
3. Unsweetened canned pumpkin (one tablespoon per 30-pound pet)
4. Slippery Elm powder—stomach soother and fiber source
5. Probiotic—*Bacillus coagulans,* lactobacillus, acidophilus can provide proper bacteria for any out-of-whack GI tract
6. Green Tripe (canned or frozen, provides bacteria and fat and easily digestible protein for a healthy gastrointestinal tract)
7. Powdered medicinal clay—aids absorption of toxins in the GI tract due to diarrhea

### MYTHCONCEPTION

*It is safe for dogs to eat cooked bones.*
**Not true.**
*Cooked bones can splinter into razor-sharp pieces and harm the GI tract.*

# I USUALLY BRING
# MY DUCK IN AT TWILIGHT

♛

*Never assume a medication is safe for a pet unless
it is prescribed for that pet—even if it is safe for a
different species.*

"**I** USUALLY BRING MY DUCK IN AT TWILIGHT," SAID THE VOICE ON
the phone, "but time got away from me and I didn't get out there,
until I heard the screaming."

It was 9 P.M. and my son was finally asleep. The man's voice was low
and mellifluous, although it sounded frantic. He described what had happened, and I told him to meet me at the clinic. My husband was already
handing me the keys and I was heading for the door.

When I arrived at the clinic, I saw the man with his pet duck. She
was a beauty. I was impressed by her wild curling head feathers and mul-
ticolored wings. But the bloody kitchen towel wrapped around her right
leg gave me a shudder. "I stopped the bleeding," he said, "with a tour-
niquet."

Rutger was the man's name. He was a tall, gentle man with salt-and-
pepper hair.

A raccoon had taken hold of Vaya's leg and tried to pull her whole
body through the chicken wire of her outdoor enclosure. Rutger had heard
the squawking and was outside before the raccoon could really pull, but

the damage had already been done. Rutger said there was a brief stare-down before the hungry bandit let go and loped out of sight.

Vaya was in shock. Rutger had scooped her up, wrapped the leg, called me, and come right over. He had tears in his eyes as he said, "You think we ought to just put her out of her misery?"

It was a mess of a leg. The webbing was torn in several directions and bloody skin and muscles were lacerated around the thigh from the chicken wire. There were no punctures or bite wounds—which was good. "No, I think we can fix this. Let's take an X-ray to check for fractures." It was going to be a long night.

In those days, there was no ER for animals. There were few vets who would handle a duck anyway, so it was up to me.

The radiograph I took showed a fracture. Luckily it wasn't displaced, and there were no fragments. I started to feel more confident. It seemed unlikely that she would lose the leg. I recalled a duck at the Stillman Nature Center, in Illinois, that had one leg and was still able to swim normally. I was relieved that Vaya's leg looked as if it might heal, if we could keep it from getting infected.

I anesthetized the duck by putting her face in a cone of isoflurane gas anesthetic. Rutger would have to be the anesthetist. He was a fast learner. Vaya was snoozing in seconds.

I had already given fluids for shock. I thought through the medicines I'd need. I had to carefully consider the safety of each one for a duck. There weren't a lot of safe, medical options at the time, nor were there many books or resources available on duck leg injuries. With any exotic animal, I worried about reactions to pharmaceutical medication. I had seen too many cases in wildlife or zoo medicine where a medication that was safe in one species was given to another, with disastrous results. A de-wormer that was given routinely for many species of animals at a local aquarium caused a deadly reaction in Beluga whales in a matter of minutes. Certain anti-inflammatories that are safe for dogs can be fatal for cats. Several antibiotics that humans can take will destroy the GI tract of a rabbit. The most glaringly obvious example is a miticide used to treat canine mange mites. Miticide will not only kill a mite infestation in a pet tarantula's cage, but will also kill the tarantula. Spiders and mites are, in fact, closely related.

That rule also applies to herbal medicines. For example, full-strength tea tree oil that is generally safe to use on fungal or bacterial skin infections on humans and dogs can cause neurologic dysfunction and even death when applied topically on a cat. However, it can be used on cats when significantly diluted.

Birds, fish, mammals, and insects have developed their own tolerances for medications. When giving medications that have never been tried in a species, we must proceed with caution. And then, based on the severity of the condition, it is wise to use only what is absolutely essential.

> *"Be like a duck. Calm on the surface, but always paddling like the dickens underneath."*
> —MICHAEL CAINE

For Vaya, I used only medications that I knew were safe for ducks. My first priority was alleviating pain. I injected her with a morphine derivative. For the topical preparation, I decided to go with a diluted herbal preparation mixed with an old-fashioned burn cream. This would help heal the skin. I added yarrow to stop the bleeding and as an antiseptic, comfrey to help heal the bone, and calendula as an antibacterial. With the leg healing in a splint, the immune system would need to be supported by supplements. There were other herbs I considered, but I didn't have them at 10 P.M. on a Saturday night. I used what I had, confident that it was a good, safe combination. I didn't want any infection under the wrap.

A duck's leg doesn't have a lot of extra tissue, and what it does have is not easy to sew. I cleaned the area with some diluted Betadine (antiseptic povidine-iodine). I had to pluck some of the damaged feathers. Rutger watched without flinching. He was a real trouper. Then I started sewing things back together over the leg. It was like a jigsaw puzzle.

As for the rubbery webbing, I sewed it up with tiny sutures, and then I took out my trusty superglue. Once the leg was put back together, it looked like a Frankenstein body part.

Something like a splint would have to be fashioned to keep the leg still, but in a natural, slightly bent position. The tongue depressors I'd set out didn't quite fit the bill. I looked around for an object I could make into a curve that was lightweight but stiff. A plastic detergent bottle on the counter would serve nicely. After emptying the detergent, I cut out a curved portion of the bottom. It was perfect. I wrapped it in soft cotton wrap and covered it with tape.

Covering the wounds with my concoction of herbal cream, I wrapped a Telfa pad and thin cotton over the whole leg. I anchored the plastic splint to a couple of feathers, and then to the leg with a cotton wrap. One more wrap with cotton gauze—it couldn't be too bulky, too tight, or allow any bending of the leg, but it had to be light and durable—and the rig was finished. Now it was up to Vaya's natural ability to heal.

I remembered dealing with duck patients at the end of my time at vet school. I had gone to a wildlife field course in Oregon instead of going on a honeymoon with my husband. Only he, being an ecologist, could have understood why this might be more important than drinking margaritas by the pool in St. Croix. There were fourteen vet students in the course, and we called it the Wildlife Honeymoon Course.

One part of the course involved detoxifying wildlife in oil-spill situations—particularly waterfowl. Local ducks from a nearby nature center were volunteered to be dipped into nontoxic oil and we had to clean them. Dawn dish detergent is what we used. It is donated to wildlife rescues for oil spills. When you start to scrub, it's easy to soak the feathers with water and soap because they are saturated with oil, and the natural ability of the feathers to repel water is destroyed. But the more you wash, the more you can see the water beading up on the feathers, being repelled. We were literally washing them dry.

It was amazing to see it up close. I had never appreciated how well constructed the feathers of waterfowl are. They are perfectly suited for living in their environment. I would wash until washing was not possible—because the water just bounced off. Then the protective beading mechanism was restored—exactly like water off a duck's back. I had a new appreciation for the magic of nature.

We learned how toxic oil spills really are, and what is done (much too little) to safeguard against them. We studied various other toxin sources: effluents, paper companies, strip mining, factories, roads, dry cleaning, and simple littering. We discussed the role of pollution laws and the Environmental Protection Agency and what protection—again, inadequate in my opinion—it offers for the environment.

The class was also taken to an enormous building that held acres of confiscated animal parts. We saw firsthand the many species of wild animals that are poached. They are all gratuitously killed for useless reasons. We gaped, distressed and horrified at gorilla-hand ashtrays, elephant-leg tables, the rhino-horn aphrodisiac, feathers of endangered birds, cheetah furs for hats and fashion, and much more.

The course that summer taught me many invaluable things, but learning directly what happens to wildlife when their world is filled with toxic oil and inhabited by poachers had a powerful effect on me.

Flash forward to when little Vaya woke up, blinked, and shook her feathery head like a slightly drunk duck. She was extremely lovey-ducky with Rutger, and their reunion was beautiful and happy. For the next few days he had to carry her outside and in; he had to help her eat and clean her leg and feathers. If he hadn't she would have had to sit in her own mess because she was unable to stand on her own. We worried for three days, talking daily on the phone. Then suddenly she tried to walk. It still seemed painful, but her instinct to survive was strong. I was impressed by her efforts.

Six weeks later, after six rebandagings and much thoughtful care by Rutger, I went to his house for another recheck. He led me to her little outdoor pen, where she was happily walking on the lightly wrapped leg. This was the day we were to take off the last wrap. She was used to me by now, and quacked softly when I came over. We brought her inside, and I cut the bandage off. Her feathers had grown in and you could only see a scarred ridge where I had glued the webbing together. She was healed.

She walked outside, shook herself, and went straight to the pool as if she knew her six-week no-water sentence had been lifted. She waited while Rutger opened the gate and she hopped right in. She looked like a duck in water.

Vaya was in and out of her pond with no problem. There was no sign of infection or other lasting injury. I could hear her quiet quacking as Rutger walked me to the door.

I asked him, in passing, about her name, "Why Vaya?"

"Vaya Duck!" He answered. "Don't you know Groucho Marx?"

I couldn't believe I hadn't caught that one.

"Yes," I said, "I love to quote him. 'Outside of a dog, a book is a man's best friend. Inside of a dog, it's too dark to read.'"

We both laughed and shared a quick look of relief as I got in my car and he headed back to Vaya in the pool. It was just about twilight, and I knew he wouldn't forget to bring her in.

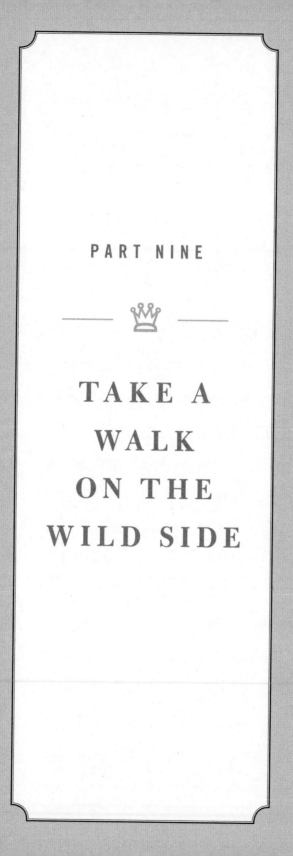

PART NINE

TAKE A
WALK
ON THE
WILD SIDE

# REHAB AND THE COYOTE

In wildness is the preservation of the world.
—HENRY DAVID THOREAU

MY FIANCÉ AND FUTURE HUSBAND, MATT, WAS THE CARETAKER of the Stillman Nature Center, where nature bloomed, chirped, splashed, and burrowed with wildlife. The eighty-acre estate in South Barrington, Illinois, owned by millionaire Alexander Stillman, was donated, and for educational purposes the grounds were allowed to go wild. Most of the nonnative plants withered. Matt worked hard cutting back buckthorn, which aggressively encroached on the developing indigenous foliage.

The center had become an oasis for animals pushed out by urbanization. The feathered and the furry, the hoppers and the trotters, the compact and the lanky, had all made their way to our little haven. In the late afternoon and evening, waterfowl held cocktail parties on the pond. Mergansers, teal, and my favored grebes chattered shrilly while we read or just sat on the deck.

When I woke in the mornings it was as if I were in a Disney film. Birds nested on every ledge, bees made honey, spiderwebs gleamed in the morning dew, and shiny turtles floated by on logs. Even Bambi could be found cavorting outside my window on the edge of the wood. And, joy! His mother was alive here in my own movie.

Nature worked her unerring magic day and night there. I fell asleep to the hooting of the great horned owl and the fine whine of bat radar zipping

## TAFFY

Five weeks before he came to me, Taffy, a dachshund, had suddenly been unable to walk or even get up without crying. He would drag his rear feet and walk on his knuckles. According to the surgeon, the spinal procedure he had done on Taffy was routine. He should be walking by now. But he wasn't. He didn't even try.

Taffy was obese. He had started off overweight, and his parents, worried and feeling sorry for him, had been feeding him every time he lifted his brown eyes to look into theirs. He ate a high-carb diet and lots of it. I could see that his weight kept him from lifting himself off the ground. But why didn't he even try? His back pain should have been improved.

My exam didn't reveal any reason for his inability to walk. He had good reflexes, and could feel me pinch his foot. But he would not use any of the muscles in his rear legs. He looked paralyzed, but why? The owners were thinking about a cart for him, or even euthanasia.

I started with a diet change, blood-moving homeopathic supplements, herbal anti-inflammatories, and electro-acupuncture treatments. I received active responses from the needles, and he even lost a little weight. After a few treatments he still wasn't walking. Puzzlingly, nothing. He didn't even seem to want to try. I wondered if he would try to move if he were hungry and were forced to find food. I figured probably not until he had consumed all of his own "food" stored in his body fat. There was very little to motivate him.

At that time, my underwater treadmill was bare-bones and didn't have bubbling jet-stream machinery. Yet I wanted to stimulate the skin and muscles on this fellow. The only place we had jets was in a four-foot-deep metal pool. I filled it and put him in it in a little orange life vest. His mom was holding his vest handle while he floated, his rear legs limp. As I reached for the on switch for the jet, she lost hold and he sank for a second. She screamed, he bobbed, and I reached to grab the vest, but not before I noticed his rear legs kicking furiously. His instinct to survive had overridden his worry about his weak legs. Without the heavy weight of his overweight body, it might have even felt good. At least it didn't hurt, and he kept on kicking.

With that information, his owners, with renewed hope, helped him to lose weight on a great diet. We only had to "float" him a few times to spur his instincts before he started to half-float, half-walk on the water treadmill voluntarily. Within four weeks he was trimmed down, and started walking on land. After four months of therapy, he was fully active, running, and even healthier than his overweight self had been prior to the surgery.

## MAX

Max is a Sealyham terrier who was brought to me because he couldn't walk after his surgery for disc disease. Max was able to drag himself around with his front legs, barely using the rear ones. The underwater treadmill would be just what he needed, but he needed to focus for it to work. He was easily distracted and didn't seem to even try to walk. Unless there was lettuce in the room. Then he was a laser. A ninja warrior. A champ. He would walk for miles in the treadmill, step lightly over Cavaletti hurdles, and weave like a dancer around any obstacle, all for a green leafy treat. Even though his parents had been told it was unlikely he would ever walk, Max relearned to walk for the love of the romaine.

So the lesson here is that every animal has its thing.

## LANCE

A young cat named Lance had fallen three stories and had a spinal contusion. There was no surgery that would help him walk again. His rear leg muscles were atrophying and he could only drag them around. Acupuncture with electrostimulation could reconnect the signals to the rear and clear away some inflammation. But how could I get a cat to exercise weakened muscles when he got around just fine with two legs?

Lance was put in the dry chamber (all nails trimmed) with a technician, without a life vest. Cats generally do not suffer clothing gladly. They can exhibit "bandage paralysis"—a condition where they just won't move if anything is wrapped, Velcro'd, or taped to them.

As the water was filling the chamber, the tech held

Lance. We saw Lance tensing. He was a lovely, gentle, and trusting cat, but he was starting to worry. As the water rose, he seemed to be thinking about escape. That's when his sink-or-swim instincts kicked in and we turned on the treadmill below him. His front legs start moving, and miraculously his rears as well. They were uncoordinated, floppy, and irregular, but striding along. He was a genius at healing. Over time, he relearned, reconnected, regained strength, and could walk again. He was clumsy at first, but eventually he could jump and run.

## TRAPPER

Trapper, a Labrador with severe hip dysplasia, had significant behavior problems, so his owners didn't want to consider acupuncture. However, physical rehabilitation in the underwater treadmill made sense to them to treat the muscle atrophy and weakness in his rear legs. It would help with his weight and improve his joint function. I also added a subcutaneous injection of Adequan, the joint supplement, to improve the quality of joint fluid, which helps with pain and motion.

Trapper's behavior problems were different from the ones I see in most dogs. He was terrified by anything and always walked around the periphery of the room. He didn't like to be petted by anyone except his owners. He avoided lying down in the center of a room and tried to snuggle up tightly against the walls.

Once he had done just four treadmill sessions, this terrified behavior completely stopped. He had conquered the underwater treadmill, and perhaps regular rooms weren't a challenge anymore. He also improved in strength and comfort in his hips. He even let me do acupuncture for his hips. We had no idea this would happen. Naturally, the owners were as happy about this beneficial side effect as the improved walking!

## TOPDOG

Topdog was an older Rottweiler who had undergone neck surgery for ruptured discs. He was stubborn and overweight and he didn't want to get up at all. Again, my exam said he should be able to walk, but his mind said no. His owners were worried. After a few weeks of carrying this big dog around and trying to entice him to walk, their backs were suffering. They were exhausted and had lost hope. If they couldn't get him to walk, Topdog would have to be put down. We started acupuncture treatments with electrostimulation. His pain and neck guarding disappeared, but he didn't walk.

I could see him reposition his legs when he was lying down, so I knew he could move them. He was understandably afraid of the pain, and he didn't want to move. And he didn't have to because dinner came on a tray. Recovery and rehab was too hard and it was not something he wanted to do. He wasn't a big eater, so he couldn't even be motivated by yummy food. But survival is a potent, age-old motivator, and his survival instinct literally kicked in.

First we tried my trick of "pretend dunking," but he was too smart for me. He pointedly looked at his dad and let himself be dunked, floating like a jellyfish. No motion. He never even looked at me. His gaze was directed at his parents. He knew they would save him.

"He can't do it!" his mom said, her eyes filled with tears. I felt for her. "Let's really give this a try. He's expecting you to be good cop to my bad. I've still got some tricks in my bag." I asked them to go to lunch and come back later. They looked at him, at me, and then they left.

His countenance changed completely when they had left the building. He was at the mercy of the doctor. Back in the treadmill, the poor guy searched for a savior. I had him lying in the bottom of the tank as I filled it with water. He started to float and the water rose to his neck. His head swiveled all around, his eyes got wide, and I could see him shift into a wild thing. He had to get out. He had to find his parents. He stood up on his own. There wasn't a dry eye in my clinic, and I think I actually whooped. We started the treadmill. He walked like a drunken sailor, but he walked. He had to.

I had videotaped the event of Topdog using his legs because I knew his parents would want to see it. Little did I know that they had pulled up in front of my picture window and watched the whole drama. By the time he was strutting like a waterlogged peacock, his owners were back inside hugging and jumping. Topdog was so busy concentrating on walking that he barely looked at them. He was finding his courage, and his legs.

invisibly through the air, scooping up thousands of mosquitos (thank you, bats!) for their dinner.

One late spring evening I saw a coyote drinking on the edge of the pond. Although alert as he walked in shallow water, he was visibly lame on his left rear leg. When he came out of the water, I saw him hobble back into the woods.

I saw him regularly for the next few weeks. Clearly unable to rest the limb, he would be out at twilight, hunting and scavenging for food. The pond was a great source of edibles as he walked in the shallows, weaving through the water weeds. All the exercise kept him thin, but not overly thin, and the leg seemed to be improving quickly. I would see him lifting the leg over roots and maneuvering through the shifting mud at the water's edge. He needed the fourth leg for balance and used it increasingly. He had to keep going. The leg soon looked stronger. It seemed as if he had done his own rehab regimen, water therapy, resistance, and balance work.

A few weeks later in early winter, with a light snow covering the frozen pond, I saw him again. Just after dawn, I looked out our kitchen window and there he was, still showing signs of a slight limp, but getting along well. He was moving along the edge of the pond, as usual. As his paws slid onto the frozen white surface, I realized he was a she. The coyote mother was bringing her pups to play on the pond. Three coyote youngsters cautiously stepped onto the ice, grabbing at each other and roughhousing in circles around their mom. The pups' survival depended on her ability to navigate in her world. She stood watchful, on all four legs.

I believe her recovery would have been slowed if she been brought her food and walked on smooth paths. I suspect there is something in the struggle that also heals us. Most likely after her injury, she had rested. But to survive in the wild, she had to get moving again.

I tailor a milder version of this "struggle to survive" idea in rehab with my patients. I use instinctual reactions as an impetus to make them want to use their limbs again. It can be as simple as sink or swim. At least that's what they think.

Your pet may not live on the edge of the wilderness; he may only need to get from the couch to the dinner bowl. But there is an inner wild furry child that can be tapped into for healing. Healing can be aided by rest and recuperation, but it can also require action. And sometimes, just as in nature, that action can appear ruthless.

# CHAMELEONS
# AND COLD LASER

♛

C HAMELEONS IN CAPTIVITY ARE HIGH-MAINTENANCE. INTENSE
husbandry is needed to properly monitor their food, humidity, temperature, and overall health. They are easily stressed by captivity. This is
because their adaptation in the wild is tailored to a specific treetop environment.

Their leaflike bodies are compressed vertically to appear two-dimen-
sional, and they have independently moving eyes perched on little turrets
for a 300-degree field of vision. They hunt with a sticky tongue that grabs
prey like a projectile on elastic. It moves faster than the eye can see and
extends longer than 50 percent of their body length. Their prehensile tail
and mitten-like grabbing toes keep them safe on the branches, or in human
hands.

The chameleon I was holding, named Leif, was not showing obvious signs of stress. Other than the chronic lumpy abscesses left from old
injuries along the jaw and the ulcerated toe, this green, black, and white
chameleon looked well fed and relaxed. But his infection persisted.

Antibiotics, surgical flushing, and topical treatments had been tried
and had not worked. The cold or "low-level laser light therapy" (LLLLT)
was a treatment that had not been tried. I set the machine on 10 joules, cov-

ered the chameleon's telescoping, individually moving eyes and pressed the button. The red light covered the jaw and I waited the ten seconds for it to finish. Then we repeated this on the toe lesion. After a brief training session, I left the laser with the veterinarian. For a few weeks, she treated his chronic infection until it healed. The laser was what made the difference. I suspect he needed some extra help to recover from an infection he most likely wouldn't have encountered in his natural environment.

The FDA has approved laser to improve circulation and decrease inflammation locally. It also helps reduce scarring at incision sites, and improves the body's ability to heal from even resistant infections. I use it so frequently, I have two of them. Light therapy is not new. We all can feel the cheering effect of the sun's rays after days of clouds, and surgeons use laser to actually cut through tissue. The LLLLT that I use in rehab does not cut, or feel warm, but it does have power. The joules of light that penetrate through the skin stimulate the mitochondria in the cells to produce the proteins that will call in more circulation. This can increase lymphatic drainage and decrease inflammation and scarring where you place the beam. It is clinically effective and the research on it is persuasive. It is used both in human and veterinary medicine.

In addition to the chameleon, I have used laser on elephant foot lesions, meerkat tail wounds, nonhealing bone fractures in a Rodriguez fruit bat, a lame fennec fox, arthritic camels, zebras with swollen joints, and dogs and cats for a gazillion issues. I have even used it on myself to treat a worrisome cat bite that, as a result, healed better than any cat bite I've ever seen. I was a guinea pig for laser before I used it on a wounded guinea pig.

Cold laser and *all* of the healing equipment in my practice assist the body to heal itself. This includes the underwater treadmills, therapeutic ultrasound (deep heat), electrostimulation, acupuncture needles, and even our five-digit hands—massage, chiropractic, and acupressure. I wouldn't want to practice medicine any other way.

# TARANTULA GLUE

WHEN CLIENTS ARE CONCERNED ABOUT WHETHER THEIR SERIously ill pets will ever regain their health, I want to tell them the tarantula story. But I usually don't. Everyone connects to nature in different ways. I have to remember that not everyone likes spiders. I am one of those strange people who see Charlotte in every web.

Most people drop tarantulas—even if they are prepared to have the rose-colored toes tapping on their hand. They are excited by the prospect of holding the embodiment of dangerous and creepy, but then the creepy part strikes a reflexive cord in their psyche. The next thing that happens is the spider hits the ground. Small spiders can handle this, but not the tarantula, whose pendulous abdomen tears and breaks open upon impact.

A tarantula's skin is papery and inelastic. When it rips, it needs to be put back together. Sewing papery spider skin together is an impossible task. The edges don't close well and the mended skin does not withstand movement. Tissue glue and a steady hand are required. The first time I undertook this minuscule surgery, it was in the dark ages before tissue glue, so I used plain old superglue. But I have to admit, it worked well, and the spider owners were delighted with the results. Their pet spider—yes, named Charlotte—went on to have babies of her own.

# REJUVENATING
# YOUR OLDER PET

O UR DOGS AND CATS ARE PRECIOUS TO US. WE WANT THEM TO live forever, but we don't like to see them show any signs of age. People often explain problems with arthritis or other illness by saying, "She's just getting old." But that is not a diagnosis; it is just an assessment of how long the pet has been here.

When my dog Tundra was eleven, I felt she was "just getting old." I had originally rescued her as a puppy from a shelter, so I wasn't certain of her breed. She looked mostly like a German shepherd and I knew that breed's life span averages around twelve years. I wanted her to live longer than that and so I searched for something to do about it.

I have since refined the strategies I used for Tundra and applied them to all of my aging patients. These include a high-protein diet with proper moisture content, supplements as they apply to each case, acupuncture where needed, exercise, and simple ideas for home care. I was thrilled that Tundra lived another six years—playing on the beach and living a wonderful life. Supporting animals as they age is something I look forward to, because my clients and I consider aging an asset rather than a disease.

Here are some tips to assist you in your goal of a long and active life for your pets.

# AMBULATION: THESE FEET
# ARE MADE FOR WALKING

**Just because animals are older doesn't mean they shouldn't exercise.** Becoming sedentary with arthritis is a dangerous downward spiral. Arthritic animals that don't exercise will deteriorate rapidly. Disuse atrophy of leg and back muscles destabilizes joints and the spine, causing unbalanced, hesitant, or stilted gait patterns and increasing discomfort. Even gentle weight-bearing exercise strengthens muscles and circulates nutritive synovial fluid over the surfaces of the joint. Confidence in the limbs comes from using the limbs, pure and simple.

And older animals require enough good-quality meat protein in their diet to maintain the muscles they are working to improve. Underwater treadmill treatments can make a big difference in muscle mass and coordination.

**Take a walk on the wild side.** Go places on your walks where your pet can experience, smell, or see something new. Keep his mind lively and his body will follow suit. Don't neglect the daily outing. Take it slow if you have to, but take it—and make it interesting.

**Try moving off the beaten track.** Dogs and cats benefit from challenging terrain. If you only walk on flat surfaces, it may soon be the only surface your pet can navigate. Make games include varying surfaces for indoor pets, or when outdoors maneuver your pet over tree roots, gravel, and irregular ground. Step up and down curbs, go around posts, walk in short figure-eight patterns, and go up or down inclines or driveways.

**Massage the feet of older dogs and cats.** Once a day, gently squeeze the feet and slowly pull down the toes of your geriatric dog or cat. Take care to avoid getting bitten by foot-sensitive animals. This physical therapy trick can improve the neurological connection from the brain to the foot, improving leg mobility and foot placement, called *conscious proprioception*.

**Place toys or treats in places where it requires some effort to retrieve them, and don't forget to play with your aging cats.** People play games with dogs in many life stages, but mature cats are often left to sleep all day. Don't just put treats under their noses; make them do a little work for them. Place treats up a flight of stairs or on top of some climbing toy. Your cat will have to exercise to get to it. Those wire-bouncing fobs and little mouse toys are not just for kittens. And your cat may shed some unwanted weight as well.

**Place carpets, runners, nonskid tape or paint, rubber mats, or even yoga mats in slippery spots.** Pads of older canine and feline feet can slip more on smooth surfaces. Adding area rugs and other nonskid floor coverings can help them get up and move more confidently.

Adhesive foot pads, waxes, or nonslip booties, if they aren't too bulky, can also help.

And make sure to provide good lighting to help failing eyesight.

## SPINE AND TAIL

**Massage small circles with fingertips on either side of the spine to improve overall circulation, lymphatic drainage, and spinal health.** Little massage circles up and down the sides of the spine may invigorate circulation. Gentle traction in a smooth massaging stroke down the tail can help to stretch the spine and stimulate inter-vertebral circulation. A supple spine can mean a more active dog or cat.

316 🐾 Dr. Barbara Royal

# BREATH

## Laryngeal Paralysis

Older dogs, such as Labradors, German shepherds, golden retrievers, and many other large breeds can make more breathing noise as they age. It may be normal panting or old-dog breathing, or it can be a sign of laryngeal paralysis. This means that the larynx, which normally will open and close all day long, has more and more trouble doing its job. It doesn't close completely to cover the trachea during swallowing and can't open wide for a big breath.

These animals will often wake up and have to cough out saliva that has pooled around the slightly open trachea and dripped down toward the bronchi (the "old man cough"). They will also have trouble thermoregulating (keeping cool), as open-mouth panting with the larynx wide open is the main mechanism dogs have to cool down. This can be a life-threatening problem for dogs in summertime. Make sure to monitor their temperature, and keep plenty of water on hand in hot weather.

This condition can progress slowly, so it may be hard to notice that the respiratory noise has increased. It may be accompanied by low thyroid function, so when I hear a loud-breathing dog, I'll usually run a test to check the thyroid gland.

Treating the thyroid deficiency won't reverse the breathing problem, but it may help slow the progression of the paralysis, and it will certainly make the animal healthier in general. I use acupuncture and proper nutrition to help with laryngeal paralysis. Some people have had good results using a tricyclic antidepressant, doxepin, to help treat the laryngeal paralysis and accompanying spasms. It is not always successful, but worth a try if your vet recommends it.

The surgical fix works, but it is typically only used when the condition is severe. It is a difficult surgery for an older animal, and recovery can be stressful. The method is essentially the tying back of a side of the larynx to leave it open wide all the time. The dog will be less likely to overheat this way, and will breathe easier, since their breath is not restricted by a small opening. This surgery does increase the risk of aspiration pneumonia.

## ON THE NOSE

### Dryness and Crustiness

Crusty noses can be a sign of a significant autoimmune condition or nutritional deficiency, but sometimes older dogs just have dry noses. After ruling out any underlying medical cause, there are a few options to try.

My clients and I feel that Vaseline on the nose is the most reliably effective topical treatment for an elderly dog's dry nose. I have also had some success with shea butter or coconut oil topically. Vitamin E or fish oils make the nose sticky, not smooth. Bag balm can be too irritating, and its pungent odor can irritate a dog's keen sense of smell. Coconut oil taken orally (about 1 tsp daily per 30–50 pound dog) can ameliorate dry noses, dandruff, and dull hair coats and can improve general gastrointestinal health.

### Nosing the Bowl—Avoid Plastics

Change plastic bowls to ceramic, metal, or glass bowls, and clean them regularly. Plastic bowls may be an irritant to sensitive nasal skin. Inflamed skin on the mouth, chin, or nose of a dog or cat can improve once plastic food or water bowls are removed.

### Under Your Nose—You've Got to Smell It to Want It

If your furry friend doesn't seem hungry and is looking thin, it may be that they simply can't smell the food. Some older animals lose weight because of eating less. A pet that seems to lose interest in food as they age may be showing signs of some significant illness such as cancer, systemic diseases, or dental problems, or the answer may be under their nose. If you've been to the vet and there's no apparent medical reason, keep in mind that smell is an important appetite stimulant. Aging animals can have trouble with their sense of smell due to many causes, including previous respiratory disease, or side effects of medication—some anti-inflammatory meds can decrease sense of smell. This is why I don't use them in working pets that are search and rescue or drug sniffers or FBI explosives detectives. Animals with a poor sense of smell may be wondering what scentless clumps are in their food dish, but dinner is not on their mind—or olfactory lobe. To enhance smell, try warming up the food, or mix in some hot water, chicken broth, some tripe, or a slurry of meat baby food that doesn't contain onion or onion powder. They'll more likely come running for supper if you supersize the aroma.

## Breakfast May Be Optional

I've noticed that many aging dogs skip their morning meal. Even with enticement and fabulous-smelling food, they just say no. Yet by supper, they quickly clean the bowl. As long as everything else seems normal—and there's no vomiting or other signs—many older dogs can do just fine skipping breakfast, if that's what they choose.

## DO YOU HEAR WHAT I HEAR?

**Use clapping or high-pitched tones to get the attention of your pet.** Dogs and cats, like humans, lose their hearing, especially when you are asking them to do something they don't want to do. Hand-clapping or high-pitched tones are of a frequency that seems to be the last to go as hearing fades. This can be used to your and the animal's advantage. An elder dog will be less startled from a deep sleep if you clap or use a high-pitched tone before you touch them. You may also want to try acupuncture for hearing loss, as this can improve circulation to the ear mechanism.

Gently massage circles at the base of the ear, and rotate the earflap (pinna) a few times a week like a windmill as another way to help improve circulation.

## THE EYES HAVE IT

**Put in an extra light fixture over the stairs, and perhaps carpet them too.** This may sound like a home-decorating solution, not a veterinary one, but it can be crucial for an aging pet with a vision problem. When a pet seems hesitant to go up or down stairs, the first thought is arthritis. However, arthritis isn't always the problem. Your pet's vision may be worsening. *Lenticular sclerosis* is the name for a typical change in the lens of a dog or cat's eye that manifests itself in that bluish haze you see as they age. It creates a mild vision issue, like looking through shower glass, giving a slightly hazy vision that obscures depth perception. In twilight conditions, difficulty seeing is even more pronounced. Better lighting on stairs, and making surface edges easy to see, will help your aging pet gauge their steps better and improve their ability to walk on uneven surfaces.

**If your pet has vision issues, avoid rearranging water and food bowls, furniture, or litter boxes.** Confusion causes stress and can also cause accidents. If your pet is losing his vision, make sure he knows where things are if you have to rearrange.

Too much light or bright sunshine on light surfaces such as snow or white sand is irritating for an older animal, particularly cats and smaller dogs. Elderly animals with *iris atrophy* have trouble fully closing the opening of their iris to protect from bright light. Because of this light sensitivity, they may seem unable to see well when the light is intense. Give them some time to adjust, or get to the shade where possible.

🐾 **Q.** *Why is my dog squinting?*

**A.** It could be that your dog is trying to psych you out with his Clint Eastwood impression. Either that or his eyes are bothering him. Ocular problems can be as mild as an irritant in a tear duct or as serious as glaucoma or a corneal ulcer. Eyes that are uncomfortable enough to cause squinting in a dog or a cat can be an emergency.

## WHAT GOES IN MUST COME OUT

### Incontinence—Fecal:
### Give Your Dog the "Double Walk"

After giving your dog a walk, he comes in the house and poops on the carpet. Sound familiar? Pet incontinence is the bane of many pet owners' existence. There are many causes and, fortunately, many solutions. Here are some typical problems and solutions (once you've ruled out any underlying medical problems, as usual).

"The Double Walk" can get the dog to focus on the job at hand. After the first walk, come in for a few seconds. Then head back out the door. The second walk will be less interesting. The walking will have stimulated the colon, and the dog may have more success.

### The Four F's of Fecal Incontinence

You may immediately think of an F-word that I will not mention here, when fecal incontinence is discovered. It is often the first word uttered, but here are four other F-words that can help you recover your sanity and your dog's dignity.

1. Food
2. Frequency
3. Focus
4. Floor

**Food.** You will see a decrease in the amount of feces if you can decrease the amount of filler (prevalent in kibble) in your dog's food. This is where canned and raw food excel.

**Frequency.** Animals that are fed more than once a day will have more trouble with incontinence. When they digest their food all at once, an animal will more likely know in advance that she's ready to defecate. This is because the amount in the colon can send a good signal.

**Focus.** There are constant distractions from the outside world when an animal goes on a walk. The signal to defecate may not be strong enough to override all the fun stimuli to the brain during a walk.

**Floor.** This technique is based on the principle that you can cause a dog to defecate by taking their temperature rectally. Before your last bedtime walk, use a thermometer, or a gloved finger or a Q-tip to stimulate the pelvic floor. Sometimes it just takes a mild tapping around the anal opening to make a dog poop. Be ready to go right outside. If you're not squeamish, this is an effective method to prepare you and your dog for a good night's sleep.

### Feed once a day and feed canned, home-cooked, or pre-prepared raw food, if possible.

"She doesn't know when she is defecating—although it can be several times a day—and often wakes lying in her poop."

I hear this scenario from owners with pets that are very arthritic and losing sensation in their rear end. After an exam ruling out anything more serious, this common problem can be resolved with a change in diet. Canned, home-cooked, and pre-prepared raw foods have less filler and fewer carbs. You'll find smaller, firmer, less frequent poop. If the main meal only comes down the throat once a day, that is how it may come out in poop—once a day. You can work out a predictable schedule for your lives.

Psyllium fiber helps keep stool even more regular and firm (about 1 tsp mixed in wet food for a 50-pound dog, or ⅛ tsp per wet meal for a 10-pound cat).

## Incontinence—Urinary

There are many medical reasons for urinary incontinence, but once they are ruled out, feeding a diet with proper moisture content can help avoid overdrinking. There's a huge advantage to evening out water intake with moist foods. Unlike dry food, canned, home-cooked, or raw foods don't require a gallon chaser. Bladders don't bulge, and urinary accidents decrease.

## KEEPING THEIR FIGURE— WATCH THEIR WEIGHT!

FRIENDS DON'T LET PETS get overweight!

To recap: In addition to watching your pet's weight, actively make him slim. If your dog is overweight, believe me, it's the food. Decrease the amount you feed. Even cut the amount in *half*.

An overweight pet faces many health, mobility, energy, and mental issues. Remember, for every pound your dog loses, they feel four pounds less torque on each leg. This is a good incentive to keep your older pet thin. Every pound truly counts!

## HARNESS THE BODY'S ENERGY

USE A COMFORTABLE HARNESS to help your dog on walks and stairs and to help your own back. I recommend harnesses that support along the chest and have two straps that go around the chest in front and back of the leg. These straps are best when they attach to two separate points on the strap that goes down the back. If they meet at the same place on the back and make a triangle around the front leg, they can cinch around the base of the leg when pulled (not good!) and press on a nerve plexus in the armpit. You'll find that moving them more like a suitcase helps save your back. This is more sustainable than trying to lift them with your arms and carrying them up and down stairs multiple times a day.

We can't make our pets live forever, or extend their life span to match ours. However, there are many simple, commonsense actions we can take to mitigate the effects of old age. I still miss Tundra, but I am comforted to know that she enjoyed her golden years.

---

### MYTHCONCEPTION

*You can't teach an old dog new tricks.*
**Not true.**
*Dogs, like most species, can learn throughout their
lives, at any age.*

PART TEN

WILD
CIRCLE

# EUTHANASIA,
# THE HEART OF THE MATTER

♛

MANY OF US HAVE AN ANIMAL IN OUR LIVES THAT IS "THE one"—unlike any other animal we have ever had. Tundra was mine. She was smart, sleek, fast, athletic, and vigilant. She spent much of her time either checking the perimeter or circling me. I never knew her genetics, but she looked like a German shepherd bred with a Belgian Malinois and maybe some coyote in the mix as well. She was about sixty-five pounds, with ears long enough for a donkey. Her intense dark brown eyes were set in a black mask that turned gray over the years. Always thin, she was built for efficiency. She had impeccable bone structure, although her long back developed arthritis as she aged. She loved to play Frisbee and do the Sunday crossword puzzle with me.

Tundra had gone to vet school with me, and I attribute that to why she lived such a long life. She spent hundreds of hours under my desk in class and in the vet school library, but she was equally at home on the foot of my bed or at the foot of a mountain. Always ready for adventure, she was my girl.

Wherever I went, people expected her to be there. She knew how to run along my bicycle when I biked to school; she'd frantically swim out to me if I went for a dip, pulling at my arm and pointing to the safety of the shore. Her nudging and circling during thunderstorms meant "would everyone please just follow me into the basement."

She aged elegantly—from twelve, to thirteen, to fourteen. It seemed incomprehensible and unfair that her life span, like all canines', would be shorter than a human's. I knew that when the time came, I wouldn't be able to face the decision myself. I enlisted the backup of two veterinarian friends. They knew I would need help and agreed to be there for us both. I felt as prepared as I could be.

Another year went by, and another, and then, at seventeen, her fate became obvious. Although the week before she had been happy to totter along the wet sand by the lake, I could see that things were changing drastically. She had all the clinical signs of an endgame. An inability to get up on her own and once up, suddenly falling over, standing and staring into corners of the room, walking with her spine hunched as if in pain, a sudden disinterest in her surroundings, stomach partially bloating several times in one day, and lack of control over bowels or bladder. The signs were there. But even being aware of this, and being well versed in veterinary geriatric medicine, making that final decision was still torture. It felt as if I were deciding to remove my own soul.

I desperately wanted someone to tell me what to do. But I knew what to do.

I made the calls. It was a holiday and my friends were out of town. No one could come. I felt surprisingly calm and unfazed. Tundra and I had been through so much together. In the end, it was only fitting that I would have to do this for her myself.

I thought about the first time I saw her. I was living with my fiancé, Matt, at the eighty-acre nature center. We often were called upon to pick up wildlife and release them into the relative wild of the sanctuary. This day it was a wayward screech owl at the Anti-Cruelty Society in downtown Chicago, hoping for a ride back to nature.

I was pacing around waiting for the owl's paperwork when I caught her eye from the back of her cage. She was watching me. I went up to the cage and saw an angular, fluffy, shy, and adorable puppy. She walked up to the bars and licked my nose.

The attendant said, "Wow, she didn't growl at you!" I thought she was kidding, but she told me this unfriendly little puppy was slated to be euthanized. Her gentle brothers had long been adopted. All four of them had been in a box found in the middle of a street on the city's South Side.

I stepped away, forcing myself to think about what I was there for—the owl. I had to get back before traffic hit. Was the owl ready? They were just copying the paperwork. It would only be a few more minutes. I thought of waiting in the outer lobby area. But I could still feel the puppy's bright eyes on me and we exchanged another intense glance.

I asked if I could hold her. How mean could that little pup be? The attendant said she didn't think it was a good idea; but when I insisted, she carefully opened the cage door and stepped back. I could barely make out the puppy's silhouette crouched in the back of her cage. She did look like a wild thing until she leaped off her blanket and into my arms, where she stayed for the next two hours of more paperwork—this time for a puppy adoption. She sat happily in my lap as we drove the owl, and now Tundra.

I had planned to get a dog later, once I was settled into a routine at vet school and had a better idea of what I was up against. That would have been the sensible way to go. But Matt was learning that I wasn't afraid to let my heart lead the way.

After that moment of instant recognition through the cage bars, my life was never without my little brown friend. In a misguided attempt to be kind to her, I tried a gentle house-training method of positive reinforcement (no crating), which basically meant she had the run of the house. I would never recommend this method to anyone. It doesn't work. After I gave in and finally crate-trained the little puppy (as suggested by everyone I knew, including Matt), she was practically perfect in every way.

She saved my life literally and figuratively, in so many ways. One time, she became a snarling wolf when a street gang surrounded my truck and threatened me. Her bony body helped me through vet school by teaching me and my classmates every landmark in anatomy. She brought joy in my saddest moments with her flying leaps returning all tossed Frisbees, high or low. During the day, her motions were fluid and continuous like a shark, but at night she was like a sleepy kitten, quietly curled up in the crook of my knee, spooning with me all night.

It was only right that I would be the one to help her through that final moment, as painful as it was going to be. After all, it's a part of what I do.

My husband, Matt, and my children, sisters, and parents were there. She was on her bed surrounded by a circle of love. I was the conduit for her now. I had to help her leave us. The unbearable tension between being her mom and being her vet felt like a brick on my heart. But I thought I could manage by myself.

When the time came to inject, I couldn't breathe. I couldn't do it. I froze. Kneeling beside her with a shaking syringe, I could barely see or hear because of my emotions and tears. That's when Tundra came through for me again. She never was one for histrionics—a definite "get-it-done" kind of gal. She leaned forward with her long nose and nudged me, as she used to do when she wanted to go outside. Then, for added punctuation, she lifted her paw—in an unusual move—and smacked my hand. Our life together passed between us in a final glance, and then she pointedly closed her eyes.

I took my first breath in what seemed like hours, and became my other self—the veterinarian. After administering the injection, I put my stethoscope to her chest, blocking out everything but my connection to her beating heart.

Still infused with life, her heartbeat suddenly changed direction, carrying life away. At first the rhythm picked up speed and became louder, getting closer like a fast train. But as I listened, it grew more faint, moving off into the distance. My own Tundra, the single passenger on this train, who had followed me everywhere, was leading the way. But I wouldn't call her back this time. She was free to go on ahead.

With my eyes closed, I held the stethoscope steady. It was the moment of departure. I heard the slowing beats fade like far-off gasps of steam as her train rounded the last curve, passing out of sight and finally out of sound.

# FINDING THE RIGHT TIME
## TO SAY GOODBYE

*Have the courage of your convictions—*
*only you can decide when it is "time" for your pet.*

ELPING AN OWNER DECIDE IF IT IS FINALLY "TIME" FOR THEIR
beloved pet is a blessing and a curse of my profession. Veterinarians
are able to alleviate unremitting suffering, but choosing the right time to
say goodbye can be agonizing. While there is no template that fits every
situation, the main goal should be to treat each unique pet and owner with
the compassion and dignity they deserve.

Even though death is a normal part of every life, it is never easy to face
the death of someone you love. *Euthanasia* comes from the Greek, *eu*
meaning good and *thanatos* meaning death. Fortunately, we are able to
provide "a good death" for our pets. Extreme and unnecessary suffering is
heartbreaking—especially when the suffering continues without hope of
recovery. But determining if an animal is at that point can be unbearably
difficult.

Euthanasia, the last component of wild health, while unalterably sad,
must be looked at as another duty we have as stewards of our animals.
This is an aspect in which we may have some control. In nature, their
final days would be different than it is for them in our homes. Often we
keep them alive long past what would have happened in a more natural

environment—just by feeding, cleaning, and keeping them safe. While this is an advantage for pets in our care, it can become a liability when a pet is terminally ill. For that reason, we are responsible for their humane treatment at this last stage.

## BORIS

One of the saddest things I've done was to euthanize Boris, a sweet little pug who had squamous cell carcinoma on his jaw. I'd only had him as a patient for a couple of weeks. His mom and I had a serious conversation.

She was unsure of what to do, but she was unbearably sad and overwhelmed by her pet's condition. We talked about that "sad and overwhelmed" feeling. How it is a sign that means your dog is incredibly sad and overwhelmed, too. That feeling is an expression of the intense bond between a loved dog and a loving owner.

We began with the question "How bad does he have to get before we can let him go?" and continued from there. We talked about what he must feel like, how his cheerful nature kept him from showing any pain, how the tumor had degraded his jaw in a horrific way, and how he was becoming anemic from constant bleeding.

Her husband was with us that last day and we all shared a box of Kleenex, including some for adorable Boris because of his bloody drool while he sat in her lap as we talked and cried. There was such a loving bond in this sweet little family.

In my integrative practice, I treat many geriatric pets. With this approach, many are able to enjoy a good quality of life without invasive surgeries or side effects from harsh medications. My clients tell me that our alternative approach made their course of action more apparent, and when the time came, they felt less guilt. My clients feel empowered by improving not just the quantity but the quality of their pet's life. The final decision for their pet is therefore made with a clearer conscience.

> *How do the geese know when to fly to the sun? Who tells them the seasons? How do we humans know when it is time to move on? As with the migrant birds, so surely with us. There is a voice within, if only we would listen to it, that tells us so certainly when to go forth into the unknown.*
> —ELISABETH KÜBLER-ROSS

When dealing with chronically ill, significantly geriatric, or disabled pets, owners can quickly become overwhelmed. They can become mired in information about diagnostic tests, prognosis, possible medications, diet changes, and alternative medical options. They try to make sense of it all. Contriving ways to give medications, new foods, or to assist in procedures changes the owner-pet relationship, and sadly, it's not a change for the better. Financial and time constraints as well as the diminishment of their pet's physical abilities can cause owners to lose sight of their own needs. As they struggle to keep their pet alive, they say, often in the same breath, the same three things.

"I am so overwhelmed by what has to be done for my pet every day."

"I will not make the decision to end my pet's life just because my life is falling apart."

"I wish my pet would just go quietly in his sleep."

These seemingly conflicting statements are understandable because in these situations emotions are complicated. The amount of care required to keep a chronically ill animal is intense. Stress has an accumulative effect on an owner's ability to care for an animal that is near the end. The empathy between pet and owner is often so strong that feelings overlap. When an owner is feeling overwhelmed, it could be because the pet is feeling the same way. If it's too hard for you, it may be too hard for your pet as well.

> *It is crucial for owners to be aware that if they are feeling overwhelmed, chances are their pet is feeling the same way.*

People will judge you and offer their opinions. As a vet, I've certainly heard some preposterous comments from well-meaning people. Stand firm about your decision, have the courage of your conviction, and maintain your own integrity. Only you know when it is time. Everyone thinks their way is the best, but in life-and-death dilemmas, your decision is imminently personal.

The amount of care required to keep an animal going can frustrate an owner. It is common for them to feel resentment, followed by guilt. Guilt builds a small prison in our heart. We feel trapped and can't see a way out. Normal emotions are subverted. We know it is not our pet's fault—soiling things, requiring lots of time, needing constant physical help, keeping us up at night—but we still feel annoyed. Especially if there is no end in sight. Pretending you aren't feeling these things makes matters even worse. It is okay to let these feelings have a part in our decision-making process.

### A SAD, BUT GOOD, RULE OF THUMB

> *If you feel you are performing practically all the duties a life support system might do in an ICU in order to keep a pet alive, and there is little hope for recovery, it's probably time to let your pet go.*

If you really don't know what to do, I advise owners to notice if the pet has more bad days than good ones. It helps to keep a simple daily diary—noting just one word on each day—"Good" or "Bad" as an overall grade for the day. Although "good" versus "bad" is a subjective matter, there are a few factors to monitor.

It is extremely important to be aware of *any medications* that could also cause any of these signs. For example, I often see geriatric animals that are having increasing trouble walking and have apparently lost their will to live. However, these signs can also be side effects of a medication called tramadol, an opiate derivative that changes the way the brain perceives pain. In geriatric pets, careful dosing is essential. Overmedicating can make them more uncoordinated, cause depression, and dull their motivating energy. When I stop or significantly decrease the tramadol, they regain their spark and mobility. The next step is pain management, using more natural methods like acupuncture or herbs or changing meds. Tramadol can work as a sleep aid in some animals.

## CONSIDER THESE QUESTIONS

### Is your pet in chronic pain?

Surprisingly, pets in chronic pain will not show it by crying or vocalizing. That would not be effective from an evolutionary standpoint. An animal would not want to announce pain to a predator. Short-term acute pain is a different matter—an inadvertent step on a paw causes your pet to yelp to get you off his foot.

> *Chronic pain can best be determined by assessing subtle signs and behavioral changes.*

Signs of chronic pain: panting, pacing, stilted gait, short strides, head held low, lamenesses, falling over, inability to get up or lie down, inability to move about freely, decreased appetite, increased thirst (sometimes due to panting), behavior changes (usually either more ornery or hiding more, sometimes suddenly overly needy), touch sensitivity, increased heart rate, decreased interest in their surroundings caused by focusing inward on the pain.

## Does your pet still enjoy the basic routines of the day?

Is she excited by a walk? Interested in your actions? Responding to stimuli? Or do you notice her pulling away from family activities? Hiding in unusual places, avoiding play and contact?

## Do you recognize your pet's personality?

Does he seem chronically depressed? Is there some evidence of cognitive dysfunction—standing, staring into space, walking into the hinge side of the door instead of the opening side? Does your pet stand with his head pressed against a wall or corner? Again, remember to consider the possibility of this being caused by overmedication—especially if your pet is taking pain meds.

## Does your pet still eat regularly?

Refusal to eat can be a definitive indication that a pet has given up. But there's a difference between skipping a meal here and there—particularly the morning meal, which I find many older pets like to skip—and losing interest in all food. Make sure you've offered plenty of different options. Is it just food, or treats as well? Sense of smell or appetite can be significantly decreased either because of age or because of certain medications. Try warming food by adding warm water or low sodium chicken broth. You can also mix in some meat baby food, a small amount of canned cat food, or some tripe to enhance the odor of the food. A pet that feels bad enough to stop eating even fun foods may be seriously ill. It may not mean it's "time" but if you know the end is near, it can be a sign. (See the diet chapters for tips on getting your pet to eat when he doesn't have an appetite.)

## Has your pet lost the control of his bladder and bowels?

Normally fastidious animals that are unable to control urination and defecation can become stressed by this problem. This can also be a health hazard, causing urine scald or infections from repeated soiling. If the animal has lost control of these functions, it makes life extremely challenging for everyone. But check with your vet. Urinary tract infections are more common as animals age and can be treated. Food or treat increases or changes, excessive water drinking, medications, or GI parasites can also cause incontinence.

## Do you think your pet is giving you "the Look"?

Many clients tell me that they knew it was time because of "the Look" their pet was giving them. Their eyes show that they have "left the building." They may be looking inward and have lost their will to live. This can be a good clue that it's time. However, again, look carefully into any medication that could be causing them to seem dazed out. If this is the case, reassess the need for that medication. Some pain medications will do this. Try decreasing pain meds like tramadol to half doses, only at night, or even stopping them, and see if the pain is manageable.

## Are you changing your assessment about whether "it's time" from moment to moment?

In a decision this grave, consider asking for a second veterinary opinion. While your regular veterinarian, who has known your pet for years, may be an excellent judge, a fresh set of eyes may clarify things. It's even acceptable to ask your vet who they would recommend. Most vets don't mind a consult when there's a difficult decision to be made.

If you notice many of the above signs, you might want to discuss the options with your vet.

With an integrative approach to chronic care, many injured, sickly, or geriatric pets can become rejuvenated. Because animals have bounced back, even several times, often with just a minor tweaking of supplements or treatments, owners may cling to the hope that this time, they will bounce back again. It can be hard to determine the difference between a setback and the end. In some cases, animals can regain a good quality of life before their last days. Many owners have told me that they felt greatly relieved about the decision to euthanize—when the time did finally come—because their pet had so enjoyed life with them before becoming incapacitated.

Even one good day before death can be a cause for joy.

## SUE THE ELEPHANT'S
## LAST DAY ON EARTH

SUE, AN AGING INDIAN elephant, had been kept for years in deplorable conditions by a private owner who rented her out to circuses. The U.S. Department of Agriculture finally enforced elephant management laws and cited violations for this owner. An agreement was reached that she would go to a shelter in Tennessee.

Sue had been down for several days after collapsing when her regular vet had tried to sedate her for a blood sample. A "down elephant" is considered an emergency situation, as they usually can't survive more than a couple of days. The weight of their own organs crushes other organs. The rescue team asked me to come and provide acupuncture for Sue, in a last-ditch effort to get her back on her feet. It was close to Christmas, snowing and cold, but I drove the two hours there to see what I could do.

When I came to the property, Sue was chained up in the foul-smelling barn. The barn staff, their vet, as well as the staff and vet from the sanctuary that called me had all been working together, night and day, to keep her going. There were an assortment of tractor tires for support, a forklift, huge canvas straps, pulleys and chains and ropes, all over the barn floor. Medical equipment, boxes of topical and injectable medications, IV bags, and medical instruments were strewn everywhere like a makeshift hospital.

A homemade canvas sling/vest contraption was rigged under her belly and she was suspended with the pulleys and the forklift to shift her weight regularly every few hours. Pressure sores on her hips, shoulders, and face were tended, and she was being given fluids and hand-feedings all day. It was an exhausting, dangerous task. At any time she could toss a person into a wall if she felt like it. We worked in a radius around her, just out of reach of her trunk, whenever possible.

Because of all the intense effort, with each day Sue had shown some signs of recovery. Every morning brought new hope—her blood work improved, she behaved in a more animated way, took more food, and ate more readily. We offered her anything she would eat. There were piles of options in boxes all around—from peanut butter and jelly sandwiches to the typical fruits and vegetables, to hay. Just the fact that she was still eating was encouraging. Everyone was hoping for an unlikely holiday miracle.

I treated her with acupuncture and she also let me treat her ulcerated eye. At one point she grabbed my arm with her trunk. I wondered if she was going to splatter me against the wall. But she just calmly looked at me, apparently decided I was there to help her, and gently let go.

I wished we could do more for her and I mentioned how ideal it would be if we could build a pool to float her in. Sue hadn't been in water for decades and it would be a great present for her. The rescue team quickly mobilized and procured a huge Dumpster that could be made into Sue's pool—if only she would survive until it was made.

Sue did live long enough to be lifted by crane into the makeshift watering hole. Warm water was poured over her. As soon as she was partially submerged, she started to splash about happily and began to play, filling her trunk with water and spraying and trumpeting playfully. No one could believe the transformation.

And then—after an hour of sheer joy—she died.

Years of mistreatment and poor nutrition had debilitated her to the point of no return. It was a small but potent consolation to us that we had brought her some relief before she left this planet. After such suffering, she still had the urge to play, and in the end, the water allowed her a final moment of happiness.

## WHERE DO YOU GO, NOW THAT THE DECISION IS MADE?

ONCE YOU HAVE DETERMINED that it is time, you may have the option to choose where to euthanize—at home or in a veterinary hospital. Another option is choosing a veterinarian who will do a home euthanasia. Owners can decide what is right for them. For some people, just the thought of "the room where it was done" is too painful and is reason enough to not have it done in your own home. Also, animals may urinate or defecate at the end, which may be a trial for some owners.

I recommend that owners *not* watch the handling of the body, after the actual euthanasia is finished. It's not horrible, but it is an image you don't need to remember. If these don't seem like worries for you, an in-home euthanasia can be a lovely sendoff. However, a clinic can offer a neutral environment.

## BEING THERE

WHO IS TO BE present for the procedure is a personal matter and can only be decided by the owner. Not everyone is able to deal with being there. It is not advisable to have very young children (under five) present, but, again, this is the owner's call. Be careful using the term "put to sleep" around young children who may be confused by this. Using honest, clear language with children is best. They will probably understand more easily than you think.

It is advisable to *bring the other pets* so that they know what happened and do not search for the missing pet.

## EUTHANASIA: THE CLINICAL VERSION OF WHAT HAPPENS

SOMETIMES KNOWING WHAT TO expect can help ease the stress of an already overwhelming situation. The vet team will place an IV catheter to use as a port to be ready for the injection. The veterinarian injects an overdose of an anesthetic agent or a mixture of anesthetic compounds directly into the vein. These usually cause cardiac function to cease. Typically all the owner sees is a peaceful release, with in seconds or minutes, after the injection.

Things that might happen:

- ❧ The agent itself can cause a slight stinging sensation, especially in older veins, as it is injected, somewhat like lidocaine, but the sensation quickly disappears. This is less likely if there is an IV catheter in place.
- ❧ Dogs and cats don't generally close their eyes in death.
- ❧ They will sometimes release the contents of their bladder and colon.
- ❧ There can be a reflex, a gasp-like muscle spasm or vocalization as they move through planes of anesthesia.
- ❧ They may have muscle twitching after the heart has stopped.
- ❧ More than one injection may be needed to complete the euthanasia.
- ❧ Chemotherapy or multiple IV injections, blood draws, or catheters in leg veins may hamper efforts to find a suitable vein and alternative methods may be required.

Disposition of the body is up to the owner. Most people use the cremation service recommended by their veterinarian, unless they have a permanent place to bury their pet. Many cities do not allow burials within city limits unless it is in a cemetery. If you do plan to bury a pet, remember that you must dig down to six feet to prevent scavenger wildlife from interfering with the body.

## MEMENTOS

DECIDE IF YOU CAN in advance if you'd like to have the ashes back after cremation, or other remembrances like a clay mold of the pawprint, or some of the fur. There are companies that will take some of the ashes and make a piece of jewelry from it. If you are getting ashes back, it's good to know if you plan to retain them permanently in an urn or scatter them somewhere. Cremation companies offer several urns to choose from. Some urns once sealed cannot be opened easily. You can also have the ashes placed in an urn that can later be transferred into a container you purchase yourself.

It is imperative to ask your vet if she is confident that the cremation service is reputable and the ashes are reliably returned.

## CONSOLATION

BEFORE THE ACTUAL EUTHANASIA, make sure to have a designated friend or relative call you to check up on you afterward and to inform your loved ones that your pet has passed. It can be hard to call people and tell them the news, but it's nice to hear from friends who already know.

Grieving over an animal is one of the hardest things to get over, especially if it is the sole pet. The echoes of the empty house are haunting. I try to remind owners to be extra nice to themselves for the days following the loss of a pet. Many people won't understand why losing a pet can be so devastating, but it certainly can be.

Untended grief in any form can be debilitating. Our dogs and cats, with their compact life span, seem born to teach us about love and loss. When we lose a pet, it is important not only to grieve, but also to temper the destructive side of sadness with happy memories of our pet's life with us.

As DIFFICULT AS THIS final decision is, we make it with love. All of us grieve in different ways. Grief does not ever go away—it's a permanent resident in your heart. But it does make your heart bigger. It is okay to feel relief at the unburdening because your pet is now also unburdened. You have made a difficult, heartbreaking decision—but it was the right one.

With time, the acute pain of loss may diminish and we can find joy in our memories, and, perhaps, in a new pet.

# BABY ANIMALS

♟

*When you get a new puppy, whatever you do,*
*don't name it "Lucky." I'm serious.*

ELEPHANT BABY SOUNDS LIKE A BIT OF AN OXYMORON. AND rightly so. Elephant calves are bigger than an oven. I know because I saw the birth of an elephant at the Lincoln Park Zoo.

We'd been waiting for a month. The mother elephant, Indie, had come to the end of her two-year term and we knew the birth would be soon. Everyone was exhausted. We wanted to be there when it happened because Indie didn't have midwives of her own species, as she would have had in the wild. We didn't want her to be alone when she gave birth. We were on call and on edge.

Even when I went home to sleep, after working all day in the zoo hospital, I slept fitfully, awaiting the call that I knew would most likely come in the middle of the night. And it did. I lived only a few blocks away from the zoo and so I ran over to witness the mysterious and happy event. It was surprisingly quiet in the elephant house, but as I approached the mother elephant's enclosure, I could hear her unusual, low-pitched rumbling that vibrated the walls all around. We knew to keep quiet and remain a respectful distance away.

I could see a shift in her belly as she paced, moaning and trumpeting. Every so often she'd make a low rumble and almost do a cha-cha-cha across her stall. Three steps forward, two steps back. Her undercurrent rumble was answered by two other elephants in the adjacent stalls. Their trumpeting sounded like a fanfare announcing the event to the world. I wished they could have all been together.

Indie's belly became even tauter. Then, with no preamble, what looked like a gray beach ball appeared from under her and fell to the ground. It was the placenta-covered baby elephant all curled up inside the amniotic sac. The pacing movement of the mother's legs rolled it carefully as if it were a fragile soccer ball. The sac broke open, revealing the fuzzy square head of the baby elephant. Then the entire baby unfolded and lay on her side. She slowly moved her pewter-colored legs, arms, and trunk.

It was a girl. A little soft-skinned, dark gray chunk of perfect girl elephant. She had rolled over nearly onto the feet of the head vet, Dr. Meehan. The veterinary team quickly checked her. She looked terrific. With long-lashed dark eyes, she was cartoonesque. Her trunk was smaller and her legs stockier than I expected. She was much more beautiful than I could have imagined. As the keepers and medical staff stepped away, the mother, tired but happy, stepped in close. Using her trunk to hold her newborn, she seemed to memorize every inch of her.

It was difficult to do anything for the mother or the baby—nature had taken care of everything. None of us could remain detached; we were all connected in a new and profound way.

I could not suppress a sob of joy. I looked around, taking in the scene in the dimmed lights. Those whose eyes met mine were filled with tears. Others were hiding their eyes. I realized every single person in the room was crying.

Perhaps our tears were inspired by the beauty of childbirth, the incredible elation of witnessing creation. But for me it was tinged with the sadness of the zoo setting—that this mammoth creature was not surrounded by her own relatives in the jungle. I wished there was an untamed place for her and her new baby.

The zookeepers opened the enclosure and let the other elephants in.

Their gentleness astonished us. Each elephant, in turn, ran the tip of their trunks over every part of the baby's body, as if they were reading braille. The baby seemed to bask in their tender attention. Then the sweet hunk of baby sought out her mother and their trunks entwined.

It was a miracle, nothing short of it. And we all were there to see it.

WITNESSING THE MOMENT OF birth for any creature is intense. The sisters in my family have all acted as midwife-helpers for each other. With fourteen children between the five of us, we have learned a lot. But nothing prepared me for the singular way a giraffe comes into the world.

It is a very peculiar thing to see. When the mother giraffe is about to give birth, she walks around in a distracted sort of way, but doesn't seem to be in pain. From under her tail, two baby feet stick out and dangle, waving like batons. Then a balloon type thing appears and it seems incredible that the whole thing will just fall from such a great height. The mother giraffe has such long legs and she doesn't squat during birth.

The nose comes out next and the giraffe baby looks like a diver getting ready to dive. The whole giraffe body pokes out of the sac and plummets out, hits the ground, unimpeded, in a heap. I worried that the new giraffe would be broken. They say the jarring landing causes the baby to take a big first breath. It looked to me like someone dropped a set of tangled hoses—tail, legs, neck. Then, as if an antigravity lever had been switched, the little giraffe stood up. Indeed, if he were in the wild, his life would depend on him getting up immediately. The long neck was the last thing to straighten and the head came up in a drunken motion.

Only seconds ago this giraffe baby had been folded like origami, and now he was already walking with his mother. At one point the baby's legs were wobbling and the mother wedged her baby in between her two front legs to stabilize him and keep him standing, with the gentleness of motherly love.

We recently added a black Labrador puppy, Darwin, to our home. I have to admit that I didn't relish the idea of revisiting puppyhood. I remembered all the long nights, needle-sharp puppy teeth, accidents to clean up, long hours of training, chewed-up favorite shoes, books, computers, and remotes strewn about the house. For that reason, I am usually a big fan of adopting older dogs because they are already somewhat trained and are grateful to be with a family. But ever since losing Tundra, we felt our house could use another family member. My husband overruled me and Darwin arrived, to the delight of our children.

A puppy brings youthful energy into a house, which you will need for those long nights and early mornings. To my surprise, I've found myself waking effortlessly to take Darwin out. I could not contain the happiness I felt just thinking about him and his adorable little self.

After a beloved pet dies, many people feel they will never want another pet again. While I respect and understand this sentiment fully, I would urge anyone who has lost a pet and is unsure of what to do, to visit an animal shelter. There are so many great pets out there waiting for a home. Connections happen quickly.

My lovely and ingenious friend Tamar Geller loves dogs. She loves them so much that she's written some fantastic books, *The Loved Dog*, and *30 Days to a Well-Mannered Dog*, about the best way to train them. (She's Oprah Winfrey's dog trainer.)

Here are Tamar's top-ten tips for making life with your pooch a pleasure for both of you.

### DOG TRAINER TAMAR GELLER'S TEN RULES FOR HAPPY CANINE COHABITATION

1. **There is no bad behavior.** A dog behaves in a way that is appropriate for a dog. Dogs say "It's so good to see you!" by jumping up and touching you with their paws. Angrily saying "Bad dog" when that happens will be confusing, to say the least. Like a toddler, a dog is guided solely by natural instinct. Unlike a toddler, they remain in that state for life. They can learn what is expected of them, but instinct is a tough thing to control. It

never goes away. We have to understand that and coach them with lots of patience. It's up to us to be good dog coaches!

2.  **Establish the rules early—and consistently.** Sit down and think ahead. Do you want your puppy to be the sort of dog who jumps up and greets you when you walk in the door? If not, then do not encourage or reinforce jumping—even during the cute puppy phase. The same goes for feeding from the dinner table, sleeping in your bed, etc. Establishing the ground rules early is especially important in families. Everyone in the family must have united agreement on rules, so your dog will be able to follow them and be well mannered.

3.  **Learn your dog's seven basic needs.** Your dog has a good reason for his behavior or misbehavior. Seven good reasons, in fact. Everything he does is motivated by the need for one of these:

    ❧  *Security. Your dog will feel secure if your rules are consistent and reinforced by praise.*

    ❧  *Companionship. Mere coexistence is not enough. Taking walks, playing games, doing things together—that's companionship.*

    ❧  *Hierarchy. Your dog will feel safe knowing he has a benevolent leader in charge of the pack. Dictators are counterproductive.*

    ❧  *Excitement. If your dog is bored, it will entertain itself by digging, chewing, barking, etc., so plan at least one exciting activity each day: a hike, a new route for a walk, a new toy, or making a new friend.*

    ❧  *Physical stimulation. Your dog needs physical exercise daily, preferably wolf games (chasing, wrestling, tug-of-war) with other dogs in a dog park, a doggie day care, or a canine playdate.*

    ❧  *Mental stimulation. Dogs love to learn and they learn language easily. Keep teaching them new words for toys and activities.*

    ❧  *Love and connection. All his life, your dog has the emotional needs of a toddler.*

4. **Improve vocabulary.** Your relationship with your dog, like any other, requires mutual understanding—so be clear about what you want. Dogs can learn up to 150 words. Start saying "drink" when it's drinking, "go to bed" when it's in bed, "come" when it's right next to you. Teach it the way you would teach a toddler: wait for a behavior, and then give it a name. Soon you'll be on the same wavelength.

5. **Teach with patience and fun and games, not dominance.** Instead of training by intimidation, inspire trust and love so your dog will want to do the things that will please you. From studying wolves in the wild, I can tell you that the leader of the pack is there to serve his pack, not to serve his ego.

6. **Recognize, Redirect, and Reward.** If you want to change your dog's behavior, learn the three *R*'s.
   - 🐾 **R**ecognize *what basic need your dog is trying to meet with that behavior.*
   - 🐾 **R**edirect *by showing him a more appropriate way to meet that basic need.*
   - 🐾 **R**eward *the new behavior.*

7. **Socialize early.** Nervous aggression (far more common than dominance aggression) stems from a dog being too sheltered when he was young. Expose your dog early to everything he might encounter in life and associate those things with pleasure. Carry treats and use them, with words of encouragement, to ease your dog through any scary encounters. Teach it "safe words" like "friend" and "take it."

8. **Teach the Big Three important behaviors first.**
   **"Sit"** *is basic manners, the equivalent of teaching a child to say please.*
   **"Come"** *is for safety and should be fun!*
   **"Leave it"** *means stop what you're doing and is considered advanced behavior, but I teach it right away—it could save the dog's life.*

*The key is to teach all three behaviors in a way the dog will associate with fun.*

9. **Wolf games are a daily must.** Dogs crave games of chase, wrestle, and tug-of-war. Most "bad" behaviors (nipping, tugging on your robe, stealing something to initiate a chase) come from dogs being deprived of wolf play, which is a basic need. Play tug-of-war many times a day to relax your dog and make him look at you like you're the best thing that ever happened. This will increase your dog's feeling of love and connection and make him happy to be in your control.

10. **Save "Heel" for later.** It's difficult to teach a dog to stay by your side during walks when he is very young, because you have to fight the outdoors for his attention. Teach him to sit first, while you are standing, kneeling, and lying down—using hand signal and verbal request. He must associate saying please before getting what he wants: a treat, a toy, a walk. Both of you will be happier when that hierarchy is established.

## ROYAL TREATMENT QUICK DOG TRAINING LESSON

I LIKE WHAT TAMAR has to say. I also tell all my clients to teach "Drop it" right away. (Tamar Geller uses a similar phrase, "Leave it.") This command is essential for all dogs and particularly for puppies. For their safety, they must learn to drop anything they have in their mouth in an instant. It is easy to teach, but takes persistence. Because it is such an important command, I will tell you how I taught my puppy Darwin to "drop it."

### "Drop It"

🐾 Put something your dog doesn't care about in his mouth, like a spoon or a chopstick.

🐾 Put your hand over the top of the muzzle and use your fingers at the sides of the mouth to open the mouth fully.

🐾 Say at the same time, "Drop it!"

🐾 Because of gravity and your hand opening their mouth, your dog will drop the item.

🐾 This is the time, as Tamar says, to "make a party" by showing excitement and happiness that he has dropped the chopstick.

🐾 Your dog won't know what he did but will understand quickly.

🐾 Training is in the repetition. Do this several times a day for a few days.

🐾 Do not say the command unless your hand is on their muzzle, making the mouth open.

🐾 After a few days, you will notice that his mouth slackens as you are saying the command.

🐾 Let him start dropping before you press the mouth open. Stay near the puppy, ready to open the mouth if he doesn't.

🐾 Gradually become less and less involved with the opening of the mouth, as your dog does it himself.

🐾 Don't say "Drop it" if you're not sure he will do it or you aren't close enough to do it for him. Otherwise he will think, "When she says 'Drop it' I don't have to do anything."

> *Don't just train the dog. Train the dog to live with you.*

## Things to Do and Know That Will Make Life Easier with Your Puppy in the Long Run

🐾 Teach your puppy "Drop it" ASAP.

🐾 Do not overvaccinate (see Dr. Dodds's recommendations).

🐾 Detox with homeopathics prior to and after vaccines.

✥ Use thuja and lyssin homeopathic remedies, especially after vaccination for rabies.

✥ Feeding puppies raw food is a great idea.

✥ Play with paws. Then hold them still, as if you were trimming the nails.

✥ Hold your pet still and examine teeth, ears, skin, belly, and tail.

✥ Chew toys—buy safe, good ones that are not easy to chew open or swallow whole. No bead stuffing, long strands, or plastic eyes or noses to swallow. Just look it over with an eye toward visualizing the youngster chewing/swallowing parts or all of it.

✥ Never yell at dog while training. They hear much better than we do.

✥ Raise the kind of dog you want in your home, not the kind of dog someone else wants you to have. If you don't care about them being on the couch, let them on the couch.

✥ If it's awkward to get them to go out the door after you (for hierarchy training)—the leash gets caught in the door, and the dog is on the wrong side, and you have packages—don't stress about it. Training is there to teach a dog the manners of your home, however you want them.

✥ Do not feed "life stage foods." Just feed an excellent diet. Once weaned, a puppy eats what the pack eats, not a special puppy diet. Most puppy diets, while they might have improved nutrition compared to a typical adult formula, still have too much carbohydrate and calories and too little protein. Puppies on sugar (carbs) grow too fast and can have behavioral issues. Choose an appropriate diet for health.

*Trying to train an animal that is eating a high-carb diet is like trying to teach a child on a candy diet.*

🐾 Make sure treats, including training treats, conform to the Royal Treatment standard.

🐾 Know that until the age of six months, puppies poop 4–6 times a day.

🐾 Don't freak out if the vet finds worms in a stool sample. All puppies come with gastrointestinal worms and are usually given a de-wormer.

🐾 Heartworm disease is carried by mosquitoes and the first stage of the disease occurs when an affected mosquito bites a dog and transmits microfilaria into the blood. This stage itself does not pose a health threat; heart disease occurs when these microfilaria develop into worms that lodge in the heart about 50–60 days after infection.

🐾 Heartworm medication given monthly prevents heartworm larvae that may have infected the dog in the previous 30–60 days from becoming worms embedded in the heart. This is why we say that it "protects for the month *before* it is given."

🐾 This is also why in the Chicago-area climate, unless there is an unseasonably warm March, we give the medication from June (to protect for May and some of April) through December (to protect for November and some of October) during any possible mosquito exposure.

🐾 There is no need to give the heartworm medication if there are no mosquitoes.

🐾 If you travel with your pet where there are mosquitoes, it is important to give the heartworm medication within 30 days *after* any exposure.

🐾 Some breeds, such as collies, do better on Interceptor rather than Heartgard.

🐾 Use flea and tick medications only in the case of exposure. In most cities and suburbs you don't have to use them all year round, or even regularly if your exposure is limited. If you live in Florida, you may want to use it monthly all year. Use prevention if tick-borne diseases are prevalent in your area. In Chicago we don't really have them, but Lyme, Ehrlichia, and Rocky Mountain spotted fever are the most common tick-borne diseases found in states near Illinois.

😾 Many products combine medications to treat several things at once. But like shampoo and conditioner, it is often cleaner to do one thing at a time. You are less likely to overmedicate if you choose your purpose and then get your medications rather than the other way around. I do not recommend the sledgehammer approach. I avoid a product that takes care of fleas, stops them from reproducing, repels ticks and mosquitoes, and prevents heartworms, mites, GI parasites, and aliens.

😾 Keep meat baby food on hand in case you need to syringe-feed any baby carnivore (remember, assist-feeding is across the tongue, not straight down the mouth).

😾 Puppies can become hypoglycemic quickly, especially if they are small. It can be a real emergency. Regular eating is important. Vomiting and/or diarrhea are often an emergency. Puppies crash quickly and need fluid support from a vet. Once they are stable, keeping some powdered clay, slippery elm, and probiotics on hand help them recover from loose stool.

*Baby-proofing is not enough. You have to puppy-proof.*

Because their sense of smell is twenty-seven times better than ours and they want to smell, explore, and get to know their world, puppies get into everything! Their only real way to learn about their new world is to grab, chew, and identify with their mouth. Puppies are an equal-opportunity destructo-machine. Ferragamo shoes and Coach bags are as intriguing as old tennis shoes and underwear.

## ARE MICROCHIPS SAFE?

I PUT A MICROCHIP in each of my pets. I believe that the benefits outweigh the risks.

I am concerned about the increasing reports of possible tumors and inflammation associated with these chips, but an exact causal relationship is not yet conclusively proven. Other causes for tumors, such as vaccination, seem more likely to me, and I have not seen any tumors at the sites of microchips in my patients. All in all, I believe microchipping a pet is a good idea.

Socialization is essential to a pet's health and well-being. Make sure they know how to deal with the people and animals that may come in and out of their lives. Above all, a healthy immune system is your pet's best defense against all invaders.

### Check for Hernia

- ❦ It is located by the belly button.
- ❦ See if there is a lump that can be pushed into the belly and then pops out again. Depending on how large it is, it may need to be surgically repaired (e.g., during the puppy spay or neuter). It's usually not a big deal, but it's better if you find it before you have the dog spayed or neutered.
- ❦ Remember to learn what's normal for your pet. Look at them, feel them, smell them.
- ❦ Remember to smell the ears—you will then recognize the normal ear smell.
- ❦ If there's an odd smell in the ear, there may be an infection.
- ❦ If you see black discharge in the ears, have your vet check for mites. They are easy to treat, but won't go away on their

## DOG COLLARS

Be aware that dog collars can become too tight as puppies grow. Remember to loosen.

Be careful not to have a collar too loose. If the puppy is startled or jumps back, he can pull out of a loose collar and run into the street.

## CAT COLLARS

Kitten collars can become too tight as they grow. Remember to check them.

Use breakaway collars for cats. They need to be able to come off if the cat gets stuck.

own and can be not only irritating, but in severe cases lasting months, can cause deafness.

- 🐾 Almond oil or olive oil in the ear can help keep mites at bay. Mix in a few drops of vitamin E as well.
- 🐾 If you're trying holistic treatments for ear mites, be diligent. Make sure to treat at least every three days for six weeks.
- 🐾 Don't use concentrated tea tree oil to treat the ears, especially in cats. Just a few topical drops of undiluted tea tree oil can be toxic to a cat or kitten. I have seen it happen.
- 🐾 There are allopathic medicines that will kill the mites and their eggs, and they certainly work. Depending on how

severe the infection is, you can decide what method to use. Often the infection needs to be treated with a conventional medicine.

## A PET BY ANY OTHER NAME

NAMING A PET IS great fun because the sky's the limit. I have a cat patient named Toast (not great when your pet becomes terminally ill) and patients named Mr. President (an orange tabby) and Winston Churchill (clearly a bulldog). I love hearing my receptionist say, "You can bring Mr. President into room A." Someday . . .

Beware of scheduling snafus when you call for a vet visit if you name your pet Tuesday. This is an email my staff received from a wonderful client whose dog has that name.

> Hi guys,
>
> was wondering if I can bring tuesday in next week for treadmill/ laser treatment on tuesday around 3 and thurs around 3. Tuesday could use two treatments this week. Next week Tuesday can't come on Tuesday, but Thursday would be great. See you Tuesday.
>
> Tuesday and Heidi

Once the new pet is home, you'll have the fun of coming up with the perfect name for it, whether it's a dog, a cat, a mouse, or a chimpanzee.

### FABULOUS PET NAMES I HAVE KNOWN

| | |
|---|---|
| Vagabond | Frog |
| Solomon | Holiday |
| The Flash | Midas |
| Gandalf | Willard |
| Diesel | Deluxe |
| Quincy | Polaire |

| | |
|---|---|
| Wallace | Bogie |
| Luna | Bubba |
| MoneyPenny | Percy Plushbottom |
| Chaplain | Piewacket |
| Moxie | Tuesday |
| Ratzo | Zoe |
| Darwin | Numbers |
| Prexious | Skeeter |
| YoodleDoodle | Spartacus |
| Hugo | Nutjob |
| Hudson | Sadie |
| Copper | Sonny |
| Mr. Belvedere | Lauren |
| Wolfgang | Snickerdoodle |
| Max | Jemima |
| Harrison Ford | Shakespaw |
| Ariana Fluffington | Freaky |
| PennyLane | Mydarling |
| Sculley | Chickaboom |
| Cosmo | Osiris |
| Cricket | Coquette |
| Charlemagne | Huckleberry |
| Ditto | Pippin |
| Gizmo | Slinky |
| Albatross | Beebop-alula |
| Doc | Princess Leia |
| Harp | Princess Augusta Jones |
| Coco Taylor Crime Fighter | InterContinentalBallistic-Missile ("Icy") |
| Ringo | Pancake |
| Yojimbo | |

Whatever you call your new pet, I know that animal will grow into its name with personality and love. They always do.

# A ROYAL TREAT: FROZEN CUPCAKES FOR YOUR PET'S FIRST BIRTHDAY (AND EVERY YEAR THEREAFTER)

ONE OF THE BEST things about having animals around the house is birthday parties!

Since you can't have a birthday party without birthday cake, here's an easy recipe for frozen birthday cupcakes that are healthy but still delicious. Your pooch will love you for it.

- ❧ First, mix up a batch of canine "cake"—mostly chicken baby food, with some cooked oatmeal, plain yogurt, and a bit of pumpkin for pizazz.
- ❧ Pour the goop in a muffin pan or mini-muffin tins and freeze them.
- ❧ Frost with yogurt mixed with a little cream cheese for stiffness. (You can use natural food coloring, if you like, but remember it will color your puppy's tongue.)
- ❧ You might even top it off with some small rawhide twists or tiny twigs for candles—but resist the urge to light them on fire!
- ❧ Frozen cake is yummy (especially in summer) and less likely to cause tummy upset than other treats or recipes requiring wheat, corn, peanut butter, and sugars.

*Happy Birthday!*

# AFTER THE FIRE

‎♚

I DON'T REMEMBER THE TWO WEEKS AFTER I LOST MY PETS IN THE house fire. But I do remember coming out of my fog because of the support and love that came to me from many unexpected directions.

When I think about my life before the fire, I remember feeling useful and involved. I was practicing medicine and making my own way. I assumed then that most of my clients saw our relationship as strictly professional. I was someone they hired to heal their animals, nothing more. I wasn't fully aware of the connective web of community that had already been woven.

After the fire, my clients came out of the woodwork and brought me back to life. The word spread, and I was awash in so many thoughtful gifts. These animal-loving people seemed to feel that I had made a difference in their lives, and they wanted to help me recover mine. I felt my life's purpose come back to me. Although the sadness of that day will always be remembered, the shock of it was washed away by the kindness of people I barely knew, and their pets that I knew so well. Through their animals, we all connected.

Because my clients love the animals I care for and correctly assume that I care about their animals as well, they seem to think of me as part of the family. That could explain some of the strange late-night phone calls I've had over the years.

One time at 2 A.M., I was awakened by a call from a woman.

"If a mouse bit my chinchilla," she said, "would there be anything you could do?" I pinched my wrist; no, I wasn't dreaming.

"Did a mouse bite your chinchilla?" I cautiously (and sleepily) asked.

"No," she said, "but I just wanted your opinion."

We all know how the night can inspire hypothetical situations and magnify our fears. Besides, what if someday a mouse *did* bite her chinchilla? I wouldn't want her to despair.

"Well, that depends on how big the mouse is," I said. "If it's bigger than your chinchilla . . . I mean, if it's a monster mouse, we could have a problem. If it's not, I could handle it."

She thanked me, hung up, and presumably had a good night's sleep.

It's nice to know that even half asleep, in the middle of the night, I can allay an owner's fears, and at least hypothetically cure a chinchilla.

# CURE AND RELEASE

I HAVE NO IDEA IF SHE WAS A SHE, BUT I CALLED HER ARWEN. I WAS twelve and she was only about a week away from being old enough to fly when I found her after a storm. There were trees down everywhere in our neighborhood. High winds had picked up souvenirs from everyone's yards and scattered them all over the county. Our backyard got someone's maple tree branches, a soggy book of poems, a bent watering can, and Arwen, the baby blue jay.

She was alive, cold, and lovely. She had black eyes, big, gangly feet, dark feathers with blue ends poking out from their growing tubes, a dark band of soft feathers like a necklace around her neck, and grayish white fluff underneath, all matted and wet. She smelled musty and wild and I wanted to save her.

I took her home, dried her off, and put her in a box. I gave her a hot-water bottle, a towel, a cup of water, and some shredded newspaper. Then I made a mash of worms and water and fed them to her with a dropper. She was a champ at eating and made me look like a pro. My friends came over to watch. I was a celebrity.

When she was hungry, Arwen made a lot of noise. That was okay. I was one of seven children, and everyone made a lot of noise. There was usually someone hollering for something, singing, organizing yard games, or playing piano. Amid all this cacophony, the little raspy squawks of the blue orphan under my bed floated unnoticed out of my bedroom window. Except by me.

On her diet of fat worms and bugs Arwen grew quickly, and even took the bugs whole. I realized it was time for her first flight. I climbed a tree with her and placed her on a small branch. Her feathers were ready, and she seemed strong. She had been wildly stretching her wings around my room, and now seemed excited by the limitlessness of the yard. Flapping while she held on for an extra second, she let go and glided off. I will never forget the way I felt watching her fly. She was my secret self.

She stayed in the yard the whole summer, and begged for food even though she was fully capable of finding her own. She would call out with her raspy voice when I came into the yard, but she slowly chose a bird's life. I felt the loss, but I understood. My friends and school and civilization pulled me away from her as well.

Arwen is still with me in a sense. Whenever I'm involved in the rehabilitation and release of an animal back into the wild, I am often reminded of the wild joy of that first free flight of my adopted blue bird.

ONE SUNNY MORNING IN northern California about fifteen years ago, Pacifica the sea lion shot out of her kennel and onto the beach as if she were coming out of a starting block. Ungainly on land, she made the sand fly with her flippers as she galumphed her way toward the shore. She was full grown and her scars had healed. She knew just where to go and what to do today and forever. The water sprayed in a sparkling arch as she dove in. After she was a safe distance away, her head bobbed up in the slow rolling waves and looked back at us.

We had been her nurses for nearly two weeks, but this was not a look of thanks or even goodbye. She had moved on and this was more like hello. A proper hello from a healthy, curious sea lion to those of us on land. Even more, she was saying, I'm home.

I had been working as an intern at the Marine Mammal Center in northern California. We took care of any injured and sick marine mammals—elephant seals, sea lions, seals, dolphins, otters, whales, whatever needed help—and then reintroduced them to their habitat. They were often quite ill from some bullet or man-made toxin, or injured trying to free themselves from a net or a snare of plastic encircling their neck or flippers. Extremely intelligent, they responded to the routines of treatment and often became accustomed to us. There was never any doubt, though, that they were wild and wanted to stay that way.

The sea lions were large and dangerous, requiring restraint methods ranging from a light towel wrap to large wooden baffle boards used as shields. That was how we herded the crabby sea creatures into a corner for a blood sample or a treatment. There were hundreds of fish to prepare for meals, some carefully stuffed with medications and supplements. Many animals ate on their own, but some had to be coaxed or tube-fed. The conditions at the center were often cold and wet, and the work was physically grueling. A constant smell of fish and seawater stayed in my hair and hands even after showering.

The facilities were spare, but the resources were not. Dr. Frances Gulland, the devoted head veterinarian, monitored every case with intensity. She had an overflowing, healing energy and her enthusiasm was contagious. She ensured that our laboratory equipment, staff, and volunteers were all top-notch. Each animal had the support of a team of volunteers and staff intent on their release day.

All the hours and hard work were rewarded when we watched that wild splash during the climactic sendoff back to the ocean. I felt overwhelmingly delighted and relieved knowing that those sea animals I had cared for were once again in open waters. They would be fully provided for by their real caretaker, the planet.

*    *    *

LOVE OF ANIMALS HAS always been as deeply rooted in me as my love of people. Animals comfort us as we take on their rhythm and they calm us when nothing else does. They can be unobtrusive in ways humans cannot. Nonhuman language is rich; we understand it instinctively, making us feel profoundly connected to a broader, deeper, better-integrated life.

An elderly client once confided to me, "I cried harder when my dog died than when my own father died." He said there wouldn't be enough handkerchiefs in the world to wipe away the tears when he started thinking about his dog. Perhaps he was tapping into unshed tears for his dad, too, but I have heard similar stories from many people over the years.

Our love of animals rejuvenates us every day. Perhaps the ancestry of our pets resonates with the wild that remains in us. Reminding us of the animal way we were born, tumbling into the world; of the way our untamed heart beats as we run with our dogs, of the way we fall asleep with our cat nestled in the crook of our arm or our dog warming our back, and of the uncharted unknown that awaits us when we are finished on this earth.

Spotting a flying bird in a clogged cityscape sets us free. There is an elegance and grace to the soaring—above all the traffic of our minds and troubles of our hearts—that lifts us higher than our wildest dreams.

# ACKNOWLEDGMENTS

This book, like my veterinary practice, is a result of fusion and collaboration. My sister and cowriter Anastasia Royal's vision, endless talents, late-night humor, and generous contributions made the shaping of my story possible, and kept the creative process on fire.

So many people have taken the sting out of any bite and have added love and laughter to my life. Together with their animals, they have been instrumental to the completion of this book.

I single out the following with gratitude:

My angel investors, Kevin Demaret, Fran Tuite, Judy Keitz, Kurt Dorner, Doreen Parish, and Michelle Cullom, whose spontaneous generosity made my dream reality. All of the clients and patients who fill my days.

Everyone on staff at the Royal Treatment Veterinary Center, especially Veronica Vazquez, Zoe Magierek, Alex Kislaitis, Kate Shears, Tashyia Fields, Janelle Davila, Jessica Ahrens-Noel, Kerry Bolger, Nancy Schulz, Pam Kuhn, and Sara Watson.

Oprah Winfrey for giving me the opportunity to foster the wild health in her beautiful dogs. The producers and employees at Harpo Studios: Bridgette Theriault, Hilary Robe, Caroline Ziv, Tracey Carter, Pam Barnes, Pier Smith, Libby Moore, Angelique McFarland, and Chris Hill. My friends Tamar Geller, Billy Corgan, Larry and Shawn King, Ted and Dr. Natasha Lilly, and Dr. Rick Palmquist for helping to get the word out about my work.

The keepers and staff at Brookfield Zoo, the Shedd Aquarium, and the Lincoln Park Zoo, especially Joel Pond, Penny Reidy, and my first zoo bosses, Dr. Peregrine Wolff and Dr. Tom Meehan. Everyone involved in the Chicago Peregrine Program.

Dr. Jean Dodds, my friend, colleague, and mentor. The veterinarians and staff at Woodstock Veterinary Clinic, especially Dr. Charles Charmichael, Dr. Deb Grude, and Dr. Lloyd Shaw, my friend and veterinary idol.

My incomparable mother, Charlotte Royal, my sister Char Walker and brother Mark Royal for insightful editorial comments. My father, William Royal, my East Coast siblings William Royal, Jr., Madeleine Walker, and Mary Therese Royal de Martinez for their sweet support. My brothers-in-law Bruce Ingram—for his editorial wit and encouragement—Jonathan Walker, Matthew Walker, and Ronald Martinez. My niece Dorothee Royal-Hedinger and Mark Boyer for their many efforts on my behalf. My nephew Hans Royal-Hedinger for his editing skill and humor. My nephew and godson Thomas Walker, and Daniella Conrad, for taking care of my pets. The Gies, Kennedy, and Dogan families, Kimberly Penfold, and Brian Komei Dempster for continuous enthusiasm. The late Ernest Dunbar for his literary wisdom.

Dr. M. Patricia Faber, my chemistry professor, mentor, and dear friend, who encouraged the latent scientist in me; Dr. Joe Dorner, who taught me to see beyond numbers; and Dr. Leslie Kordecki, who taught me to read between the lines.

Pat Shepard, my honorary sister; Jeannie Pollack; and Steve Hames, for generosity and useful ideas. Brian Hanley, Craig Thorstenson, the Winchesters and Chismans (particularly Diane and Dora) for enduring friendship. My power girlfriends: Karen Stevenson for her keen literary eye, Sondra Brigandi, and Dr. Julia Sturm. Lisa McMath and Walter Garschagen, my lifelong friends. Sweet Jake's dad, Karl Brummel, the late Billie Webster and her family, and Rita Wiggins and Mary Denigan.

The Fasseas family (especially Paula and Alexis), Chris Tardio and Charles Day, Aaron Charfoos, Joan Gunn, and Sir Ken Robinson for being there at the right time with interest and guidance.

My friends at Family Pet Animal Hospital—especially Dr. Jane

Lohmar, Dr. Kathi Berman, Dr. Amy Ujiki, Dr. Rae Ann Van Pelt, and Dr. Marla Minuskin; and the dedicated zoo and wildlife vets Dr. Darin Collins, Dr. Frances Gulland, Dr. Nan Schaffer, and Dr. Curtis Eng. Mentors Dr. Steve Marsden and Dr. Mona Boudreaux, and friends Dr. Elaine Holt, Julie Kreiner, and Harriet Coles. Richard Martin, Dr. Elisabeth Girard, Dr. Renee Leveille, Dr. John Hintermeister, Dr. Cindy Charlier, Dr. Susan Fife, Dr. Karen Becker, Dr. Mimi Noonan, Dr. Laura Hungerford, Mike Meehan, Andrea Kane, Caroline Porter, and Kate Cetrulo for their encouragement and support.

My colleagues and friends at the AHVMA, the Veterinary Specialty Center, Hinsdale Pet Cemetery, Chicago Veterinary Emergency and Specialty Service, Animal Emergency and Treatment Center, and Darwin's Natural Pet Products.

The late and beloved Reverend Thaddeus J. Neckerman, who taught me to sail through life but to never let go of the tiller.

I am indebted to Peter Miller, my literary agent, for his expertise and for telling me, many years ago, that I had a book in me.

I am fortunate to have Emily Bestler as my editor. She intuitively understood the scope and content of my first manuscript and deftly facilitated the writing of this book.

My children, Sean and Sophie, lights of my life, and my husband, Matthew, whom I love for his kindness to animals and people.

# PROFESSIONAL ACKNOWLEDGMENTS

American Academy of Veterinary Acupuncture (AAVA)

American Association of Wildlife Veterinarians (AAWV)

American Botanical Council (ABC)

American Holistic Veterinary Medical Association (AHVMA)

Animal Emergency and Treatment Center, Chicago

Animal 911, Skokie, IL

Antech Diagnostics, Irvine, CA

Barat College, Lake Forest, IL

Brookfield Zoo, Chicago

Chicago Peregrine Program

Chicago Veterinary Emergency Services, Chicago

*Chicagoland Tails* magazine

Creative CoWorking, Evanston, IL

Cummings School of Veterinary Medicine at Tufts University

Darwin's Natural Pet Products, Seattle, WA

Family Pet Animal Hospital, Chicago

Ferno Company/Hudson Aquatics

Greyhounds Only, Inc., Carol Stream, IL

Hartigan's Ice Cream, Evanston, IL

Hemopet, Garden Grove, California

The Huffington Post

Idexx Veterinary Laboratories, Westbrook, ME

International Veterinary Acupuncture Society (IVAS)

John G. Shedd Aquarium, Chicago

Lincoln Park Zoo, Chicago

Marine Mammal Center, Golden Gate Park, CA

Natural Path Clinic, Edmonton, Alberta, Canada

Noah's Ark, Winnetka, IL

North Shore Community Bank, Wilmette, IL

PAWS Chicago—Humane and Adoption Center, Chicago

Ruff Haus Pets, Chicago, IL

Sirius Cooks, Oak Park, IL

STAY Dog Hotel, Chicago

Stella and Chewy's, Milwaukee, WI

Tops Veterinary Rehabilitation, Grays Lake, IL

University of Florida, Gainesville

University of Illinois College of Veterinary Medicine

University of Tennessee, Knoxville

Veterinary Specialty Center, Buffalo Grove, IL

Woodland Park Zoo, Seattle, WA

Woods Hole Oceanographic Institution, Woods Hole, MA

Woodstock Veterinary Clinic, Woodstock, IL

# SUGGESTED READING

*The End of Illness*, by David B. Agus, MD

"Mythology of Protein Restriction for Dogs with Reduced Renal Function," by Kenneth C. Bovée, DVM

"Cat Food for Aardvarks, and Other Zoo Diets," by Jane E. Brody, *New York Times*, June 18, 2002

*The Lost Language of Plants*, by Stephen Harrod Buhner

*Dharma, The Revenant, Another Reason I Don't Own a Gun*, and any other work of poetry by Billy Collins

*Anatomy of an Illness*, by Norman Cousins

*The Dog Cancer Survival Guide*, by Demian Dressler, DVM and Susan Ettinger, DVM, ACVIM

*Sacred Economics*, by Charles Eisenstein

*Complications*, by Atul Gawande

*The Loved Dog* and *30 Days to a Well-Mannered Dog*, by Tamar Geller

*Animals in Translation: Using the Mysteries of Autism to Decode Animal Behavior* and *Animals Make Us Human: Creating the Best Life for Animals*, by Temple Grandin (with Catherine Johnson)

*The Horse Boy*, by Rupert Isaacson

*Animal, Vegetable, Miracle*, by Barbara Kingsolver

*When Antibiotics Fail*, by Marc Lappé

*A Sand County Almanac*, by Aldo Leopold

*Food Pets Die For: Shocking Facts About Pet Food*, by Ann Martin

*A Ring of Bright Water*, by Gavin Maxwell

*Born to Run*, by Christopher McDougall

*Brain Rules: 12 Principles for Surviving and Thriving at Work, Home, and School,* by Dr. John J. Medina

*The Jungle Effect,* by Dr. Daphne Miller

*The Cosmic Serpent,* by Jeremy Narby

*Earthing,* by Clinton Ober, Stephen T. Sinatra, MD, and Martin Zucker

*Raw & Natural Nutrition for Dogs,* by Lew Olson, PhD

*Releasing Your Pet's Hidden Health Potential,* by Dr. Richard Palmquist

*The Omnivore's Dilemma, Food Rules,* and *In Defense of Food,* by Michael Pollan

*The Tell-Tale Brain,* by V. S. Ramachandran

*The Element,* by Sir Ken Robinson

*Dog Heaven,* by Cynthia Rylant

*Musicophilia: Tales of Music and the Brain,* by Oliver Sacks

*The Little Prince,* by Antoine de Saint-Exupéry

*Four Paws, Five Directions,* by Cheryl Schwartz

*Dogs That Know When Their Owners Are Coming Home: And Other Unexplained Powers of Animals,* by Rupert Sheldrake

*The Natural Remedy Book for Dogs & Cats,* by Diane Stein

*The Thurber Carnival* (anthology), by James Thurber

*Options: The Alternative Cancer Therapy Book,* by Richard Walters

*Spontaneous Healing,* by Dr. Andrew Weil

*Charlotte's Web* and *The Trumpet of the Swan,* by E. B. White

*In Defense of Dolphins: The New Moral Frontier,* by Thomas I. White, PhD

*Manual of Natural Veterinary Medicine, Science and Tradition,* by Dr. Susan G. Wynn and Dr. Steve Marsden

# INDEX